Integration and co-operation in Europe

Western Europe after World War II saw the establishment of structures and institutions designed to bring about political, social and economic co-operation. Now the political and economic conditions which shaped organizations such as the EC, the Council of Europe and EFTA have radically changed with the collapse of the communist regimes in Eastern Europe.

Brigid Laffan explains the evolution and extent of this post-war framework. She examines the ability of the major institutions of 'Euracracy' to cope with the demands of Eastern European states for political integration and economic assistance and she surveys the current state of military, economic, cultural and policy co-operation.

Issues such as the 1992 programme are dealt with in the context of the new Europe and the effect of the EEC on the evolution of other European organizations is assessed.

Brigid Laffan is Jean Monnet Professor of European Politics at University College, Dublin.

The Routledge/University Association for Contemporary European Studies series

Series editor: Clive Church, University of Kent

Integration and co-operation in Europe

Brigid Laffan

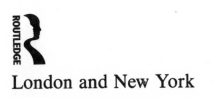

London and New York

First published 1992
by Routledge
11 New Fetter Lane, London EC4P 4EE

Simultaneously published in the USA and Canada
by Routledge
29 West 35th Street, New York, NY 10001

Reprinted 1993

Typeset in 10/12pt Baskerville by
Falcon Typographic Art Ltd, Fife, Scotland
Printed and bound in Great Britain by
Mackays of Chatham PLC, Chatham, Kent

British Library Cataloguing in Publication Data
Laffan, Brigid
  Integration and co-operation in Europe. – (UACES)
  I. Title II. Series
  337.142

Library of Congress Cataloging in Publication Data
Laffan, Brigid.
  Integration and co-operation in Europe / Brigid Laffan.
  p. cm. – (The Routledge/University Association for
  Contemporary European Studies series)
  Includes bibliographical references and index.
  1. European Economic Community. 2. Europe–Economic integration.
  3. Europe 1992. 4. World politics – 1989 – I. Title. II. Series.
  HC241.2.L33   1992
  337.1´4–dc20   91–41474 CIP

ISBN 0–415–06338–8
ISBN 0–415–06339–6 pbk

For Aileen and Con

Contents

Figures

Tables

Preface

The purpose of this book is to assess the extent and nature of integration and co-operation in Western Europe. When I began writing it in late 1989, I was immediately confronted with the changing realities of Europe, realities that forced Western Europe to look beyond its own narrow confines to the Continent as a whole. I have throughout the text used the term 'European Community', rather than the more legally exact term 'the European Communities'. The term 'European Community' is more accurate in describing the level of integration achieved among the twelve EC states. I also adopted the term 'European Economic Area' rather than 'European Economic Space' to denote EC-EFTA negotiations. Both sides in the negotiations now agree that the term 'area' is more appropriate to what they are trying to achieve.

I must thank many people for their assistance and encouragement while I wrote this book. A year spent as Newman Scholar in the Department of Politics, University College Dublin, enabled me to complete this work. My thanks to Senator Maurice Manning, who was responsible for the administration of the fellowships during this time, and to Professor John Whyte, who made me so welcome in his department. My thanks also to Peter Brew and Brian Howlett, of Irish Pensions Trust, who financed my fellowship and therefore gave me sufficient time to complete the book. My appreciation to many academic colleagues who read various drafts – Patrick Keatinge, Rory O Donnell and Richard Sinnott – and to a number of officials in the Department of Foreign Affairs and the Prime Minister's Department in Dublin. Trevor Salmon, of St Andrews University, in Scotland, deserves a special mention, not only for reading the text but for stimulating my interest in this field as an undergraduate at the University of Limerick. My thanks also to the staff of the Commission

Office in Dublin and of various libraries for invaluable help with sources. A special thanks to a small group of former students at the University of Limerick, who now work in Brussels, for their ready assistance – Anna Murphy, Liz-Anne Scott and Fiona Hayes. I am indebted to Clive Church and the UACES editorial board for asking me to undertake this work.

Agus le mór grá, I reserve the final thanks for Michael, who was always ready with encouragement, and for Diarmuid and Kate, whose 'Will this book ever be finished?' was a great spur.

Brigid Laffan
Dublin

Acronyms, abbreviations and glossary of terms

ACP African Caribbean Pacific: Sixty-eight Third World countries associated with the EC by the Lomé Conventions

Acquis communautaire a term used to describe the corpus of Community legislation and commitments among the member states arising from the Treaties and subsequent legislation. At the beginning of 1991, the *acquis communautaire* consisted of over 10,000 pages of text

Acquis politique a term used to describe agreements in European Political Co-operation

Dirigisme a term used to describe French economic policy

EBRD European Bank for Reconstruction and Development: founded in 1990 and aimed at assisting East European countries

BRITE Basic Research in Industrial Technologies in Europe: EC programme for advanced material technologies

CAP Common Agricultural Policy: price and structural support for agriculture in the EC

CCT Common Customs Tariff: tariff on goods entering the EC

CEN European Committee for standardization: standards body including EC and EFTA states

CENELEC European Committee for Electro-technical standardization: EC/EFTA standards body

COMECON Council for Mutual Economic Assistance

COMETT Community Action Programme for Education and Training for Technology: EC high technology co-operation

COREPER Committee of Permanent Representatives: member States' ambassadors to the EC

COST Committee on European Co-operation in the field of Scientific and Technical Research

CSCE Conference on Security and Co-operation in Europe: forum established in 1975 for East-West dialogue. Now one of the main elements in the new European architecture

CSF Community Support Framework: statement of EC financial support for each lesser-developed area under the structural funds

DG Directorate General: name for departments within the Commission

EAGGF European Agricultural Guidance and Guarantee Fund: agricultural support fund

EC European Community

ECHR European Court of Human Rights

ECJ European Court of Justice

ECOFIN EC Economic and Finance Council

ECSC European Coal and Steel Community: founded in 1951 with six original members.

ECU European Currency Unit: basket of twelve EC currencies used in all matters relating to the EC budget

EDF European Development Fund: financial aid for ACP states

EEA European Economic Area: proposed treaty between EC and EFTA

EEC European Economic Community: one of the original three communities

EEIG European Economic Interest Grouping: legal framework for EC joint ventures

EES European Economic Space: original term for EC-EFTA negotiations

EFTA European Free Trade Association

EIAD Environmental Impact Assessment Directive

EIB European Investment Bank: independent EC bank

EMS European Monetary System: exchange – rate system in the EC

EMU Economic and Monetary Union

EPA Environmental Protection Agency

EP European Parliament

EPC European Political Co-operation: system of foreign policy co-operation started in 1970

ERASMUS European Community Action Scheme for the Mobility of University Students

ERM Exchange Rate Mechanism: instrument linking EMS currencies

ESF European Social Fund: community training and labour market fund

ESPRIT European Strategic Programme for Research and Development in Information Technology

ETUC European Trade Union Confederation: trade union umbrella group

EUI European University Institute

EUREKA European Research Co-ordination Agency: technological research community involving 18 countries

Eurofed putative European central bank

FAST Forecasting and Assessment in Science and Technology: EC programme

GATT General Agreement on Tariffs and Trade: international forum for trade negotiations

GEMU German Economic and Monetary Union

IEA International Energy Agency

IGC Intergovernmental Conference: formal conference to negotiate treaty change in the EC

IMF International Monetary Fund

IMP Integrated Mediterranean Programme: EC programmes for the Mediterranean regions

JESSI Joint-European Sub-Micron Silicon project: high technology research

JET Joint European Torus. Research on thermonuclear fusion

LINGUA Promotion of the Teaching and Learning of Foreign languages in the EC: EC educational programme

MAGHREB Algeria, Morocco, Tunisia

MASHREK Egypt, Lebanon, Jordan and Syria

MEP European Parliament Member

NATO North Atlantic Treaty Organization

NORDEN refers to the totality of Nordic institutions

OECD Organization for Economic Co-operation and Development: twenty-four industrialized states

PHARE Poland and Hungary Assistance for Economic Restructuring Programme; now covers all of Eastern/Central Europe

RACE Research and Development in Advanced Communications Technology in Europe: integration of telecommunications systems

SAD Single Administrative Document: EC customs document since 1978

SEA Single European Act

STABEX System of Stabilization of Export Earnings; Lomé Convention

SYSMIN System for safeguarding and developing mineral production: Lomé Convention

TEMPUS Trans-European Mobility Programme for University Studies: university exchange scheme for Eastern Europe

UN United Nations

UNICE Union of Industries of the EC

WEU Western European Union: Western European defence organization

Introduction

The year 1989 will go down in the history of Europe as an *annus mirabilis*: the year when the post-war order came crashing down, bringing with it not only democratic freedoms for the peoples of Eastern Europe, but also great uncertainty about the nature of Europe's political and security structures in the 1990s. The profound changes in Eastern Europe came at a time when the core regional organization in Western Europe, the European Community (EC), was itself undergoing significant change. The EC is simultaneously attempting to complete its main policy objective of the 1980s – the achievement of a barrier-free internal market by 1992 – and to deepen the level of integration by setting off on the road towards economic, monetary and, perhaps, political union. At the same time the Community is faced with pressing demands from European non-member states for new forms of co-operation. The notion of a 'European Economic Area' is at the heart of discussions with the European Free Trade Association (EFTA). Mikhail Gorbachev's evocative suggestion of a 'common European home' and US Secretary of State James Baker's call for a 'new European architecture' testify to the fact that Europe is searching for a new pan-European system to manage inter-state relations for the continent as a whole. The EC is faced with the enormous challenge of deepening the level of integration, while at the same time coming to terms with the revolutionary changes in Eastern Europe and with the fact of German unification.

After World War II, Western Europe evolved as a distinct region in international politics, characterized by liberal democratic forms of government and market economies, tempered by a strong commitment to social welfare. The post-war divide led to the establishment of very different economic, political and social systems in the two parts of Europe. In Western Europe, a plethora of formal regional institutions took root, leading to a profusion of political and economic ties across borders. Because the European Community emerged as the core regional organization, there is a tendency to regard the Community as synonymous with Western Europe and even with Europe as a whole. This view ignores the existence and role of organizations such as the European Free Trade Association, the Council of Europe, the Nordic Council and the Western European Union (WEU). In Eastern Europe, the Warsaw Pact and COMECON provided the formal multilateral context for inter-state relations until the collapse of communism. The UN Economic Commission for Europe and the process that evolved under the auspices of the Conference on Security and Co-operation in Europe (CSCE) provide an embryonic pan-European system. A large number of organizations with overlapping membership and scope mould inter-state relations in Western Europe.

Although the European Community and the other Western European organizations are the product of a specific set of recent geopolitical circumstances, the ideal of European unity through co-operation, rather than hegemony, actually predates World War II. Proposals from political leaders and intellectuals for a European 'diet' or 'senate' have a long tradition. However, such ideas were not the stuff of practical politics when national integration was the dominant political impulse. After the carnage of World War I, the Austrian Count Coudenhove-Kalergi set up the Pan-Europe Union in 1922; the following year, he published a book entitled *Pan-Europe*[1] A formal proposal from the French government to establish a federal union in Europe was made to the League of Nations in May 1930. In the memorandum, Aristide Briand, the French Foreign Minister, advocated the establishment of a 'permanent regime of joint responsibility for the rational organization of Europe'.[2] His proposals fell on deaf ears. Hitler's rise to power in Germany meant that Europe had to fight one more fratricidal war before co-operative organizations were established at regional level.

CO-OPERATION AND INTEGRATION

The purpose of this book is to examine the extent and nature of integration and co-operation between states in Western Europe at the beginning of the 1990s. This is an opportune time to assess the transformation of Western Europe in the post-war era because

Western Europe is now forced to look beyond its own narrow confines to the continent as a whole. In these pages we shall be tracing the evolution of a myriad Western European organizations: the Council of Europe, the European Community, EFTA and the Nordic Council. Although some attention is paid to institutions, the focus of the book is on the web of relationships that bind the states of Western Europe together in different policy areas. Before embarking on this analysis, it is necessary to probe what is meant in the literature by integration and co-operation.

International co-operation and integration both involve states in collective action, but the latter can be distinguished from the former by the intensity of relations between the participating states and the manner in which those relations are organized and managed. Intergovernmental co-operation occurs within clearly defined limits and is controlled by the member states. In other words, organizations characterized by intergovernmental co-operation are not intended to impinge greatly on national sovereignty. Organizations designed to promote intergovernmental co-operation do not create a centre of power and authority independent of the participating states. By contrast, integration is, according to Haas, 'a process for the creation of political communities',[3] or, according to Deutsch, a process of transforming 'previously separate units into components of a coherent system'.[4] The study of regional integration is concerned

> With explaining how and why states cease to be wholly sovereign, how and why they voluntarily mingle, merge, and mix with their neighbours so as to lose the factual attributes of sovereignty while acquiring new techniques for resolving conflict between themselves. Regional co-operation, organization, systems and sub-systems may help describe steps on the way; but they should not be confused with the resulting condition.[5]

The notion of sovereignty in international law implies that a recognized state has jurisdiction over a particular people and territory and that within its jurisdiction, state authorities have control over the legitimate use of coercive power. When states engage in integration, they cede some part of their individual sovereignty in favour of its joint exercise with other states.

Wallace distinguishes between formal and informal integration. Formal integration is defined as 'deliberate actions by authoritative policy-makers to create and adjust rules, to establish common institutions and to work with and through those institutions', whereas informal integration consists of those 'intense patterns of interaction' that follow the dynamics of markets, technology, communications networks and social exchange without the intervention of public authorities.[6]

From the outset, European integration has been the subject of much academic analysis, as scholars sought to explain the pattern of co-operation and predict the outcome of integration. The European Community, in particular, excites considerable scholarly interest because the ultimate aim of the member states is,[7] according to the Preamble of the Single European Act of 1987, to 'transform relations as a whole among their States into a European Union'. Although the precise nature of this union has not been articulated, the goal itself provides the European Community with a strong ideological underpinning and is used by those who wish to widen the scope and deepen the level of integration to pressurize recalcitrant states into further collective action. The Council of Europe, the OECD, EFTA, the Nordic Council and the Western European Union receive far less scholarly attention. This is unfortunate because all these organizations contribute to the profusion of political, economic and social ties that bind together the states of Western Europe.

Formal economic integration assumed a central place on the post-war agenda in Western Europe. There was a widespread recognition that 'beggar thy neighbour' policies, or autarky, exacerbated the Depression of the 1930s. The US was committed to the creation of an integrated economy modelled on the large American home market; and sustained economic growth, achieved through increased openness in national economies, was essential to Western Europe's search for political and social stability. Economic integration in Western Europe has gone hand in hand with an acceleration of the states' role in economic management and the provision of welfare services. Integration among advanced mixed economies is intensely political because economic performance is a key factor in electoral competition between parties.[8] Potential economic benefits arising from increased specialization, economies of scale, improved terms of trade and increased competition provide the economic rationale for integration.[9] Once a regional economic grouping is established, market access, through either membership or association, becomes a major priority for all non-member states.

In 1968, John Pinder applied two concepts developed by Tinbergen to the study of economic integration: negative integration and positive integration. Negative integration consists of the removal of barriers that hamper the free flow of goods, capital and labour, whereas positive integration involves the formation of common policies and laws. According to Pinder, negative integration is more easily achieved than positive integration. It is relatively easy to define discrimination and to legislate for its removal in a treaty, whereas it is difficult to make provision for a common policy which can take many different forms.[10]

Economists have identified different levels of economic integration, namely a free trade area, a customs union, a common market, economic and monetary union and total economic integration:

Free trade area Tariffs and quotas are eliminated on trade between the participating countries but maintained on trade with third countries.

Customs union Countries remove barriers to trade and adopt a common external tariff *vis-à-vis* third countries.

Common market involves the free movement of all factors of production – labour, capital and services – in addition to the free flow of goods.

Economic and monetary union A stage further than a common market, economic and monetary union implies the harmonization of some national economic policies and a single currency or irrevocably fixed exchange rates.

Total economic integration involves not just product and factor integration, but the integration of economic policies.[11]

Free trade areas and customs unions are usually associated with negative integration or the removal of obstacles to the free movement of goods, capital and labour. Advanced stages of economic integration, even a common market, require considerable positive integration. Pinder agrues that joint structures of government are needed for advanced stages of economic integration.[12] There is a complex interaction between political and economic considerations when states embark upon and intensify economic integration.

Political integration has many facets, but is usually taken to describe the emergence of a political community based on trust, loyalty and shared values.[13] It is useful to distinguish between four different aspects of political integration.[14]

Institutional integration refers to the growth of collective decision-making among a group of states. Common institutions are necessary to develop and administer the rules and regulations required for economic integration. Decision-making must be governed by a set of formal rules about the role and powers of individual institutions. The extent to which common institutions are or should be supranational in character is the subject of much debate in the literature on integration. Supranational institutions can engage the citizens of the member states directly, and can take decisions independently of, and in some cases against, the wishes of the member states.

Policy integration focuses on the extent to which responsibility for particular policies is transfered to a higher level of government or jointly exercised or co-ordinated by more than one level. The scope, extent and salience of common policies is of major political significance to integration. The appropriate level of government for the exercise of different functions is a key issue in the design of advanced forms of economic integration, notably an economic and monetary union.

Attitudinal integration is concerned with the sources of support for regional integration among the public at large and among the political and economic élites. Attitudes effect the development of institutional and policy integration. There is no consensus in the literature about the relative importance of public opinion, other than a recognition that in liberal democracies the actions of governments both within and outside the domestic jurisdiction must be seen to be legitimate. Developments in formal integration sometimes require the active involvement of the general public through the holding of referenda.

Political and economic élites are given an important role in integration theory. It is widely accepted that political leadership has played an important part in the development of integration efforts in Western Europe since the war. A large number of political leaders championed the cause of integration by sponsoring policy and institutional initiatives from the early 1950s. The absence of political will is sometimes used to explain stagnation in the process of integration. However, political capacity, no less than political will, is critical. If, for domestic political reasons, governments find it difficult to accommodate the views of partners integration will stall.[15]

Security integration applies to Deutsch's notion of a 'security community' characterized by a well-established expectation of nonviolent inter-state relations. According to Deutsch there are two types of 'security community' – an amalgamated security community which achieves a common government, and a pluralistic community which preserves peace but falls short of a common government.[16]

Although there have been many approaches and perspectives on integration as a political phenomenon, no one approach has ever achieved complete prominence. Rather, different approaches have dominated during various stages of the development of the European Community. In the mid-1970s, when the Community was experiencing a period of stagnation, one of the seminal integration theorists, Haas, concluded that regional integration theory was obsolescent.[17] The revival in the fortunes of the EC in the latter half of the 1980s has led to renewed interest in the dynamics of integration. Among the many approaches adopted by students of EC integration, the most significant can be portrayed under the following headings: federalism, neo-functionalism, intergovernmentalism and domestic politics, and interdependence.

Nordic integration is fundamentally different from EC integration because it is based largely on parallel national action which reduces the impact of boundaries in a very practical fashion. Anderen depicts Nordic integration as a 'fine-meshed net of small interdependencies that is being spun over the Nordic countries' and suggests that 'cobweb integration' offers the best metaphor of this form of integration.[18]

Federalism

Federalists, committed to the establishment of a 'United States of Europe', have an important place in the history of post-war Europe. In the immediate aftermath of the war, federalist ideas, drawn from American political experience, were very prevalent in debates about the future European order. Proponents of a federal Europe looked for a decisive act of political will to create new institutions for a European federation, based on a contract or treaty negotiated by the participating governments or a constituent assembly. Because this proved to be utopian, in so far as the establishment of the Council of Europe and the European Coal and Steel Community were not accompanied by the kind of constitutional settlement that characterized earlier federations, the relevance of federal models has been somewhat neglected in writings on integration.

Yet federalism and the experience of federal states offer useful insights into why political authority is shared between different levels of government. Federations are typically associated with heterogeneous societies because they combine the virtues of collective endeavour with local autonomy. Various terms are used to define unions of states – most notably, confederation and federation, or *staatenbund* and *bundesstaat*, to use the German terms. The distinction between a confederation and a federation lies in the degree of sovereignty surrendered. In a confederation the participating states accept the collective discharge of limited functions while maintaining a high degree of autonomy and sovereignty, whereas in a federation there is one sovereign state, and the locus of external sovereignty is at the higher level. Historically, confederations have been stepping stones to federations; the US and Swiss confederations, based on security and defence, became federations, as did the German *Zollverein*, an economic union.[19]

Federal systems of government have a number of common characteristics. First, legislative and administrative powers are constitutionally divided between different levels of government. Second, a bicameral legislature is common, with one house, usually the upper house, representing the interests of the states in the federation. Third, federations tend to have rigid constitutions, which can be modified only by super-majorities, in order to protect the interests of the states. Fourth, judicial review, involving a constitutional court, is critical in solving disputes about powers between the different levels of government.[20]

Although a fully fledged federation may not materialize in Western Europe, federalist analogies are useful in analysing the nature of the Community's political system. 'Neo-federalism' is a useful term for describing the process of integration whereby common institutions are being established by a series of steps, rather than by a single constituent act. The federalist emphasis on the primacy of politics and on the issue of sovereignty draw our attention to the fact that the EC has established institutions of government beyond the nation-state.[21] Federalist principles are part and parcel of debates on institution-building and on the appropriate policy scope of supranational institutions.

The concept of subsidiarity, a federalist concept, is central to the debate on economic and monetary union, the Social Charter and political union. The first formal attempt to define the concept in the context of the European Community is made in the European Parliament's Draft Treaty on European Union, which reads as follows:

> The Union shall only act to carry out those tasks which may be undertaken more effectively in common than by the Member States acting separately, in particualar those whose execution requires action by the Union because their dimension or effects extend beyond national frontiers.[22]

Put simply, the higher tier should assume only functions that cannot be carried out effectively at the lower levels. But as we shall see, there is no simple formula for determining effectiveness. The transfer of policy competence or its sharing owes as much to political bargaining, values, and economic and political interests as it does to abstract formulas. However the emerging debate on subsidiarity within the EC is significant because it demonstrates that after more than thirty years of the Community's existence, the appropriate balance between the policy competences, or areas of responsibility, of the Community and the member states is being openly questioned.

Functionalism/neo-functionalism

What has come to be called neo-functionalism dominated writings on European integration up to the early 1970s and provided the most comprehensive theoretical approach to the subject matter. Neo-functionalism owed a lot to the writings of David Mitrany on functionalism. Mitrany advocated piecemeal co-operation on major social and economic issues among states because he concluded that functional co-operation had been the most successful aspect of the League of Nation. International functional agencies would eventually erode the role of national governments and states. For proponents of functionalism, 'integration is the gradual triumph of the rational and the technocratic over the political'.[23]

Neo-functionalist writers share a concern with the functionalists for the collective pursuit of welfare through inter-state co-operation but regard the process as inherently political. The power of national governments is progressively eroded because

> Political actors in several distinct national settings are persuaded to shift their loyalties, expectations and political activities towards a new and larger centre, whose institutions possess or demand jurisdiction over the pre-existing national states.[24]

But how are national actors persuaded to shift their loyalty? Co-operation on low-key, relatively non-controversial issues generates demands and pressures for co-operation on related policy areas – the inexorable logic of functional spillover. And as the actors involved in the process deal successfully with technical issues, they enhance their capacity to deal with more politically sensitive policy areas. National politicians, officials and interest group élites are gradually socialized by their participation in central institutions and joint decision-making structures. The supranational commission is endowed with a key role in the development of functional co-operation. It represents the common interest and can build-up coalitions with trans-national organized interests to overcome the resistance of national governments to further co-operation. Furthermore, the Commission can create package deals involving side-payments, if necessary, to get agreement to a particular proposal. Lindberg and Scheingold, writing in 1970, portrayed the process of integration as less automatic than that envisaged by Haas or by Lindberg himself in his earlier writings. They accept that spillback, as well as spillover, characterizes integration.[25]

Although neo-functionalism has its limits, which are dealt with below, some of the insights of this literature are applicable to the study of contemporary integration. The neo-functionalists were aware that they were dealing with a complex system of policy-making, the intricacies of which they describe with considerable accuracy. Their analysis of bargaining and negotiations, and of the manner in which issues are raised and dealt with by different networks of national and EC actors, remains apposite. An emphasis on 'rules of the game' and 'norms of behaviour' in policy-making is still relevant. So, too, is their concern with the institutional and decision-making capacity of the Community.

Neo-functionalism has been the subject of much critical appraisal, not least from some of its own proponents. The explanatory power of incremental spillover was called into question because of stagnation within the European Community and apparent limits to the willingness of governments to transfer an ever-widening range of policy responsibilities. The Commission's role as the motor force of integration disappeared. Also, so-called 'low policy' issues were not necessarily less contentious than 'high policy' issues. The expectation that national politicians and officials would transfer their loyalty to central institutions was not fulfilled. Neo-functionalist writers tended to underestimate the importance of the international political and economic environment in creating conditions that were either favourable or unfavourable to integration. Nor did they pay sufficient attention to the domestic dimension of integration.[26]

Intergovernmentalism and domestic politics

Scholars of the realist or traditional school of international relations have always been uneasy with integration by stealth, stressing the role of national governments as the main determinants of the pace of integration. For Hoffman, whose name is the one most associated with this view of integration, national authorities can 'stop or slow down the building of a central political system'.[27] He questioned the willingness of governments to allow technocratic élites to erode their sovereignty. He portrays the role of national governments as gatekeepers between the Community and the national level and emphasizes the importance of the EC in the regeneration of the Western European states after the war.[28] Hoffman's writings draw attention to the blocking power of leaders, such as General de Gaulle, who were attached to the nation-state as the highest manifestation of political order.

Intergovernmentalism was highlighted as a dominant characteristic of EC policy-making in the 1970s. The national dimension or domestic context of European integration received increasing attention in a growing literature on policy-making in the EC. The important role of national governments as participants in the Community's policy process is apparent in this literature. The formal decision-making process in Brussels is but the tip of an iceberg that extends into the national polities. Scholars concluded that the submerged part of the iceberg held many of the secrets that would help illuminate the nature of European integration. Bulmer, in reaction to the monolithic image of national governments portrayed by Hoffman, advocated a domestic politics approach to the study of integration. This approach combined five main assumptions:

1 The national polity is the basic unit in the EC.
2 Each polity has its own social and economic conditions, which shape its interests and concerns.
3 European policy represents only one facet of national policy-making.
4 National governments hold a key position at the junction of national and EC politics.
5 The concept of policy style, borrowed from public policy-making, is a useful tool for analysing national policy styles on EC issues.[29]

This approach focused attention on links between the domestic and EC levels of policy-making. It served to correct the previous concentration on Brussels-based institutions. However, it does not pay sufficient attention to the profusion of links between the Community and the national political and economic systems, on the one hand, and the growth of cross-national networks among the member states, on the other. Nor does it capture the intermingling and intermeshing of the national and Community levels of the policy process and the extent to which European issues have now been absorbed as part and parcel of public policy-making. By contrast, a focus on interdependence does allow this.

Interdependence

This approach serves to highlight one of the main weaknesses of intergovernmentalism – namely, the intensive and extensive nature of collaboration among states in the contemporary international system and the consequent constraints on national governments in an interdependent world. No one government, particularly those in Western Europe that represent small and middle-range states, can control and direct the development of co-operative organizations. In Western Europe there are a multitude of transnational organizations representing economic interests, pressure groups and political parties that have created cross-national links.

From a transnational perspective, collaboration in Western Europe is but a reflection of transnational processes in the contemporary international system and a manifestation of increasing interdependence among advanced market economies. Scholars writing on interdependence highlight the extent to which the growth of international trade, the flow of international capital, the location policies of multinational enterprises and increasing economic specialization have reduced the effective exercise of national sovereignty.[30] The need for inter-state collaboration extends well beyond economic matters to encompass the environment, public health and the problem of crime. Particularly in Western Europe, it is apposite to talk of a 'fourth level of government' based on the growth of political-administrative networks across national boundaries.[31] Few aspects of public policy escape an extra-national dimension today.

During the 1970s, when the study of integration became unfashionable, interdependence took over as the new focus of scholarly endeavour. According to Keohane and Nye, two of the major writers in this field, under conditions of 'complex interdependence', international regimes will emerge to regulate inter-state relations. In the absence of a central authority in the international system, regimes are based on coalitions between governments and involve procedures, rules, norms and institutions for the conduct of inter-state relations.[32] The interdependence literature has given rise to a renewed emphasis on the impact of the international political economy on states.

Differentiated integration

The evolution of European integration has had to face the extra-ordinary diversity of Western Europe: countries of different sizes, with varying historical experiences, political systems, levels of economic development and approaches to economic management search for ways of pursuing their common concerns within the framework of joint institutions. Within the European Community itself, notwithstanding the importance of the core policies, the need to accommodate diversity has been a feature of policy-making and a pervasive theme in the debate about the development of the Community. This debate has given rise to an array of related, though not necessarily coherent, ideas, all falling under the general rubric of 'differentiated integration'. The most important of these are

- Europe à la carte
- two-speed Europe
- graduated integration
- variable geometry
- concentric circles.[33]

Ralf Dahrendorf, in the Jean Monnet Lecture (1979) delivered to the European University Institute in Florence, offered the concept of a Europe 'à la carte' as a means of overcoming institutional failure in the Community and of making progress in new policy areas. Dahrendorf decried the Community orthodoxy that does not allow 'those members of the Community who want to go along with certain policies to do so, and those who are not interested to stay put'.[34] Dahrendorf favoured common policies where there are common interests, but envisaged wide scope for action à la carte.

The notion of a 'two-speed' Europe was first suggested by the German Chancellor Willy Brandt in 1974, and was taken up by Leo Tindemans in the Tindemans Report on European Union in 1975.

Because of economic divergence, Brandt felt that the member states of the Community should be divided into two camps; the first camp would move more speedily towards greater co-operation in economic matters, with members of the second camp eventually participating. The Tindemans Report makes a plea for the development of a common concept of European Union but with varying time-scales for the achievement of agreed objectives, thus enabling states that were able to make progress to go ahead of others. The Community would then provide assistance for the lagging states to catch up.[35] Fears that a 'two-speed' Europe might result in a permanent 'two-tier' Europe gave rise to considerable opposition to the Tindemans formula.

Graduated integration, a German concept, evolved from a major study published in 1984 which examined the range of policy sectors within the Community. The study found that there was considerable differentiation in the harmonization of EC laws, with special provisions for temporary and even permanent derogations for some member states with regard to some laws. The authors argue that 'graduated integration' provides a flexible means of expanding the scope of integration into new policy areas while keeping the core policies intact.[36] The following steps characterize 'graduated integration':

1 EC objectives are set for all member states in relation to the broad goals of integration.
2 There is acceptance that in some cases only a sub-group of countries will adopt measures to achieve these objectives.
3 A series of measures to reduce the socio-economic differences that prevent full participation are agreed upon.[37]

The notion of 'graduated integration' was put forward as a means for the Community to take responsibility for policy problems of interest to a number of member states, given the stagnation of the early 1980s.

The French came up with the idea of 'variable geometry', which was also an attempt to enable the Community to take on additional policy responsibilities, particularly in relation to industrial, technological and energy policy. A group of member states would be free to participate in and develop collaborative projects with the possible participation of non-member states.[38] A Europe of concentric circles, portrayed by the former British Commissioner Christopher Tugendhat, gives structure to the notion of 'variable geometry'. The Community here would be the centre of European collaboration, with other forms of co-operation radiating out from it.[39] The concepts have continued relevance as the EC attempts to achieve EMU, political union and new forms of relationship with non-member states.

ANALYSING INTEGRATION AT THE BEGINNING OF THE 1990s

No one theory or approach to the study of integration can capture the complex interaction of political, economic and social forces that mould inter-state relations in Western Europe. The rich literature on the subject suggests that three levels of analysis are critical to a balanced assessment of integration. These are

- the international environment
- the domestic dimension of integration
- the dynamics of regional organizations.

The literature on interdependence and the international political economy draw attention to the challenge posed to the small and medium-sized states of Western Europe by the international political and economic environment. National autonomy is increasingly constrained by the international character of production, financial markets and technology. The neo-realist school of international politics continues to emphasize the importance of security and defence in international politics.[40] The literature on domestic politics reminds us that states remain powerful economic, political and social actors. It is important to assess the manner in which domestic concerns impinge on integration. Intergovernmental bargains are essential to changes in formal integration. However, we need to go beyond domestic politics because formal integration is built on common institutions that rest on the political systems of the member states but that have an independent dynamic of their own. Here neo-functionalism tells us much about the importance of common institutions and the tendency of functional problems to spill over from one policy area to another.

Federalism deals in the most overt manner with the question of government in advanced integration. Bulmer and Wessels coined the term 'co-operative federalism' to capture the 'pooling' or sharing of sovereignty in the EC. In this system the EC level and the national level share responsibility for problem-solving because 'neither has adequate legal authority and policy instruments to tackle the challenges they meet'.[41] National governments are torn between the need to enlarge EC competences so as to fulfil economic and welfare needs and the desire to maintain autonomy and freedom of action. There is thus a constant tension between pressures towards integration and forces wishing to maintain sovereignty. Although intergovernmental co-operation continues to be an important facet of inter-state relations in Western Europe, the emergence of the EC as the core regional organisation gives integration the upper-hand.

THE MAIN THEMES OF THIS BOOK

In order to explain why there are so many international organizations in Western Europe today and their pattern of membership, it is necessary to place these organizations in their historical context. The tapestry of Western European organizations cannot be understood without reference to the political and economic forces that moulded them in the aftermath of World War II.

Chapter 1 traces the emergence of a myriad organizations in the political, economic and military spheres between 1945 and 1960. By 1955, the contours of defence collaboration were defined and collective defence was consolidated, whereas it took until 1960 for the shape of economic integration to emerge. It becomes clear that changes in the international environment and the preferences of the Western European states themselves moulded the contours of the system that emerged.

Chapter 2 continues the main themes of Chapter 1 by giving a synopsis of how the main organizations have evolved since 1960. The different approaches to the study of integration are used to analyse the dynamics of regional institutions. The main conclusion of this chapter is that the European Community is the core regional organization.

Chapter 3 examines the agenda of economic integration in the 1980s, namely the 1992 programme. During the early years of the decade, the Community was faced with time-consuming and divisive disputes about budgetary matters and the Common Agricultural Policy. The Community's apparent inability to move beyond the initial compact between the member states meant that it risked becoming irrelevant as the member states sought ways of combatting economic stagnation. The 1992 programme emerged as a powerful symbol of renewed vigor and relevance. This chapter highlights the importance of adopting a multi-levelled approach to integration. Profound changes in the international political economy challenged Western Europe's economic competitiveness. A convergence of economic policies around economic liberalism allowed the EC member states to respond to the international challenge. Community institutions, notably the Commission, played a key role in fostering a consensus about the completion of the internal market.

Although the completion of the internal market is primarily a matter of negative integration, common policies or positive integration is also necessary. Chapter 4 examines the array of positive policies, notably research and development, the structural funds and the EC budget, that accompanied the internal market programme. The 1992 programme introduced a new element into the politics of redistribution and led to increases in financial resources for the lesser-developed regions. So-called flanking policies were central to the political bargains that led to the Single European Act. The opening of an intergovernmental conference in December 1990 to negotiate a treaty on economic and monetary union constitutes the economic agenda for the 1990s.

Chapter 5 focuses on the activities of European organizations aimed at protecting the environment and individual rights and establishing social rights for the citizens of the Western European states. This chapter also discusses the legitimacy of the European Community and the democratic deficit – a perceived weakness of political accountability. EC policies on education and in the social domain serve to increase cross-national mobility among students and young workers. These policies complement the 1992 programme and attempt to reverse the traditional migration of European university students towards the United States.

Chapter 6 looks at relations between the European Community and the wider international system. The first part of the chapter highlights the instruments that are available to the Community in the external sphere, notably the external competences of the Rome Treaties and European Political Co-operation. The revolutions in Eastern and Central Europe bring increasing pressures on the EC to work out a new political and security order for the Continent, which entails changes in relations with the two superpowers and the countries of Eastern Europe. The architecture of a 'common European home' is explored.

Chapter 7 moves the level of analysis to the domestic dimension of European integration. This chapter highlights the priorities and interests pursued by individual countries, with particular emphasis on the larger countries. The inclusion of a separate chapter on the member states acknowledges the importance of this level of analysis for a balanced analysis of integration and co-operation.

Chapter **8**, the concluding chapter, draws the strands of the book together. It assesses the prospects for economic, political and security integration and co-operation for Western Europe and the continent as a whole.

NOTES

1 For a brief synopsis of pre-World War II proposals for co-operation, see W. Nicoll and T.C. Salmon, *Understanding the European Communities* (London: Philip Allen, 1990), pp.1–5.

2 Text of the Briand Memorandum can be found in R. Vaughan, *Post-War Integration in Europe* (London: Edward Arnold, 1986), pp.11–12.

3 E.B. Haas, 'The Study of Regional Integration: Reflections on the Joys and Anguish of Pretheoryizing', in L.N. Lindberg and S.A. Scheingold (eds), *Regional Integration: Theory and Research* (Cambridge, Mass: Harvard University Press, 1971), p.6.

4 K. Deutsch, *The Analysis of International Relations* (Englewood Cliffs, N.J.: Prentice-Hall), 1971, p.158.

5 Haas, op. cit., p.6.

6 W. Wallace, *The Transformation of Western Europe* (London: Frances Pinter, 1990), p.54.

7 Preamble, Single European Act, EC Bulletin, Supplement 2/86.

8 J. Pelkmans, 'Economic theories of integration revisited', *Journal of Common Market Studies*, 1980, vol.18, pp.333–54.

9 P. Robson, *The Economics of International Integration* (London: Allen and Unwin, 3rd ed., 1989), pp.1–4.

10 J. Pinder, 'Positive integration and negative integration: some problems of economic union in the EC', in M. Hodges (ed.)., *European Integration* (Harmondsworth, Middlesex: Penguin, 1970), pp.124–50.

11 B. Balassa *The Theory of Economic Integration* (London: Allen and Unwin, 1962).

12 J. Pinder, 'Democracy and integration', IPSA Research Committee on European Unification, *Newsletter*, 1, 1990.

13 K. Deutsch, *Political Community and the North Atlantic Area* (Princeton, N.J.: Princeton University Press, 1957).

14 This categorization is taken from R.S. Jordan and W J. Feld, *Europe in the Balance* (London: Faber & Faber, 1986), p.91. The different categories are elaborated on by J.S. Nye, *Peace in Parts: Integration and Conflict in Regional Organization* (New York: University Press of America, 1987), pp.21–54.

15 The distinction between political will and political capacity is developed by D.J. Puchala, *Fiscal Harmonizaton in the European Communities* (London: Frances Pinter, 1984), pp.4–9.

16 K.W. Deutsch, 'Attaining and Maintaining Integration', in M. Hodges (ed.), op. cit., pp.108–23.
17 E.B. Haas, *The Obsolescence of Regional Integration Theory*, Research Series, Institute of International Studies, paper no. 25, Berkeley, California, 1975.
18 N. Anderen, 'Nordic integration: aspects and problems', *Co-operation and Conflict*, 1967, vol.2, p.17.
19 M. Forsyth, *Unions of States* (Leicester: Leicester University Press, 1981).
20 D.P. Kommers, 'Federalism and European integration: a commentary', in M. Cappelletti, M. Seccombe and J. Weiler (eds), *Integration Through Law: A Political, Legal and Economic Overview* (Berlin: Walter de Gruyter, 1986), pp.605–16.
21 J. Pinder op. cit., 1990.
22 Article 12, EP Draft Treaty on European Union, 1984.
23 C. Pentland, 'Political theories of European integration: between science and ideology', in D. Lasok and P. Soldatos (eds), *The European Communities in Action* (Brussels: Bruylant, 1981), p.551.
24 E.B. Haas, *The Uniting of Europe: Political, Social, and Economic Forces, 1950-1957* (Stanford, California: Stanford University Press, 1958), p.16.
25 L.N. Lindberg and S.A. Scheingold, *Europe's Would-Be Polity*, (Englewood Cliffs, N.J.: Prentice-Hall, 1970), p.137.
26 S. George, *Politics and Policy in the European Community* (Oxford: Clarendon Press, 1985), pp.21–4.
27 S. Hoffman, 'Obstinate or obsolete: the fate of the nation state and the case of Western Europe', *Daedalus*, 1966, vol.95, pp.862–915, and S. Hoffman, 'Reflections on the nation state in Western Europe Today' *Journal of Common Market Studies*, 1982, vol.21, p.30.
28 Ibid.
29 S. Bulmer, 'Domestic politics and European Community policy-making', *Journal of Common Market Studies*, 1983, vol.21, pp.349–63.
30 H. Sprout and M. Sprout, 'Tribal Sovereignty vs. Interdependence' in M. Smith, R. Little and M. Shackleton (eds), *Perspectives on World Politics* (London: Croom Helm, 1981), pp.249–51.
31 M. Egeberg, 'The Fourth level of government: on the standardization of public policy within international regimes', *Scandinavian Political Studies*, 1980, vol.3, pp.135–48.
32 R.O. Keohane and J.S. Nye, *Power and Interdependence: World Politics in Transition* (Boston: Little, Brown, 1977).
33 H. Wallace with A. Ridley, *Europe: The Challenge of Diversity* Chatham House Paper, no. 29 London, 1985.
34 R. Dahrendorf, 'A Third Europe', Jean Monnet Lecture, EUI, Florence, 1979.
35 Report on European Union, the Tindemans Report, EC Bulletin, Supplement 1/76.
36 For a summary of the findings of the study see B. Langeheine and U. Weinstock, 'Graduated integration: a modest path towards progress', *Journal of Common Market Studies*, 1985, vol.23, pp.185–97.

37 Wallace and Ridley, op. cit., pp.40–1.
38 Ibid, pp.36–7.
39 C. Tugendhat, 'How to get Europe moving again', *International Affairs*, 1985, vol.61, pp.421–9.
40 The best-known theorist on neo-realism is K. Waltz, author of *Theory of International Politics* (Reading, Mass., 1979).
41 S. Bulmer and W. Wessels, *The European Council* (London: Macmillan, 1987), p.10.

TOPICS FOR DISCUSSION

1 Which approach to the study of integration offers the best insights to integration in the 1990s?
2 What is the difference between integration and intergovernmental co-operation?
3 What is meant by supranationalism?
4 Discuss different forms of differentiated integration.

FURTHER READING

There is an extensive literature on integration as a political, economic and social phenomenon. The following titles are a small selection of readings that will allow the student to delve deeper into the subject.

Andern, N. (1967) 'Nordic integration: aspects and problems', *Co-operation and Conflict*, vol.2, pp.1–25.

Bulmer, S. (1983) 'Domestic politics and EC policy-making', *Journal of Common Market Studies*, 1983, vol.21, pp.350–63.

Forsyth, M. *Unions of States*, Leicester; Leicester University Press, 1981. A historical analysis of the concept of unions between states.

Hoffman, S. 'Obstinate or obsolete: the fate of the nation state and the case of Western Europe', *Daedalus*, 1966, vol.95, pp.862–915. The classic statement of intergovernmentalism. See Hoffman's 1989 article cited in Chapter 2.

Nye, J.S. *Peace In Parts: Integration and Conflict in Regional Organization*, New York: University Press of America, 1987, 2nd ed. This volume examines economic and political integration and discusses the utility of different approaches to the study of integration.

Pentland, C. 'Political theories of European integration: between science and ideology', in D. Lasok and P. Soldatos (eds), *The European Communities in Action*, Brussels: Bruylant, 1981. Pentland has written widely on integration theory. This chapter gives a useful overview of integration theory at the end of the 1970s.

Pryce R. *The Dynamics of European integration*, London: Croom Helm, 1987. The first chapter of this book provides a framework for the analysis of formal integration.

Wallace H. with Ridley A. *Europe: the Challenge of Diversity*, London:

Chatham House Paper, no. 29, 1985. An overview of differentiated integration.

Wallace W. (ed.) *The Dynamics of European Integration*, London: Frances Pinter, 1990. This book is better suited to the specialist undergraduate or graduate student. However, the first and final chapters give useful insights into the dynamics of integration at the end of the 1980s.

Chapter 1

A rich tapestry of organizations

By 1945, beyond the joy and frenzy of liberation, beyond the panic of defeat and conquest, much of the continent shared a grim uniformity. Europe, and above all, central and eastern Europe, was a land laid waste.[1]

Although the European idea has its roots in European political discourse, it was not until the aftermath of World War II that serious thought was given to the construction of a 'permanent regime of joint responsibility' for the management of inter-state relations, as suggested by Aristide Briand to the League of Nations in 1930. The shape of the Western European regional system that evolved between 1945 and 1960 was moulded by the priorities of the superpowers, the need to reach an accommodation on the 'German Question', and the imperatives of economic, social and political reconstruction. The states of Western Europe had strongly held but differing views about the kind of regional organizations they were willing to endorse. The tension between sovereignty and integration, still characteristic of European integration, was apparent in the early years of the post-war era. For Western Europe, however, there could be no return to the world before the war. There was a perceived need among West European political élites to establish formal institutions to manage inter-state relations. This chapter analyses the challenges facing Western Europe after the war, in the light of the new strategic landscape. These challenges were to establish a security system that could balance growing Soviet power, to deal with demands for some form of European unity and to achieve economic reconstruction.

THE LEGACY OF THE WAR

World War II devastated both the victors and the vanquished. There was an urgent need to reconstruct basic infrastructure and housing, to transform the economies from a war footing to peacetime, to provide sufficient food to feed a war-weary population, to deal with wartime refugees and to re-establish political systems in those states where a complete or near-complete breakdown had occurred. The task of reconstruction took place against the emergence of an international system dominated by two superpowers, the United States and the Soviet Union. After World War I, the United States' retreat to 'Fortress America' and a policy of quasi-isolationism, together with Stalin's preoccupation with creating a state controlled economy in the USSR, served to disguise the extent to which European dominance of the international state system was weakening. Although fragile, the European state system, which was based on a delicate balance of power, did not collapse until World War II.

After 1945, Europe's weakness could not be hidden; its future was dominated by relations with and between the superpowers. By the end of the war, a new strategic landscape, characterized by a high degree of bi-polarity, was in place.[2] The United States was both a military and an economic superpower, whereas Soviet power was based entirely on its awesome military strength. After the war, the United States set out to establish a system of international economic management based on a multilateral system of free trade. American policy-makers were convinced that a liberal economic system would enhance economic prosperity and political stability. The International Monetary Fund (IMF), the International Bank for Reconstruction and Development (World Bank) and the General Agreement on Tariffs and Trade (GATT) provided the global institutions for the post-war capitalist economic system. Fear of communism led the US to conclude a series of multilateral defence arrangements, a 'Pax Americana', with states throughout the world. The competitive nature of relations between the two superpowers, reinforced by a deep ideological conflict, ensured that there would be no retreat to 'Fortress America' after the war.

The Soviet Union, although less powerful than the United States, made considerable strategic gains as a result of the war, and the Red Army was to remain the most powerful military establishment on the European continent. Stalin's desire to provide the

Soviet Union with a *cordon sanitaire* around its borders led him to dominate those states where the Red Army held sway in 1945 by engineering Communist control in one Eastern European state after another. Eastern Europe was locked into a Soviet sphere of influence. The USSR exercised its hegemony by establishing political systems controlled by Communist Parties and by creating command economies based on state ownership, modelled on the Soviet system. A related Soviet goal was to isolate the East European states from economic interaction with the Western World. The USSR refused to join the multilateral economic institutions that grew up after the war and prevented its satellites from doing so. A rival socialist economic system based on the Council for Mutual Economic Assistance (COMECON), was set up in 1949.[3]

Between 1945 and 1947, the wartime alliance between the United States, Britain and the Soviet Union gradually gave way to increasing hostility and suspicion which crystallized into the cold war. Europe became a continent of two halves. Germany, at the centre of this divide, represented the most delicate challenge facing the post-war order. Because Germany had gone to war against its neighbours twice in less than thirty years, occupying much of Europe, the need to contain German militarism loomed large in the debate about the post-war order. After its defeat, Germany was divided initially into four zones of occupation under American, Soviet, British and French control.

In 1949, as relations between the West and its wartime ally, the USSR, continued to deteriorate, two German states were constituted: the Federal Republic of Germany (FRG), consisting of the American, British and French zones, and the German Democratic Republic (GDR), made up of the remaining territory, under Soviet control. Berlin, at the centre of the GDR, was controlled under separate arrangements by the four occupying powers. The partition of Germany was the centrepiece of the European post-war order. After 1949, the incorporation of the FRG into the emerging Western European order became a major priority for the United States and France.

During World War II there had been much debate among the fighters of the Resistance movements about Europe's future political order. The model favoured by many in the movements was a 'United States of Europe'. The following attitudes dominated their writings:

- Worship of the state and extreme nationalism was the primary source of strife in Europe.
- The weakness of the intergovernmental League of Nations led many of the Resistance fighters to favour supranational federal institutions.
- A federal Europe was the best solution to the German Question.
- Economic integration was justified on the basis of the small size of individual European states.
- A federal Europe would enable the European states to resist domination by the Soviet Union and the United States.[4]

Although the utopian vision of the Resistance fighters did not prevail, the ideal of a united Europe had a powerful emotive appeal in the immediate post-war era. Nationalism was seen as a powerful but irrational and dangerous ideology which had contributed to the rise of fascism.

Western European states had to respond to the multiple challenges of fashioning a new security order that could deal with the German Question and growing East-West conflict, of establishing structures to foster economic recovery, and of responding to the trauma of the war by creating new institutions to manage inter-state relations. The system was fashioned by a number of key states. The United States, as the Western superpower, spurred on by its policy of containment *vis-à-vis* the Soviet Union, largely determined the nature of the security regime and influenced, but did not fashion, the political/economic institutions. Britain and France became the key Western European states in the development of the new order. The Federal Republic of Germany was the subject of much of the post-war system-building, but it was also a participant from 1949 onwards. The smaller states had to work out their responses to proposals and policy designs emanating from these key states.

THE SECURITY DILEMMA

The task of assuring their own defence and territorial integrity led the states of Western Europe into a highly institutionalized and multilateral defence system designed to counterbalance the military might of the USSR. Yet in the immediate post-war years, fear of German militarism was rampant. The Dunkirk Treaty, signed by France and Britain in 1947, cited the German threat as its *raison d'être*. In time, anxiety about Soviet military power would replace fears of Germany and would impel the states of Western Europe to accept German rearmament. A keenly fought civil war in Greece led to fears of a communist take-over of that country. Britain, traditionally the policeman of the Mediterranean, informed the US that it could not come to the aid of the Greek government. The US responded with what is known as the 'Truman Doctrine', a pledge by President Truman of American aid for 'free peoples who are resisting attempted subjugation by armed minorities or outside pressures'.[5] The United States was willing to accept global responsibilities in its effort to contain communism and its rival superpower.

In 1948 a series of events strengthened the perception of a Soviet threat to Western Europe. A *coup* in Prague ended a multi-party system as Czechoslovakia fell under the yoke of communism. In July 1948, the Soviet Union began the Berlin blockade by refusing West Berlin supplies of food, energy and other necessities. The blockade lasted from July 1948 to May 1949. Rather than respond by force, and thereby increase the possibility of major conflict, the US and Britain kept Berlin supplied from the air until the USSR finally abandoned the blockade. Fear of communist subversion in France and Italy was rife during this period because both had sizeable communist parties and trade unions with strong links to Moscow.[6]

The Western European states first resorted to regional multilateral defence arrangements and later to an integrated defence structure linked to and dependent upon the United States. Although the Brussels Treaty Organization (BTO), established in 1948 between France, Britain, and The Netherlands, Belgium and Luxemburg (Benelux states), identified Germany as a potential aggressor, it was also a response to the Soviet threat. The Western European states, faced with the size of the Red Army (175 divisions), felt the need for a US involvement in their defence.[7] In 1949 the US signed the North Atlantic Treaty with the Brussels Treaty states, Canada, Italy, Portugal, and three Scandinavian states (Denmark, Norway and Iceland). Greece and Turkey joined in 1952, followed by the Federal Republic in 1955 and Spain in 1982. Although France withdrew from the integrated command in 1965, it remains a member of the Atlantic Alliance. A number of Western European states are outside the system of collective defence; these are Switzerland, Sweden, Austria, Finland and Ireland.[8]

When discussions began on the establishment of NATO in 1948, Sweden, in an attempt to keep all of Scandinavia outside the Atlantic defence system, proposed a Defence Union of Denmark, Norway and

Sweden. However, the three countries had very different views of their security interests. Denmark and Norway opted for membership of NATO. A delicate Nordic balance was struck between the two members of NATO, and the neutrals – Sweden and Finland. Sweden opted for its traditional policy of neutrality, whereas Finland's relationship with its neighbour, the Soviet Union, was regulated by the 1948 Treaty of Friendship.[9]

The question of German rearmament came to the fore with the onset of the Korean War in 1950. Given increasing commitments in Asia, the US was determined to foster the rearming of West Germany as a contribution to the defence of Western Europe. For its neighbours, ever fearful of a resurgent Germany, the imperative was to find a means of acquiescing to the demands of the United States while controlling a rearmed Germany. The French proposed a solution modelled on the European Coal and Steel Community (ECSC) (discussed below) of establishing a European Defence Community (EDC); the Pleven Plan in which German contingents would form part of a European army within NATO. The EDC Treaty was signed in May 1952 by the six states that had participated in the European Coal and Steel Community. As a corollary to the EDC, a companion European Political Community (EPC) Treaty was drafted some six months after the EDC Treaty. In 1954, the French National Assembly rejected the EDC on a procedural vote because of communist and Gaullist opposition. The international environment following the death of Stalin in 1953 was less conducive to bold initiatives such as the EDC and the EPC which implied the establishment of federal institutions and an advanced level of political integration.[10]

The rearming of Germany was accomplished by the reorganization of the Brussels Treaty Organization (BTO) into the Western European Union (WEU) in 1954. It made provision for a West German army and for that nation's membership of NATO in 1955. After the failure of the EDC, Britain, which had refused to become part of a European defence organization with a supranational character, took the lead in establishing the WEU. The latter was not envisaged as a European defence arrangement in its own right; it was simply a device to integrate the Federal Republic of Germany into NATO and, by specific measures, to control German rearmament. By 1955, Western Europe's security order was in place. The challenge of European unity remained.

A UNITED EUROPE

In 1947 a variety of groups committed to European union formed the 'International Committee of the Movements for European Unity,' with the intention of convening a Congress of Europe. This was held at The Hague in 1948 under the chairmanship of Winston Churchill. The resolutions of the Hague Congress were a mixture of idealism and rhetoric. Among the most important claims and demands were

- the duty of the nations of Europe to create an economic and political union
- that European nations must transfer and merge some portion of their sovereign rights
- the convening of a European assembly
- the drafting of a charter of human rights
- the establishment of a court of justice
- the integration of Germany into a united or federated Europe.[11]

The French Foreign Minister, Georges Bidault, suggested that the Advisory Council of the BTO should study the possibility of setting up a European assembly among its member states and other states wishing to take part. This led to the Council of Europe.

Tension emerged in the Committee between the French and Benelux representatives, on the one hand, and Britain, on the other, about the role and powers of a European assembly. Britain was opposed to all forms of supranational integration and the transfer of sovereignty. It agreed to the establishment of a European assembly, provided that there was a controlling committee of ministers representing state interests. The Statutes of the Council of Europe were signed in May 1949 by the BTO states and by Ireland, Norway, Sweden and Denmark. The debate on the powers of the Council's institutions was the first indication of a major divergence between Britain and the continental Western European states about the transfer of powers to regional institutions. Britain favoured traditional intergovernmental arrangements, whereas the others were prepared to go beyond the existing state-system to embrace integration.[12]

The aim of the Council, as laid down in Article 1 of its Statutes, is to 'achieve a greater unity between its members' so as to safeguard Europe's common heritage.[13] From the outset, the Council of Europe has been identified with promoting the common values of Western

European democracy, especially the rule of law. The aim of the Council is achieved by 'discussion of questions of common concern and by agreements and common action in economic, social, cultural, scientific, legal and administrative matter', according to Article 1 (b) of the Statutes.[14] Apart from defence policy, the Council has a very wide policy domain. The range of the policy instruments at its disposal remain, however, very limited; it relies on conventions or intergovernmental agreements with no independent law-making power. The Council of Europe corresponds to Mitrany's functionalist approach (see p.9)

In order to meet the requirements of the two alternative views about its development, the Council has two main institutions: the Committee of Ministers, to represent the member states, and the Consultative Assembly, to represent the national parliaments. The Committee of Ministers is the central organ of the Council, with responsibility for drafting conventions and agreements among the member states under Article 15 of the Statutes. The Committee also makes unanimous recommendations and asks member governments to report back on actions taken. It makes resolutions on the internal workings of the Council and issues declarations on major issues. Eighteen Specialized Conferences of Ministers meet in an intergovernmental structure to discuss issues of mutual concern. Senior diplomats accredited to the Council take care of routine matters, and there is a small secretariat in Strasbourg. The Assembly, with 177 members, meets for not more than one month each year; it has a largely consultative role, although it has the power both to issue recommendations to the Committee of Ministers and to pass resolutions.[15] With such restricted jurisdiction, the Council of Europe was clearly not equipped to become the powerhouse of a United Europe.

ECONOMIC CO-OPERATION: LITTLE EUROPE AND THE GREAT DIVIDE

The task of economic construction after World War II was formidable. Political consensus required policies of modernization, industrialization, employment creation and increased trade.[16] By 1947, expansionist policies had led to a severe dollar deficit because the states of Western Europe did not have sufficient dollars to pay for the imports of the capital goods they needed for recovery and reconstruction, at a time when the United States was the chief source of these goods. Added to the dollar deficit, there was a shortage of food in Europe and a widespread fear of social upheaval, fuelled by the strength of the Communist Parties and trade unions in Italy and France. Although recent historical analysis suggests that fears of social and political unheaval were exaggerated, such fears played an important role in shaping the US response to developments in Europe.[17]

In 1947, the US Secretary of State, George Marshall, visited Europe to get a first-hand view of the economic crisis. On his return to the United States, the Secretary of State set out in an address at Harvard University the main lines of American policy towards the economic reconstruction of Europe. The following extract from his speech shows a US commitment to significant financial transfers to Europe:

> The truth of the matter is that Europe's requirements for the next three or four years of food and other essential products – principally from America – are so much greater than her present ability to pay that she must have substantial additional help or face economic, social, and political deterioration of a very grave character.[18]

The United States was prepared to offer Europe long-term aid only if the Europeans themselves created mechanisms to allocate any grant-aid in a co-operative manner. For Marshall, it would not be fitting for the US to 'draw up unilaterally a programme designed to place Europe on its feet economically. This is the business of the Europeans'.[19] Although George Marshall claimed that it was the 'business of the Europeans' to devise structures to administer US aid, the Americans had clear ideas about European economic reconstruction. Within the US administration, many officials advocated economic integration and customs unions as a means to greater economic efficiency and growth. And economic integration was viewed as a precursor of political integration.[20]

The Europeans responded to the US initiative by establishing a permanent organization to distribute American aid, known as the Marshall Plan, or the European Recovery Programme (ERP). The Organization of European Economic Co-operation (OEEC) came into being following the signing of a Convention in April 1948 by sixteen countries and representatives of the occupying forces in Germany. Although the Americans had not specified that Marshall Plan aid was directed only towards Western Europe, there was little likelihood that the Soviet Union would have participated in the co-operative distribution of the ERP monies or that it would have allowed its satellites to do so. For the first four years of its existence, the OEEC acted as a consultative body for the distribution of Marshall Plan aid; a total of $12.5 thousand million in grants flowed into Western Europe during the four years of the programme.[21] The US wanted the OEEC to develop beyond the administration of ERP monies to become the nucleus of economic integration. This it never did.

There was much discussion and a myriad proposals about liberalizing trade and payments among the member states. In 1950 the OEEC states agreed to the establishment of a European Payments Union (EPU) to replace the many bilateral payments agreements existing at the time. The EPU was assisted by a capital fund provided by the United States and operated on the basis of a clearing mechanism for payments among the states in the Union. The multilateralization of payments through the EPU facilitated an expansion of trade. Other proposals for limited economic integration came into being. The Stikker Plan, named after the Dutch Foreign Minister who championed it, favoured the creation of a common market in selected industries. A French plan for integration in the transport field followed, as did a proposal for a 'green pool' to market agricultural products. None of these plans came to fruition, in contrast to the success of a proposal to merge the coal and steel production of France and Germany.[22]

Little Europe: the 'inner Six'

For France, in the years immediately after the war, a major policy priority was to gain access to the coal, coke and steel resources of the Ruhr for its modernization plans. By 1949 France had to devise new ways of structuring its relationship with the newly constituted Federal Republic of Germany. In May 1950, Robert Schuman, the French Foreign Minister, proposed the creation of a European 'Coal and Steel Community', to provide a joint authority for the management of German and French coal and steel production. The Schuman Plan was based on a blueprint devised by Jean Monnet in the French Planning Commissariat and revised in the French Foreign Ministry. In October 1950, the American Secretary of State, Dean Acheson, told a meeting of American ambassadors in Europe that the 'key to progress towards integration is in French hands'.[23]

Schuman announced that the proposed authority would be open to membership of other European countries and would be 'the first concrete foundation for a European federation which is so indispensable for the preservation of peace'.[24] Thus limited sectoral integration was linked to a wider political concern with European unity. From the outset, the proposed European Coal and Steel Community (ECSC) was more than simply a functionalist organization *à la* Mitrany. It was driven by the powerful political impulse of providing a Western European shelter for the emergence of the West German state. For the Chancellor of West Germany, Konrad Adenauer, the Schuman plan offered a golden opportunity for Germany's rehabilitation into the family of Western European states. The three Benelux states and Italy also indicated their willingness to participate in negotiations based on the Schuman Plan. Britain, however, refused to accept the notion of a supranational organization and the diminution of sovereignty it implied. Its decision not to participate in the ECSC negotiations meant that France became the pacesetter in European integration and the Franco-German entente became the core relationship in the development of the EC. The signing of the Paris Treaty creating the European Coal and Steel Community in 1951 was the beginning of sectoral integration involving a restricted number of states. The Paris Treaty made provision for the creation of a common market for coal and steel over a five-year transitional period. The ECSC was accompanied by the establishment of strong institutions to manage the operation of the common market.

The new community had four institutions: the High Authority, the Council of Ministers, the Court of Justice and the Common Assembly. The High Authority was independent of the member states; it had law-making powers in a wide range of matters to do with the common market. The Paris Treaty explicitly mentions the 'supranational character of its duties'.[25] A Council of Ministers, to represent the interests of the member states, was included because the smaller states feared the power of the High Authority. The Common Assembly, with delegated members from the national parliaments, had a consultative role in law-making with a supervisory role *vis-à-vis* the High Authority. The Court of Justice acted as the judicial arm of the ECSC. The Common Assembly and the Court of Justice were merged with the equivalent institutions when the EEC and Euratom were created in 1958, whereas the High Authority and the Council retained a separate existence until a 1967 Treaty led to their merger with the Commission and the Council established by the 1958 Rome Treaties.

The institutional blueprint of the ECSC included a mixture of supranational or federal-like institutions – the Commission, the Assembly and the Court of Justice – and a traditional inter-governmental organ – the Council of Ministers. Strong supranational institutions were to constitute one of the unique features of the EC and formed a central part of the neo-functionalist approach to integration. The ECSC combined two central features of neo-functionalism, namely sectoral integration with the possibility of spillover and a supranational agency, the High Authority, to mould and lead the process.

The failure of the EDC and the EPC in 1954 did not herald the end of integration based on the 'inner Six' or 'little Europe'. In June 1955, a conference at Messina began the task of preparing further integration among this group of states. A variety of plans were on the table: a Monnet plan to bring nuclear energy under the auspices of the High Authority, Benelux plans for a customs union, and a German plan for wider economic co-operation. The three Benelux states had already been operating a mini-customs union since 1948. The Conference agreed to set up a committee under the chairmanship of Paul-Henri Spaak, the Belgian Foreign Minister, to examine the proposals.[26]

The Spaak Committee proceeded with its deliberations during 1956 on plans for both economic integration and nuclear energy. Its final report became the basis of an intergovernmental confer-ence to draft two treaties setting up a European Atomic Energy Community (Euratom) and the European Economic Community (EEC). The former was considered the more important commu-nity during the drafting stage. Britain was associated with the early work of the Spaak Committee, but it withdrew its repre-sentative because it was unwilling to consider a customs union, which would have meant an end to the system of Commonwealth preferences.[27]

The EEC and Euratom, which came into being in 1958, together with the ECSC formed the nucleus of the European communities. The establishment of a common market with broad economic policies was the central objective of the EEC. The bulk of the Rome Treaty is thus concerned with the creation of a customs union and the common market, involving the free movement of goods, services, capital and people. The choice of a customs union owes much to the expansion of trade between the countries that ultimately joined the EEC during the 1950s.

The Rome Treaty made provision for a number of common policies, particularly in relation to agriculture and transport. The inclusion of agriculture was part of the underlying bargain of the Treaty: France was willing to face German competition in the industrial arena provided there was a protected market for agricultural products. France also insisted, despite German opposition, that special provision be made in the Treaty for its overseas territories. The social aspects of establishing a common market received attention in the form of a European Social Fund and matters relating to equality and workers' rights. Although the Treaty is usually portrayed as a *laissez-faire* document, it included a policy on competition to regulate the market and allowed for state aid in lesser-developed parts of the Community. All in all, the Rome Treaty provided a framework for the early stages of economic integration but left important grey areas for future negotiations.[28]

The 'Great Divide': the Maudling Talks and EFTA

While the 'inner Six' were preparing for the next stage of integration, the Secretary-General of the OEEC, René Sergent, in an effort to avoid an economic divide in Western Europe, suggested that a mechanism should be found to allow for free trade between the states of the emerging common market and the wider membership of the OEEC. With the support of the United Kingdom, a decision was taken to set up a committee to investigate the possibility of a European free trade area. From the outset, the states that were unwilling or unable to participate in the integrationist efforts of the 'inner Six' were forced into reacting to their efforts. Negotiations on the free trade area, known as the Maudling Talks, took place between 1957 and 1959. President de Gaulle, when he assumed power in France, in 1958, supported the customs union and common market but opposed the British plans for a wider free trade association. British and Scandinavian officials anticipated that the FRG and The Netherlands might break away from the 'inner Six'. Although the Federal Republic was sympathetic to the notion of the free trade area, for political reasons it was unwilling to side with Britain against France. A trade divide was inevitable. With the failure of the free trade talks, the United States proposed the reorganization of the OEEC to give it an Atlantic dimension aimed at co-ordinating economic policies and development co-operation with the Third World. The OEEC was reconstituted as the Organization of Economic Co-operation and Development (OECD) in 1960. The OECD, with twenty-four members, is representative of the industrialized world.

As a result of the breakdown of the OEEC talks, seven of the non-EC member states began talks on a limited free trade area. This culminated in the establishment, in 1960, of the European Free Trade Association (EFTA), involving Austria, Britain, Denmark, Norway, Portugal, Sweden, and Switzerland. The Stockholm Convention, which set out the method of achieving a free trade area and its institutional structure, was a very different document from the Rome Treaty. In tone and content it concentrated on economic integration of a very limited kind. There was no underlying political ambition to go beyond a free trade area, nor any link established between economic integration and political integration. EFTA represented a 'minimalist' or purely intergovernmental approach to inter-state relations.[29]

Not unexpectedly, given the attitudes of the participating states to intergovernmental co-operation, EFTA was provided with a very light institutional framework. Provision was made for a 'Council' and 'such other organs as the Council may set up'.[30] Each member state has one representative on the Council with one vote. Unanimity is required for all Council decisions and recommendations, except in a limited number of cases when majority voting is possible. The EFTA model of integration differs fundamentally from the Monnet or EC method of integration both in institutional structure and in policy scope.

MINI-EUROPE

No review of integration and co-operation in Western Europe is complete without mentioning the Benelux and Nordic co-operation. The Benelux is an important sub-system in the European Community involving states that are committed to advanced forms of political and economic integration. Nordic co-operation is composed mainly of states that have traditionally favoured intergovernmental co-operation rather than integration that might transcend the nation-state.

The Benelux

Economic co-operation involving the three adjacent countries of Belgium, The Netherlands and Luxemburg (Benelux) was in many ways a precursor or model for economic integration among the 'inner Six'. In 1922, Belgium and Luxemburg signed an Economic Union Treaty. During the war, in 1943 and 1944, this was expanded to include The Netherlands, when the governments-in-exile of all three countries signed a monetary agreement and a customs convention. Further co-operation, such as a liberalization of capital movements and a common commercial policy, was codified by the Economic Union Treaty, signed in 1958 after the Rome Treaty came into force. The Benelux states form an important coalition of like-minded states within the Community.

Nordic co-operation

The Nordic states form a distinct geographical entity on the periphery of the European continent. The Scandinavian countries are small to medium-sized, with a strong welfare-state tradition, a political culture that values consensus and a highly deliberative system of public policy-making. Ethnic and linguistic ties give Nordic co-operation a strong normative value. Nordic co-operation has a long history. With the failure of talks on defence, (see p.27) the Nordic countries began to concentrate on co-operation in the economic sphere. In 1948 Denmark, Iceland, Norway and Sweden formed the Joint Nordic Committee for Economic Co-operation. This was followed by the creation, in 1951, of the Nordic Council, a parliamentary institution. Finland joined Norway, Sweden, Denmark and Iceland as a member in 1956.[31]

During the 1950s, the creation of a customs union dominated debate within the Nordic Council. Wider developments in Europe tended to overshadow Nordic consideration of economic integration. The decision by the 'inner Six' to create a common market with a common external tariff towards non-member countries had profound implications for other European states. As talks within the OEEC on the creation of a European-wide free trade area faltered, the Scandinavian states chose the EFTA option. The failure of both the Defence Union and the common market meant that Nordic co-operation would have to find a different and more limited focus.

Figure 1.1 Western European developments, 1945–60

Year	Military	Political	Economic
1946		Churchill 'a kind of United States of Europe'	UN Economic Commission Europe
1947	Truman Doctrine Dunkirk Treaty		Marshall Plan
1948	Brussels Treaty Organization Berlin blockade	Hague Congress	OEEC
1949	NATO	Council of Europe	
1950	Pleven Plan	Franco-German *rapproachement*	Schuman Plan
1951		Nordic Council	
1952	EDC Treaty	Political Community Treaty	ECSC
1953			
1954	EDC Treaty rejected – WEU established		
1955	FRG joins NATO		Messina Conference
1956			
1957			Maudling Talks Rome Treaties
1958			EEC/EURATOM
1959			Failure of Maudling Talks
1960			EFTA

Developments in the wider European setting continued to influence Nordic co-operation. When Denmark and Norway decided, in 1961, to follow Britain with an application to join the EEC, there were fears about the future of Nordic co-operation. This led in 1962 to the Nordic Treaty of Co-operation between Denmark, Finland, Iceland, Norway and Sweden. The Helsinki Agreement, which codified Nordic co-operation in an international agreement was not a treaty. A Norwegian member of the Nordic Council at the time said:

It is not a treaty which formally and juridically creates any new duties or rights for those who have signed it . . . It does not create new binding treaty rights. But it gives an organised expression of the desire for broad and genuine future co-operation, and is morally binding like any declaration of this type.[32]

The Agreement specified a wide range of matters for potential co-operation; provision was made for co-operation in cultural, judicial, social and economic affairs, in addition to transport and communications. Since the signing of the Helsinki Agreement, the scope of Nordic co-operation has expanded to include environmental questions, cultural co-operation and regional policy.[33]

THE FORMATION OF A REGIONAL SYSTEM

So, with all of these initiatives, between 1949 and 1960 a rich tapestry of organizations was woven in Western Europe, regulating inter-state relations in the political, economic, security and social domains. (See Figure 1.1.) The impulse for institution-building was based on the need to construct a Western European order in the atmosphere of the cold war, compounded by problems of economic and political reconstruction. The system was fashioned by a combination of internal political and economic factors in Western Europe itself and the bi-polar nature of the international system after World War II. The variety of organizations that emerged between 1945 and 1960 owed much to the complexity of the problems facing individual Western European states and their approach to the management of

Figure 1.2 The Western European regional system

Political/Military
North Atlantic Treaty Organization
Euro-group
European Independent Programme Group
Western European Union
Franco-German Defence Council
Bilateral Defence Co-operation

Political/Economic
Council of Europe
European Community
European Free Trade Association
Benelux Economic Union
Norden

Figure 1.3 Membership of European organizations

	EC	CE	EFTA	NC	WEU	NATO	OECD	G7
'Inner Six'								
Belgium	X	X	–	–	X	X	X	–
France	X	X	–	–	X	S	X	X
Germany (FR)	X	1951	–	–	X	1955	X	X
Luxemburg	X	X	–	–	X	X	X	–
Netherlands	X	X	–	–	X	X	X	–
Italy	X	X	–	–	X	X	X	X
'First Enlargement'								
Denmark	1973	X	(F)	X	–	X	X	–
Ireland	1973	X	–	–	–	–	X	–
UK	1973	X	(F)	–	X	X	X	X
'Second Enlargement'								
Greece	1981	X	–	–	–	1952	X	–
Spain	1986	X	–	–	1990	1982	X	–
Portugal	1986	1976	(F)	–	1990	X	X	–
'Other European'								
Austria	–	1956	X	–	–	–	X	–
Finland	–	1989	1961	X	–	–	1969	–
Iceland	–	1950	1970	X	–	X	X	–
Lichtenstein	–	1978	–	–	–	–	–	–
Malta	–	1965	–	–	–	–	–	–
Norway	–	X	X	X	–	X	X	–
Sweden	–	X	X	X	–	–	X	–
Switzerland	–	1962	X	X	–	–	X	–
Turkey	–	X	–	–	–	1952	X	–
Yugoslavia	–	A	–	–	–	–	–	–
Poland	–	A	–	–	–	–	–	–
Czechoslovakia	–	A	–	–	–	–	–	–
Hungary	–	–	–	–	–	–	–	–
USSR	–	A	–	–	–	–	–	–
'Others'								
United States	–	–	–	–	–	X	X	X
Canada	–	–	–	–	–	X	X	X
New Zealand	–	–	–	–	–	–	1973	–
Japan	–	–	–	–	–	–	1963	X
Australia	–	–	–	–	–	–	1971	X

Note: X: Full member/founding member
Year: date of accession
–: Non-member
(A): Associate member or special guest status
(F): Founder member who has left organization

inter-state relations. (See Figures 1.2 and 1.3.) The two major sets of institutions that evolved were the political/security institutions, on the one hand, and the political/economic institutions, on the other. The distinguishing feature between the two sets of institutions was the Atlantic nature of the political/security domain and the regional nature of the political/economic institutions.

The rationale and the institutional structure of the political/security domain were moulded by the division of the Continent, the partition of Germany, and a perceived threat to the security of Western Europe from the Soviet Union. The politics of security were dominated by Western Europe's sense of vulnerability and the desire of many Western European states to institutionalize a US commitment to their defence in a multilateral context. The US, for its part, spurred on by its ideological rivalry with the Soviet Union and its commitment to contain the spread of communism, was willing to overcome its traditional reservations about involvement in permanent alliances to become the lynchpin of NATO.

The formation and consolidation of the second set of institutions, in the political/economic sphere, was a more lengthy and conflict-ridden process. Successive US administrations promoted plans for economic and political union involving all the states of Western Europe. Marshall Plan aid, which enabled the European states to buy American capital goods for the reconstruction process, did not provide the US with sufficient leverage to achieve its preferred goal. The political forces championing a federal structure for Europe after the war did not prove sufficiently strong to translate the aspirations of the Hague Congress into reality. The Council of Europe embodied strands of the federal vision of a European Parliamentary Assembly, on the one hand, and the traditional instruments of intergovernmental co-operation, on the other. The process of European integration was launched with the creation of the ECSC, an organization that combined limited functional co-operation with an institutional structure that had both intergovernmetnal and supranational traits. The failure of the EDC and the EPC in 1954 did not represent the end of European integration. Rather, it acted as a spur for the consolidation of the 'inner Six' and the pursuit of integration in the economic arena. Britain's reservations about inter-state relations that went beyond intergovernmental co-operation gave France a predominant role in the process of economic integration and in anchoring the Federal Republic of Germany in a dense network of Western European ties.

The failure of pan-West European negotiations on a free trade area led to the formation of EFTA by those countries that did not share the approach of the 'inner Six towards integration.

NOTES

1 R. Mayne, *The Recovery of Europe* (London: Weidenfeld and Nicolson, 1970), p.29.
2 P. Kennedy, *The Rise and Fall of the Great Powers* (London: Unwin Hyman, 1988), pp.357–72.
3 R.S. Jordan and W.J. Feld, *Europe in the Balance* (London, Faber & Faber, 1986), pp.104–8.
4 W. Lipgens, *A History of European Integration: the Formation of the European Unity Movement, 1945–47* (London: Oxford University Press, 1982), pp.53–5.
5 Quoted in D.W. Urwin, *Western Europe Since 1945* (London: Longman, 1972), p.107.
6 Ibid. p.109.
7 Kennedy, op. cit., p.363.
8 O. Riste (ed.), *Western Security – The Formative Years: European and Atlantic defence 1947–1953* (Oslo: Universitetsforlaget, 1985).
9 B. Turner and G. Nordquist, *The Other European Community: Integration and Co-operation in Nordic Europe*, London, Weidenfeld & Nicolson, 1982), pp.85–90.
10 R. Cardozo, 'The Project for a political community (1952–54)', in R. Pryce (ed.), *The Dynamics of European Union* (London: Croom Helm, 1987), pp.49–77.
11 Resolution of the Political Committee of the Congress of Europe, in R. Vaughan, *Post-War Integration in Europe* (London: Edward Arnold, 1976), pp.35–7.
12 For a discussion of the tension between the 'federalists' and the 'intergovernmentalists' see P. Gerbet, 'The Origins: early attempts and the emergence of the Six (1945–52)' in R. Pryce, op. cit., pp.39–45.
13 Statutes of the Council of Europe, signed on 5 May 1949, in Vaughan, op. cit., p.43.
14 Ibid.
15 A.H. Robertson, *European Institutions: Co-operation: Integration: Unification* (London, Stevens and Sons, 1973), pp.40–5.
16 A.S. Milward, *The Reconstruction of Western Europe 1945–51* (London: Methuen, 1984), p.466.
17 A.W. De Porte, *Europe between the Superpowers: the Enduring Balance* (New Haven: Yale University Press, 1986), pp.133–6.
18 Marshall, quoted in Vaughan, op. cit., p.23.
19 Text of speech in Vaughan, op. cit., pp.23–4.
20 Milward, op. cit., p.56.
21 Ibid, p.94.
22 Gerbet, op. cit., pp.45–8.
23 Milward, op. cit., p.391.

24 Schuman Declaration 9 May 1950, in European Parliament, *Selection of Texts concerning Institutional Matters of the Community from 1950–1982*, Luxemburg, EP, 1982, p.48.
25 Text of Treaty, in Vaughan, op. cit., p.64.
26 H.J. Kuster, 'The Treaties of Rome (1955–57)' in Pryce, op. cit., pp.78–194.
27 M. Camps, *Britain and the European Community 1955–63* (London, Oxford University Press, 1964).
28 M. Hodges, 'Liberty, equality and divergency: the legacy of the Treaty of Rome?' in M. Hodges and W.Wallace (eds.), *Economic Divergence in the EC* (London: Allen & Unwin, 1981), pp.1–15.
29 V. Curson Price, 'Three models of European integration', in Ralf Dahrendorf *et al.*, *Whose Europe? Competing Visions of 1992* (London, Institute of Economic Affairs, 1989), pp.23–38.
30 Text of the Stockholm Convention establishing EFTA, 4 January 1960, in Vaughan, op. cit., p.107.
31 C. Archer, *Organising Western Europe* (Sevenoaks, Kent: Edward Arnold, 1990), pp.133–44.
32 F. Wendt, *Co-operation in the Nordic Countries* (Stockholm: Almqvist and Wiksell International, 1981), p.41.
33 Ibid., pp.213–37.

TOPICS FOR DISCUSSION

1 How far and in what ways did the United States influence the formation of the Western European regional system in the immediate post-war era?
2 Why did so many regional organizations develop in Western Europe?
3 What approach to European unity inspired the Schuman Plan, and why did that approach create divisions among Western European states?
4 Why did economic integration lead to a division between the 'inner Six' and the 'outer Seven'?

FURTHER READING

There is a vast literature on the formation of the Western European state system in the aftermath of World War II. The following titles have been selected to highlight the rationale behind its institutional structure and membership.

De Porte A.W. *Europe Between the Superpowers: the Enduring Balance*, New Haven: Yale University Press, 1986, 2nd edition. This is an excellent analysis of the breakdown of the European balance of power system and the role of the superpowers in the post-war construction of a Western European order.

Milward A.S. *The Reconstruction of Western Europe 1945–1951*, London: Methuen, 1984. Although this detailed analysis is better suited for specialized final-year students, the book is important because it challenges the 'standard' or 'accepted' interpretations of the role of the

USA in European integration and the influence of such personalities as Jean Monnet. The main arguments of the book are summarized in the conclusions, pp.462–502.

Pryce R. (ed.) *The Dynamics of European Union*, London: Croom Helm 1987. This volume provides a very useful survey of all efforts to promote formal integration from 1945 onwards.

Urwin, D.W. *Western Europe since 1945: a Political History*, London: Longman, 1989, 4th edition. This book gives a very clear and comprehensive review of the domestic and international factors that moulded the post-war system.

Vaughan R. *Post-War Integration in Europe* London: Edward Arnold, 1976. This volume gathers together the main documents, speeches and declarations that form the history of European integration.

Wallace, W. *The Transformation of Western Europe*, London: Frances Pinter, 1990. This Chatham House paper usefully combines a treatment of the institutional structure of post-war Europe and the dynamics of integration with the earlier process of national integration.

Chapter 2

The evolution of
Western European organizations
An overview

Although the tapestry of Western European organizations was woven by 1960, some of its threads have been unravelled and rewoven as states changed their perceptions of national interest. The purpose of this chapter is to provide an overview of the evolution of the different organizations and how relations between them have developed. We begin with the Council of Europe, because its broadly based membership made it a pan-Western European organization. The chapter then looks at the development of the rival economic groups, the European Community and EFTA, before examining co-operation among the Nordic states. The chapter concludes with an analysis of the unique features of the European Community and the reasons why it has emerged as the core regional organization in Western Europe.

THE COUNCIL OF EUROPE

From the outset, the Council of Europe failed to promote the federalist ideals of the Hague Congress.[1] Although its policy scope was wide, the Council had a weak institutional base and no independent law-making power. In the 1950s, the Council saw its role eroded as the EC quickly came to overshadow it. Dahrendorf argues that the Council 'settled down to a static second-rateness in limited areas of concern'.[2] Is this assessment justified?

Unspectacular functional co-operation

Described by Pentland as an 'almost invisible functionalist workshop', the Council of Europe promotes intergovernmental co-operation by means of conventions and standing conferences.[3]

Since 1950 it has reached agreement on 135 conventions, 11 of those since 1987, which suggests a steadily growing agreement among the participating states in very diverse areas of policy.[4] Multilateral conventions replace the need for a multitude of bilateral agreements which would be much more time consuming for the member states to negotiate. Intergovernmental co-operation in the Council includes the following policy areas:

- human rights and legal matters
- social policy and public health
- mass media
- education and culture
- conservation and the environment
- youth affairs.

The conventions differ greatly in their scope and influence. The Convention of Human Rights and Fundamental Freedoms of 1953 is the most important convention, as it codifies individual rights and provides a means of redress for individual citizens (see p.122). There is general agreement that the Council of Europe has carved out a unique role for itself in the area of human rights. The Social Charter, which came into force in 1965, was meant to complement the Human Rights Convention by establishing a series of social rights. It proved much more difficult to get agreement on economic and social rights than it was to establish a list of civil and political rights. The Convention on Human Rights took only one year to negotiate, whereas the Social Charter took from 1956 to 1961. There was a conflict between those states willing to agree to a binding charter and those that would accept only a declaration of intent, a debate echoed in the EC negotiations on its Social Charter in 1989.[5]

The Cultural Convention of 1955 fosters cultural exchanges among the member states. A Council on Cultural Co-operation was established in 1962, with responsibility for making recommendations to the Committee of Ministers about cultural matters, notably expenditure from the Cultural Fund. Many of the conventions deal with low-key issues that facilitate public policy-making and social exchange in Western Europe. Conventions on the placement of au pair workers, the status of migrant workers, the repatriation of corpses, the equivalence of diplomas and scholarships are necessary and useful, given the extent of social mobility throughout Western Europe today. The emphasis in the 1980s on environmental issues, the protection of the architectural heritage, football hooliganism and the mass media manifests a changing agenda of inter-state co-operation.

The process of drafting conventions and subsequent ratification is lengthy. The patchy return from this process may be seen in the uneven pattern of ratification. Only the Convention on Human Rights and the Cultural Convention have been signed and ratified by all Council of Europe member states. The member states can and do adopt an 'à la carte' approach to intergovernmental co-operation. An 1967 convention on consular functions, together with its two protocols, was signed by only eight states, and by 1987 had been ratified by only three.[6] By the end of the same year the Charter on Local Self-Government, agreed in 1985, had been ratified by only one country, Luxemburg.[7] Many of the low-policy issues dealt with in the Council of Europe do not receive high priority in the member states.

Specialized conferences

Eighteen specialized conferences of ministers meet regularly under the auspices of the Council of Europe to promote intergovernmental co-operation in various fields. The European Conference of Local Authorities, dating from 1955, is the oldest of these. Its purpose is to bring elected representatives of local government together in a European forum. The Conference used to meet every two years, but since 1976 it has met annually. A 'Steering Committee for Regional and Municipal Matters', consisting of senior officials from ministries of local government, was set up in 1970. These various forums provide national officials and local politicians with an opportunity to discuss the major issues facing local government, including regional planning, environmental protection, town planning and local democracy. From them there is a gradual diffusion of information about common concerns and possible solutions.[8] Ministers responsible for education, culture, justice and transport, also, attend specialized conferences under the auspices of the Council of Europe. Up to the 1980s, these ministers met infrequently or not at all in the EC, but this has changed with the spread of EC activity. Once the EC becomes involved in a policy area, it is likely to become the predominant forum very quickly, because its decision-making capacity and institutional structure are more effective than the non-binding commitments that characterize intergovernmental co-operation in the Council of Europe. However, EC co-operation does not cover all of the countries of Western Europe. Increasingly, non-EC states are seeking access to the Community's policies in education, research and development.

Relations between the EC and the Council of Europe

As the European Community has increased its membership and widened its policy scope, it has gradually encroached on areas in which the Council of Europe used to take the lead. For example, the Council's work on the recognition of university qualifications and on the equivalence of diplomas and periods of study abroad was superseded in the Community of Twelve by the 'mutual recognition' Directive and by its educational policies, notably Erasmus (see page 137) Town-twinning, traditionally fostered by the Council of Europe, is now the subject of an EC programme; in 1989 the EC created a system of grants for town-twinning among the member states – another example of the better-endowed EC encroaching on the more modest work of the Council. If the EC and EFTA succeed in establishing a 'European Economic Area' (see page 91), the Community's extensive body of law will have wide application in Western Europe. The future relevance of the Council of Europe's intergovernmental co-operation may well depend on the establishment of closer links with the EC.

An agreement between the Council of Europe and the Commission in June 1987 improved co-operation between the two organizations. In an exchange of letters between the Council's Secretariat and the Commission, it was agreed that the latter should be invited to participate on committees established by the Committee of Ministers and in the elaboration of draft agreements. It is envisaged that the Community will become a contracting party to conventions and will participate in the work of ministerial conferences where appropriate.[9] The first tangible evidence of this new co-operation is the Community's signing of the Convention of the Elaboration of a European Pharmacopoeia in November 1989. There are also discussions on the possibility of extending EC agreements and laws to members of the Council of Europe. Regular meetings are held between the Presidents of the Commission, the Council of Ministers, the Secretary-General of the Council of Europe and the Chairman of the Committee of Ministers. The EC Commission has been careful to protect the Community's freedom of action. It does not accept, for example, that there should be a division of labour between the two organizations. In other words, just because the Council of Europe is working in a particular policy domain should not prevent the Community from policy co-operation in the same area, if appropriate.

The Future role of the Council – a window of opportunity

Traditionally the Council of Europe acted as a meeting place for all Western European states, and it served as a useful bridge between the 'inner Six' and the 'outer Seven' in the 1960s when British membership of the EEC was turned down. Yet it never became a 'European political authority with limited functions but real powers', as envisaged by the Consultative Assembly in 1949.[10] The intensification of integration in the EC since the mid-1980s and the 1989 revolutions in the Eastern bloc led to much soul-searching in the Council of Europe about its future role in 'European Construction', a term that occurs with great frequency in Council documents.

In 1984, the Council set up a commission of eminent European personalities, known as the Colombo Commission, to assess the future of the Council. The Commission was chaired by Emilio Colombo, former Prime Minister and Foreign Minister of Italy, and included among its members Pieter Dankert, former President of the European Parliament, and Maurice Fauré, who played a critical role in the Dooge Committee which led to the Single European Act. The main theme of the report was the perceived need to ensure that 'the geographical enlargement of the Community and the progressive development of its powers must be accompanied by a reinforcement of co-operation among the Twenty-one [member states]'.[11] The report concluded that the 'gap already existing between members of the Community and other members of the Council of Europe' might widen.[12] The participants in the Colombo Commission argued that the Council of Europe should concentrate on two major priorities:

1 Involving all the countries of democratic Europe in the process of European unification by ensuring that non-members of the European Community are not neglected.
2 Developing European co-operation among the Twenty-one by providing an arena for co-operation and preparing for more ambitious and binding action in the Community at a later stage.[13]

The revolutions in Eastern Europe provide the Council of Europe with an opportunity to carve out a niche for itself in the establishment of a Europe-wide order. Relations with Eastern Europe figured prominently in the May 1989 Declaration on the future role of the Council. In welcoming the reform process, the Committee of Ministers laid claim to a role for the Council of Europe in the Conference on Security and Co-operation in Europe (CSCE) and in human rights, education and culture.[14] The Council of Europe was one of the first Western European organizations to react to the changes in the Eastern bloc. In May 1989, before the revolutions, the Consultative Assembly deliberated on the notion of 'special guest status' for European non-member states, and its September session was attended by the first 'special guests', from Hungry, Poland, the Soviet Union and Yugoslavia. Yugoslavia has been associated with the work of the Council of Europe for a number of years and is a party to several conventions.

Intergovernmental contact groups have been set up with the task of examining how the Council might co-operate with non-member European countries. The decision by President Gorbachev to address the consultative Assembly of the Council of Europe, and not its sister assembly, the European Parliament, in July 1989 highlights the Council's role as a bridge between East and West. The Secretary-General of the Council, Catherine Lalumière, undertook an extensive range of visits to Eastern and Central Europe in 1990.

The Council of Europe, uniquely placed to help the countries of Central and Eastern Europe 'rejoin Europe', is set to become a pan-European organization in the 1990s. Hungary requested full membership in November 1989 and joined in November 1990. Poland applied for membership in January 1990 and Czechoslovakia and Yugoslavia in February 1990. Full accession provides a stamp of approval for the reform processes from the organization, which prides itself on being the protector of human rights and democratic freedoms. Involvement in the Council's intergovernmental co-operation will give these states an opportunity to engage in a broad range of specialized areas of co-operation. However, the states of East/Central Europe regard the Council of Europe as a precursor to full membership of the EC and not an alternative. The development of the Council of Europe shows that functional co-operation à la Mitrany is less successful than the EC method of integration.

THE EUROPEAN COMMUNITY

The European Coal and Steel Community, an experiment in a new type of inter-state relations based on integration rather than co-operation, provided a model for the EEC and Euratom. Since 1958, when the latter organizations came into being, it is useful to analyse their development in three distinct periods: 1958 to 1972, which saw the completion of the customs union and negotiations leading to the first enlargement of the Community; 1972 to 1984, when the Community worked through the implications of enlargement, the British budgetary crisis and the economic consequences of the oil crises; and 1984 to the present day, a period characterized by a renewed desire for dynamism and relevance.

Integration in the EC is a highly dynamic process characterized by periods of stagnation and crisis, on the one hand, and renewed commitment to the EC as a forum for the management of inter-state relations, on the other. Put simply, despite setbacks the EC is a remarkably durable organization. The expansion in the Community's policy scope and changes in its institutional structure can be traced to the impact of the international environment on the Community's agenda and to the priorities and interests of the member states, especially the larger and more powerful. The Community's institutional structure and policy-making scope create a political system supported by the political systems of the member states, but with distinctive characteristics and a measure of independence of its own.

1958–72: the limits of the Community method

Integration in the 1960s took place in a very benign economic environment which made adjustments to the reduction of trade barriers less painful. Intra-Community trade grew twice as fast as trade with the rest of the world.[15] Investment rates rose substantially, as did GNP growth rates. This golden period of growth was facilitated by a relatively stable international monetary system, controlled by the USA.

During its early years, the Community appeared to fulfil neo-functionalists' expectations. A zealous Commission, led by Walter Hallstein, was the pacesetter of integration, co-opting national civil servants and the representatives of the economic interests in creating the customs union, which was achieved without major trauma in July

1968, and in establishing the main lines of the Common Agricultural Policy. Agreement on a system of valued added tax, early regulations on the free movement of people and the beginnings of a policy on competition were all part of the early successes of the Community. The Kennedy GATT Round of trade negotiations, held in the early 1960s, and a number of agreements with newly independent states marked the beginnings of the Community's external role. The relative ease with which the Commission fostered the initial policy consensus owed much to the fact that the Treaty contained very precise guidelines on the customs union and that the CAP was central to the initial bargain between France and Germany (see p. 34).

In 1965 the 'empty chair crisis', which erupted when de Gaulle withdrew all French officials from the deliberations of the Council, destroyed the illusion of automatic spillover as portrayed by the neo-functionalists. The crisis was occasioned by the Commission's proposals on the financing of the Common Agricultural Policy, since these made provision for an independent source of revenue for the Community. President de Gaulle did not want self-financing for the EC budget, nor did he want the Commission to increase its authority with an independent source of revenue. The President of the Commission, Walter Hallstein, was already acting too much like a head of government for President de Gaulle's liking. The hidden agenda of the crisis concerned the move from 1966 onwards to a system of weighted voting in the Council of Ministers. De Gaulle, deeply committed to 'l'Europe des Patries' (a Europe of nation-states), would not support a system of voting that implied a diminution of national sovereignty. Before France would agree to resume its participation in EC institutions, a gentlemen's agreement, known as the 'Luxemburg accord', was reached. The practical effect of this agreement was that on matters of vital interest to one or more member states, the Council would continue discussions until consensus was achieved. This practice became known in Community parlance as 'the veto'.[16]

The 'empty chair' crisis was followed by a second veto on British membership in 1967, with the result that further movement in the Community had to await de Gaulle's departure from French politics in 1969. The Community quickly regained its momentum with Georges Pompidou as French President and Willy Brandt as German Chancellor. The Hague Summit, in December 1969, marked the end of the transitional period in the Community's development.

The communiqué of the Summit included measures designed to strengthen the existing Community – a priority for Pompidou – and to widen the Community to include new members – a priority for Brandt. Completion, 'deepening and widening', a phrase coined by the French Government at the time, captures the issues facing the Community in 1969. 'Completion' involved the establishment of a system of 'own resources' for the budget and a reform of the Social Fund. Deepening the level of integration encompassed movement towards economic and monetary union, technological co-operation and the development of foreign policy co-operation outside the strict confines of the original treaties. The widening of the Community opened the way for accession negotiations with the four applicant states: Britain, Norway, Denmark and Ireland.

A period of intense activity followed the Hague Summit, as the implications of the communiqué were worked out. Accession negotiations with the four applicant states were finalized, and three of them went on to become full members; a negative vote in the Norwegian referendum precluded its membership. In 1970 the Foreign Ministers proposed a system of foreign policy co-operation, to be known as European Political Co-operation (EPC). The Werner report on economic and monetary union was presented to the Council and the Commission in 1970 and was followed by the Vedel report on the powers of the European Parliament in 1972.

The Paris Summit of that year was the first of the enlarged Community, as Britain, Denmark and Ireland participated in its deliberations. In a long communiqué, the participants agreed to transform their relations into a European Union, including economic and monetary union, by 1980. Regional policy, social policy, industrial policy, the environment, energy, external relations and political co-operation were all cited in the communiqué as matters requiring future attention. An ambitious agenda was set for the enlarged Community. However, increasing monetary instability from 1968 onwards and the shock of a unilateral decision by the United States in August 1971 to break the convertibility of the dollar and to impose a 10 per cent surcharge on dutiable imports heralded a turbulent period for the international economic system. Western Europe's golden period of growth had drawn to a close.

Consideration of industrial, social, regional and technological policy at the beginning of the 1970s marked the achievement of the customs union and the increased level of economic interdependence it entailed. The first enlargement of the Community was achieved.

There was thus ample evidence of policy spillover and geographical spillover. However, the role of de Gaulle in the 1960s, as leader of one of the dominant states of the Community, showed that EC integration would be neither smooth nor automatic. De Gaulle served as an extreme example of the capacity of national leaders to slow down the development of the Community and to undermine its institutional structure. The neo-functionalists had clearly underestimated the continuing strength of the Western European state as a political organization and had failed to grapple with the limits of supranationalism. The development of EPC outside the strict confines of the Treaties was a precursor of intergovernmental innovations that would characterize integration in the 1970s.

1973–84: the limits of intergovernmentalism

The rhetoric of the Paris Summit was quickly lost in the mists of recession and in the adjustment to the problems of enlargement. The 1973 Arab-Israeli war exposed Western Europe's vulnerability in energy, with almost 80 per cent of its oil supplies coming from the Middle East and North Africa. The energy crisis led neither to consensus nor to solidarity among the member states; her partners did little to help The Netherlands when confronted in 1973 with an Arab oil boycott. France refused to go along with the US policy of establishing a consumers' cartel and remained outside the International Energy Agency established in 1974 by the world's primary users of oil. Nor was Britain, with its North Sea oil, open to the development of a common policy on energy. The oil crisis highlighted the absence of a European energy policy, the limits to solidarity among the member states, and the extent to which EC integration could be undermined by turbulence in the international economic system.

A steep increase in oil prices, affecting the supply side of the Western economies, caused a deep recession, with rising unemployment, inflation and balance-of-payments problems in many of the member states. Economic performance began to diverge, with inflation in the Federal Republic of Germany running at less than 5 per cent between 1973 and 1980, in contrast to 15 per cent in the United Kingdom.[17] Unemployment rates also diverged, reaching 20 per cent in Ireland but remaining at about 10 per cent in the Federal Republic, Italy, France and Britain. The number of people in search of jobs rose from 5.9 million in 1973 to 10.6 million in 1982.[18] The second oil shock of 1979 further exacerbated the economic problems facing Western Europe.

Progress towards economic and monetary union was rendered impossible by turbulence in the international monetary system, economic divergence in the Community and domestic political agitation within the member states. Less than two years after the 1972 Paris Summit, not one of the nine heads of government who signed the communiqué was still in power.[19] The existing core of Community policies came under attack as the member states resorted to hidden protectionism and national measures to combat the crisis. The grandiose objectives of the Paris Summit were too ambitious for a recession-torn Europe. Political commitment to further integration faltered.

A series of enlargements, beginning in 1973, required painful adjustments to the Community's main policies. From an organization of six member states with a high level of development, the EC became a Community of Twelve. Ireland, Greece, Portugal and Spain were poor and underdeveloped by EC standards. Britain and Denmark could be labelled 'reluctant Europeans' with little sympathy for the grand design of European Union. Nor did most EC policies suit Britain in the 1970s. Because of its small agricultural work-force and its pattern of trade, the British contribution to the Community budget was set to increase significantly at the end of the transitional period. This sparked off a contentious budgetary crisis which prevented consideration of the wider issues of European co-operation and which brought the CAP under scrutiny because the bulk of EC monies went on this policy. The budgetary problem was finally resolved in 1984.

Although stagnation characterized the Community in the 1970s there were a number of noteworthy policy and institutional developments during this time. Conflict internally in the Community contrasted sharply with success in the foreign policy sphere. European Political Co-operation, which began with humble objectives in 1970, had by the end of the decade become a cornerstone of the member states' foreign policies. The decision in 1974 to transform the periodic summits into thrice-yearly meetings of the European Council brought the most senior national political actors into close collaboration. The first direct elections to the European Parliament in 1979 altered the barren institutional landscape and gave the parliamentary institution ample grounds for demanding greater powers. The establishment of the European Monetary System

(EMS) in 1979 was a response to the instability of the dollar. Britain's decision not to join the exchange rate mechanism of the EMS showed that it was possible to establish policy solutions based on 'variable geometry' (see page 13). Apart from direct elections to the European Parliament, the other institutional and policy innovations of the 1970s were evidence that developments in the EC might increasingly take on an extra-Treaty character and that such developments would be intergovernmental in form.

The consensus in academic writing about the European Community in the early 1980s was one of stagnation and crisis. Tsoulkalis, in a perceptive article on the future of the Community in 1982, argued that the EC had reached a state of equilibrium. It had proved capable of absorbing the internal and external shocks of the 1970s and early 1980s but not of meeting the challenges of the future. Without adjustment and a strengthening of the Community's capacity for joint economic management, it would slide towards irrelevance.[20] The very future of the Community was questioned in a major publication from the international institutes of the larger member states entitled *The European Community: Progress or Decline?* The tone of the report is worth noting because it highlights the pervasive pessimism of the period. The following extract demonstrates the motivation of those who wrote the report:

> This report is born out of a sense of alarm and urgency. The authors ... all share the conviction that Western Europe is drifting, that the existence of the European Community is under serious threat. In sharp contrast with only a decade ago, the position of Western Europe seems to be challenged from all sides. If nothing is done, we are faced with the disintegration of the most important European achievement since World War 11.[21]

Yet after 1984 the European Community entered a particularly dynamic phase in its development; common concerns were translated into common goals, and institutional and constitutional reforms were put in place. The pressures for reform in the Community showed that intergovernmentalism had its limits. Institutional reform would have to go beyond the limits of intergovernmentalism.

1984 – renewed dynamism

While the Council of Ministers was examining the Genscher-Colombo plan – a German-Italian initiative aimed at reform in the

Community – the European Parliament took up the issue of Treaty change. A long-standing federalist, Altiero Spinelli, persuaded his fellow MEPs that the European Parliament, as the representative institution, should draft a new treaty for the Union. Spinelli was convinced that only a bold initiative could overcome the stagnation in the Community. The Parliament established a Committee on Institutional Affairs to draft the new treaty. It was subsequently adopted by the Parliament by a majority of 237 votes for, 31 against, with 43 abstentions. The draft treaty was submitted to the governments and parliaments of the member states.[22] In 1984, President Mitterand of France, who was then President of the Council, stated, in an important address to the EP, his willingness to 'examine and to support' the draft treaty.[23] Although the member states were unlikely to endorse a treaty fashioned by the European Parliament, Spinelli did succeed in placing a federal concept of European Union on the agenda, at a time when constitutional reform was edging its way onto the political agenda.

At the Fontainebleau European Council of June 1984, President Mitterand took the decisive step on the road to Community reform when he got the agreement of the other member states to establish two committees to advance progress towards European Union. First, an *ad hoc* committee (the Dooge Committee) was established, consisting of the personal representatives of the heads of government, and entrusted with the task of outlining 'suggestions for the improvement of the operation of European co-operation in both the Community field and that of political or any other co-operation'. Second, the Adonnino Committee was established to examine proposals concerning a People's Europe.

The purpose of the Dooge Committee was to explore the attitudes of the member states towards institutional and policy reform. It avoided the pitfall of seeking total consensus among the participants. In the event of disagreement, reservations concerning the majority decisions were to be included in the footnotes. In practice, the committee tended to divide into the Six and Ireland, on the one hand, and Britain, Greece and Denmark, on the other. The three 'footnote' states, as they were called, did not endorse the need for Treaty reform and expected the Dooge report to suffer the same fate as previous reports on the reform of the Community. Skilful management of the agenda by the Italian Prime Minister, Signor Craxi, at the Milan European Council (1985) led to a favourable vote on the issue of an intergovernmental conference to negotiate Treaty modifications under Article 236 of the Rome Treaty; by seven votes to three (the UK, Greece and Denmark), the European Council voted in favour of an intergovernmental conference.[24] The Community was about to embark on a process of 'constitutive bargaining among the member states', an important ingredient of the integration process according to Lindberg and Scheingold.[25] Whereas a majority of states could call an intergovernmental conference, unanimity is required under the Treaties for a successful outcome. Thus all ten member states had to agree to the new compact.

A resurgence of formal integration

Six months of negotiations led to the signing, in 1986, and subsequent ratification (1987) of the Single European Act (SEA), the first major modification of the Rome Treaty (EEC). How and why was the stagnation of the 1970s and early 1980s replaced with a resurgence of formal integration, despite the reservations of three governments? The answer lies in the capacity of the negotiators to strike a new intergovernmental bargain, especially among the larger member states. This was made possible by what Keohane and Hoffman call the 'preference-convergence' model or, more specifically, a 'convergence of national interests around a new pattern of economic policy-making'.[26] Deregulation and economic liberalism began to replace Keynesian demand management as the dominant mode of economic policy in the 1980s. In the EC, deregulation was embodied in the Commission's 1985 White Paper on the completion of the internal market. The success of the White Paper depended on strengthening the Community's decision-making capacity, which in turn required institutional reform. The imminent accession of Spain and Portugal made it imperative to overcome the barriers to effective EC decision-making, and the political momentum which began with the Genscher-Colombo Plan and the draft treaty on European union created expectations of reform. Agreement between France and the Federal Republic on the necessity for reform received strong support from their original partners in the Six. The spectre of a two-speed Europe and the prospect of achieving Community-wide market liberalization were sufficient to overcome British resistance. Starting from a position of outright opposition to institutional reform, Britain entered the negotiations determined to limit its scope. Greece and Denmark, as small countries, were not in a position to prevent the negotiations.

The SEA represents the outcome of six months' negotiations among ten states. Coalitions were established and package deals fashioned from the varying interests of the member states (See Figure 2.1.) Emile Noël, former Secretary-General of the Commission, argues that the SEA is more than a 'package deal': it represents the outcome of a synergy between different facets of integration. According to Noël, developing a synergy between two or several, hitherto independent, sectors or problems has the effect that progress in any one of these sectors benefits the others, which in turn assists politically the success of the first.[27] The major synergy in the SEA was the establishment of a link between the completion of the internal market and institutional reform, notably with respect to majority voting and an enhanced role for the EP. Consensus on the 1992 programme required a side-payment to the lesser-developed parts of the EC in the form of a chapter in the SEA on economic and social cohesion.

The SEA, described by Margaret Thatcher as a 'modest decision' has proved a far more dynamic instrument than was anticipated in 1986. The Commission, and especially its President, Jacques Delors, took the initiative in defining the post-SEA agenda. In what is widely known as the Delors package, *Making a Success of the Single European Act – A New Frontier for Europe*, the Commission attempted to build on the synergy of the SEA.[28] From the outset, the Commission insisted that its proposals be treated as a whole to avoid a situation in which individual member states could select from the package those things that suited them and disagree with the rest, thereby unravelling a carefully constructed set of proposals. The Delors package was discussed at the Copenhagen European Council (4–5 December 1987), but agreement was not forthcoming. It was left to the German presidency of the Council during the first half of 1988 to ensure that the global package would be agreed to at the special European Council of February 1988. In the traditional pre-summit letter, Chancellor Kohl appealed for support by stressing the link between the Delors package and the completion of the internal market. Agreement was reached in Brussels on budgetary discipline, both for agriculture and for the EC budget as a whole, on the reform and financing of the structural funds, and on the future financing of the Community budget. The Delors package established the broad outline of the Community's budgetary strategy up to 1992 and endowed the SEA's provisions on economic and social cohesion with some substance. The renewed dynamism evident in the EC since 1987 manifested itself in spillover from the internal market programme to other policy areas, notably social policy, and in efforts to expand still further the scope of formal integration. In December 1990 two intergovernmental conferences on economic and monetary union and political union opened in Rome. Again links are being established between policy developments and institutional change.

An overcrowded agenda

Never before in the history of the European Community have so many complex issues demanded attention. Once again the EC is faced with the challenge of completion, deepening and widening, but now at a time when the post-war European political order is at an end.

The *completion agenda* is the most straightforward because it deals with the 1992 programme and the other flanking policies, notably cohesion and social policy. The SEA gave the Community sufficient decision-making capacity to put a large measure of the 1992 programme in place. Although there are disagreements about

Figure 2.1 Summary of the Single European Act

Preamble	Objective European Union:
Title 1	(Common Provisions-3 Articles)
	*European Unity
	*European Council
	*Institutions
Title 2	(Provisions Amending Treaties)
	Institutions
	*Court of first Instance
	*Co-operation Procedure
	*Extension of Qualified Majority Voting
	*EP assent
	*Commission's Implementing Powers
	Policy
	*Internal market
	*Monetary Capacity
	*Social Policy
	*Economic and Social Cohesion
	*Research and Technological Development
	*Environment
Title 3	Codifies European Political Co-operation
Title 4	Final Provisions

aspects of the programme, there is consensus on the goal. The only non-consensus item on the completion agenda is Britain's reservation about the Social Charter. Cohesion and the politics of redistribution, however, are becoming part of the EMU debate.

The *deepening* agenda is the agenda for the next five years. The completion of the internal market, especially the free movement of capital, creates pressures for a common monetary policy. The desire to replace the dominance of the Deutschmark and the Bundesbank with a system of multilateral control also fuels demands for economic and monetary union. Economic and monetary union necessitates the creation of a European system of central banks and a high degree of co-ordination of national economic policies. This is a highly contentious issue because Britain is opposed to a single European currency. Among the other member states there are divergent views about the design of other member states there are divergent views about the design of the system and the policies that should accompany EMU.

Political union appeared on the agenda of the Community in April 1990 because of the revolutions in Eastern Europe, German unification and the institutional consequences of EMU. The 'inner Six' are determined to protect the level of integration achieved so far and to deepen collaboration, in case further enlargements lead to a wider but looser Community. France sees integration as the best means of anchoring a unified Germany in the new Europe. Subsidiarity, political accountability, the international role of the EC and its institutional capacity are the dominant themes on the political union agenda.

The widening agenda is the most problematic for the EC because of turbulence in the international environment. Enlargement and relations with European non-member states dominate this agenda. The EC is faced with membership applications from Turkey and Austria. A number of central European states have indicated that rejoining Europe for them means membership of the European Community. If the negotiations with the EFTA states do not prove successful, applications will come from yet more EFTA states. This agenda poses many dilemmas for the EC and the member states, because a wider EC may mean a weaker one, and it is not clear how the EC can maintain its capacity for policy management and decision-making if the number of member states increases substantially.[29]

EFTA – CAUTIOUS INTEGRATION

EFTA was established by those states who felt unable to participate in the 'Community method' of integration characterized by
aspirations towards an advanced level of economic integration,
buttressed by strong central institutions and with an underlying
goal of political union. It was designed to allow its member states
to benefit from free trade without sacrificing national sovereignty.
Although the limited aims of the Stockholm Convention (see p. 35)
were smoothly arrived at, EFTA itself is facing an uncertain future. If
the EC/EFTA negotiations on a European Economic Area succeed,
EFTA's institutional capacity will need to be greatly strengthened so
that it can deal with Brussels as one, supervise the EFTA side of the
EEA and enforce its rules. It will be difficult for EFTA to remain a
minimalist intergovernmental organization with a light institutional
structure and, at the same time, participate as an equal in the EEA.
If, on the other hand, the negotiations fail to produce a satisfactory
outcome, the EEA will simply be a step on the road to full EC
membership.

Successful minimalist integration

In the Stockholm Convention a precise timetable was laid down for
the abolition of import duties on industrial goods by 1970. Provision
was made for Area tariff treatment so that only goods wholly or
largely produced in the EFTA states could benefit. This was to
ensure that trade deflection was kept to a minimum. The problem
of trade deflection arises where a free trade area lacks a common
commercial tariff for trade with third countries. In the absence of
agreed rules of origin, products from a third country could enter the
free trade area by means of the lowest tariff country and be traded
into higher tariff countries without further barriers. EFTA also laid
down a number of criteria for establishing what goods should get an
EFTA Certificate of Origin.[30]

EFTA achieved free trade on industrial goods by December
1966, ahead of schedule. It was generally regarded as a relatively
trouble-free experience of trade liberalization, made possible by the
buoyant economic conditions of the 1960s. States with protected
home markets were allowed transitional arrangements for some,
but not all, products. Liberalization was facilitated by the absence
of agriculture from the original agreement. The EFTA states had

very different systems of agricultural support, which would have made free trade in this area very problematic. A series of bilateral agreements giving Danish and Portuguese food exports preferential access to the markets of other states largely solved the problem of agriculture.[31] The only problem on the road to free trade occured in 1964, when an incoming Labour government in Britain imposed a 15 per cent surcharge on imports to combat a deepening deficit crisis. This action was in conflict with the provisions of the Stockholm Convention.[32]

Relations with the EC

Relations with the European Community dominated EFTA's early years. The 'Seven' thought that they could work out a collective agreement with the 'Six' – in other words, continue the OEEC discussions on a European-wide free trade area in another way. However, Britain's decision to apply for membership of the EEC in 1961 changed the environment within which EC–EFTA relations developed. The British application was followed by one from Denmark in the same year and from Norway in 1962. Austria, Sweden and Switzerland opted only for association, because of neutrality. The EFTA countries agreed among themselves to remain united in their negotiations with the Community so that each state could arrive at a satisfactory relationship with the 'Six'. President de Gaulle's veto of British membership in 1963, and again in 1967, meant that an accommodation of Britain with the EC would take time.

The EC Hague Summit of 1969 accepted that arrangements 'would be worked out with the remaining EFTA states so as to overcome the division of Western Europe into two different trading block.'[33] In 1973 EFTA lost two of its member states, including its largest one. The negative result in the Norwegian referendum on EC membership left that country in EFTA. In 1970 the Commission proposed that the remaining EFTA states should be offered an arrangement based on a free trade area agreement with the Community.

The outcome of the negotiations in the early 1970s was a series of free trade agreements between the soon-to-be-enlarged Community and Austria, Switzerland, Sweden, Iceland, Finland and, later, Norway (when its referendum on full EC membership was defeated). The agreements made provision for the complete liberalization of trade of industrial goods, in a number of successive steps, by July 1977. The agreements included rules of competition, safeguard measures, rules of origin and provision for a joint committee to meet once a year to manage the agreements. The agreements with Austria, Switzerland, Iceland, Norway and Sweden contained an evolutionary clause to enable each partner to present requests aimed at developing the scope and content of the initial agreement.

By 1977 a pan-Western European free trade area, first launched by the OEEC negotiations in the 1950s, became a reality. EC–EFTA relations settled down to the management of the agreements with some discussion on loosening the rules of origin and some expansion in their scope; additional agreements covering transport, the environment, consumer protection, research and development were negotiated. A joint EC-EFTA ministerial meeting in April 1984 was marked by a willingness to broaden and deepen co-operation between the Community and EFTA. The term 'European Economic Area' was coined to give symbolic meaning to a commitment to lay down orientations to continue, deepen and extend co-operation within the framework of, and beyond the FTAs.[34] The establishment of a High Level Contact Group, consisting of EC and EFTA officials, added a multilateral institutional basis to the relationship. Multilateral co-operation between the EC and EFTA expanded significantly after 1984 to cover some twenty policy areas.[35] None the less, the renewed political dynamism in the EC, and especially the commitment to the internal market programme, challenged the traditional integration policies of the EFTA states. Once again the EFTA states have to respond to developments in the EC.

MINI-EUROPE: NORDIC CO-OPERATION

The history of Nordic co-operation since the 1960s is one of contrasts – failure of attempts to develop global co-operation and integration, but significant institutional development and co-operation on the basis of a piecemeal sectoral approach. The failure of efforts to form a defence union in the 1940s and a customs union in the 1950s was followed by the stillbirth of the Nordek Customs Union Treaty in 1970. The Nordic states engage in co-operation across a range of policy areas when joint solutions seem appropriate to the problems facing the governments concerned. According to Sundelius, Nordic co-operation is broad in scope but with varying intensity because 'only when domestic objectives can be enhanced through collective diplomacy will the political élites commit themselves to a joint solution'.[36] Nordic co-operation offers a very different model for integration from that found in the EC. Parallel national action, facilitated by a dense network of governmental and societal ties, is the bedrock of co-operation. Unlike the EC, this is integration from the bottom up, moulded by societal linkages that build-up political relationships as they are needed.[37]

Nordic co-operation has an impressive array of policy achievements to its credit – achievements that have been built up slowly since the last century. Social policy is one of the most successful areas of co-operation. The Nordic states have established reciprocal rights for their nationals in matters of social security, old age pensions, sickness benefit and other aspects of welfare provision. A common Nordic labour market, whereby a national of one country is free to take up employment in another Nordic state without a work permit, provides the basis for co-operation in social policy matters. The principle of national treatment in matters of social security was established by parallel national laws in the Nordic states before it was introduced in the EC. A passport union, co-operation on health policy, extensive harmonization of education policy, co-ordinated cultural exchanges, and joint research institutions create the conditions and provide incentives for considerable mobility among the Nordic states.[38]

Environmental protection is an important new focus for Nordic co-operation. In 1974 three articles were inserted in the Helsinki treaty, pledging that:

1 In their own legislation and in its application, the Nordic countries must put the environmental interests of their partners on a par with their own to the utmost possible extent. (Article 30).
2 They must seek to harmonize their environmental protection rules in order to attain the greatest possible similarity in standards. (Article 31)
3 They must seek to co-ordinate matters relating to the provision of nature reserves. (Article 32.)

The extension of the Helsinki Treaty was accompanied by a Convention on the Protection of the Environment, signed in 1974 and applied from October 1976.[39] This convention gives individuals affected by environmental damage arising in another country access to the courts in the offending country. In 1978 the first action programme on environmental protection was launched; it led to a succession of such programmes. The Nordic states have some of the most stringent environmental standards in Europe.

Because of the centrifugal pull of the European Community and EFTA, economic co-operation takes place largely within a wider Western European framework. Purely Nordic co-operation includes an Industrial Fund to promote research and a Nordic Investment Bank which can provide loans and give bank guarantees for Nordic projects. Transport has been a subject of Nordic co-operation since World War II. The amalgamation of the state airlines into the Scandinavian Airline System (SAS) in 1951 is the most symbolic manifestation of co-operation in this field. Plans to centralize transoceanic container freight in Gothenburg and to create a major joint airport in Copenhagen exist, as yet, only on paper.

The expansion in the scope of Nordic co-operation in the 1970s was accompanied by a strengthening of its institutional structure. By 1986 a total of 112 different public or semi-public bodies geographically dispersed throughout the Nordic region were in place, in contrast to a bare handful twenty years earlier.[40] The creation of a Nordic Council of Ministers in 1971 provided an institution for intergovernmental co-operation in addition to the Nordic Council, a parliamentary forum dating from the early 1950s. Policy-making in the Nordic arena rests on a dialogue between the parliamentary tier and the Council of Ministers. Since its inception, the latter has assumed a central role in policy-making because of its access to budgetary resources and official back-up. More than nineteen different commissions of senior officials have been set up to prepare the agenda for Council meetings. Policy co-operation in the Nordic system is highly compartmentalized; there is no attempt to fashion 'package deals' across policy areas.[41]

Sub-regional co-operation in the Nordic region is heavily influenced by developments on the Continent as a whole. The EC's 1992 programme and the SEA have tended to focus the attention of Nordic institutions on relations between the narrow regional context of NORDEN, EFTA and the EC. A series of reports drafted by the Nordic Council and the Nordic Council of Ministers in 1988 and 1989 evaluate the impact of EC developments on NORDEN and EFTA. The reports emphasize

- the need to strengthen Nordic co-operation so that it can keep pace with EC developments
- the need for Nordic co-operation on standards to adapt to EC developments
- the need to ensure that Nordic standards in social policy and on the environment are not weakened by EC developments.[42]

There is also a concern to ensure that Nordic co-operation, based as it is on a community of language, geographical proximity and the Nordic social model, survives in the 'New Europe'. The future of Nordic co-operation depends on the integration strategies of the non-EC states. If the Nordic states all join the EC, there will be a formidable Scandinavian coalition in the Community.

THE EUROPEAN COMMUNITY IS UNIQUE

This survey of the development of the myriad Western European organizations would not be complete without acknowledging the importance of the EC as the linch-pin of co-operation and integration. The Community is *sui generis* because it goes beyond the other organizations in the extent to which its activities are embodied in a system of law and in the intensity and range of EC co-operation. The Community's aims, constitutional basis and law-making capacity, institutional structure, policy scope and international role are highlighted in the following points:

1 The main goal of co-operation in the European Community is profoundly political: to 'transform relations as a whole among their States into a European Union', according to the Preamble of the Single European Act of 1986. The Council of Europe, with its commitment to achieving 'greater unity' among its member states displays a far weaker commitment to the notion of European unity. Jacques Delors, President of the Commission, distinguishes between the 'intergovernmental Council of Europe as guardian and advocate of democratic values throughout Europe and the integrationist Community working for European Union with all who unreservedly accept the full contract'.[43] Although the precise nature of a European union has never been clearly articulated, this ideological commitment to the 'full contract' plays a powerful symbolic role in the development of the EC. It underlines the open-ended nature of the commitment when a state opts for EC membership.

2 The European Community has created a new legal order. The founding Treaties and the Single European Act of 1986 provide the EC with a constitutional base and are the primary source of EC law and policy competence. Since the Community's inception, its institutions have enacted a growing corpus of regulations, directives and decisions, the legal instruments at the disposal of the Community.

The third source of EC law lies in the judgments of the Community's judicial arm, the Court of Justice. The Court adopts a constitutional approach to the interpretation of the Treaties and subsequent laws. In two key judgments, the Court established the three important principles of EC law: direct effect, direct applicability and the primacy of EC law over national law. Regulations are always directly applicable in the member states once they have become law; they do not have to be transposed into national law. In the van Gend en Loos case of 1963, the Court issued the doctrine of direct effect, which means that national courts have to recognize the rights and obligations imposed by EC law. The Court said:

> The Community constitutes a new legal order of international law for the benefit of which the states have limited their sovereign rights, albeit within limited fields, and the subjects of which compromise not [only] Member States but also their nationals. Independently of the legislation of Member States, Community law therefore not only imposes obligations on individuals but is also intended to confer upon them rights which become part of their legal heritage.[44]

In a second crucial judgment the Court of Justice established the doctrine of the supremacy of EC law over national law by stating that 'the Treaty carries with it a permanent limitation of their sovereign rights, against which a subsequent unilateral act incompatible with the concept of the Community' cannot prevail' (Case 6/64 Costa v. Enel 1964). The Community's legal order is one of its primary supranational features. None of the other organizations has the power to create a new and independent legal order that directly constrains the sovereignty of the member states. Co-operation, in these other cases, depends on formal conventions, treaties and parallel national legislation.[45]

3 The EC is a unique political system with an institutional structure displaying 'intergovernmental' and 'supranational' traits. Membership of the Community adds an additional and complicating layer

of politics to the political systems of the Twelve. The structures and powers of Community institutions are more sophisticated than the institutions of the other organizations. The intensity and mode of decision-making is also very different. The Commission, although it has not evolved into a European Government as envisaged by the founding fathers, is much more than a secretariat of an international organisation. As a collegiate body it has real decision- and law-making powers. The seventeen Commissioners are formally independent of their national political systems and receive a mandate for four years. The current President of the Commission, Jacques Delors, is a participant in EC decision-making at the highest level. He has managed to instil a new sense of purpose into the Commission by displaying real leadership qualities. The Commission's staff of over 15,000 provides it with a much more extensive policy-making capacity than the 900 staff in the Council of Europe's Secretariat, the 120 staff in the EFTA Secretariat and the 90 staff members in the Secretariat of the Nordic Council of Ministers.[46]

The Council of Ministers meets with far greater frequency than the ministerial bodies in the other organizations. In 1987 Ministers met on 118 occasions, in contrast to 21 times in 1958. Likewise, meetings of the Council's working groups add a European dimension to the work of most civil servants. Meetings in Brussels create a web of relationships between national civil servants, Commission officials and senior politicians across the the entire spectrum of public policy. The intensity of EC business makes the Council a permanent negotiating arena. Meetings of the heads of state and government became commonplace in the 1970s and were institutionalized by the Single European Act. Meetings at the highest political level take place in Nordic co-operation and in EFTA, but not with the regularity or formality of European Council meetings.

Although all the Western European organizations have a parliamentary forum of some kind, none resembles the European Parliament in its powers. The Parliament, with 518 members and a Secretariat of around 3,000, is much larger than its counterparts in the other organizations. More importantly, direct elections since 1979 give it democratic legitimacy which enables it to make claims for greater powers and a greater say in EC policy-making. Members of the European Parliament do not sit in national delegations but in transnational political groupings.

The extensive policy competence of the Community has led to the emergence of a myriad transnational interest organizations located in Brussels. Employers, trade unions, industrialists, distributers, farming interests, consumers, womens' groups and environmentalists have established transnational interest organizations. In 1985 a census of interest organizations conducted by the Commission concluded that there were 654 Euro-groups established in Brussels.[47] They have been encouraged by the Commission because it gives formal recognition to Community-wide groups and co-opts such groups into its policy-making process. There are some 1,400 consultative committees and bodies attached to the Commission.[48] This range and intensity of interest group formation is not found in the other European organizations.

4 The policy scope of the Community is very extensive because it is engaged in an advanced form of economic integration. The customs union, the common market and, more recently, the goal of economic and monetary union bring the Community into an ever-widening range of policy integration. Although the Community has taken-over exclusive responsibility for a limited range of policy issues, an EC dimension is an important aspect of most aspects of public policy in contemporary Europe. The Community has developed a role in such diverse areas as womens' rights, health and safety in the work-place, public health, environmental issues, education and research and development, in addition to the core of economic co-operation. Although the policy scope of the Council of Europe is potentially very wide, it has very limited policy instruments. EFTA, on the other hand, does not seek involvement in a very wide range of policy issues. Nordic co-operation concentrates on limited sectoral co-operation over a wide range of policies but is not engaged in advanced forms of economic integration.

The Community's policy scope is buttressed by a budget that is based not on national contributions but on what are known as 'own resources'. Although this budget is equivalent to just 1 per cent of the Community's gross national product, it enables the EC to influence national policies by means of funds and grants. The politics of 'grantsmanship' extends beyond the national capitals to Brussels. The budgets of the other organizations are much more modest.

5 The development of the European Community as the largest single trading bloc in the world, coupled with European Political Co-operation (EPC) in matters of foreign policy, endows it with a significant role in international politics. Although the Community lacks a common foreign policy, it is an international actor in its

own right. The Community has developed association, trade and co-operation agreements with adjacent European states, states on the southern shores of the Mediterranean, and states in the Third World. The Community is a major participant in GATT negotiations on trade issues and in other international economic forums. European Political Co-operation seeks to give the EC a diplomatic profile.

None of the other Western European organizations can match the Community's authority because of its legal order, institutional capacity and policy reach. Although the EC falls well short of the attributes of a fully fledged state, it has pioneered a new approach to inter-state relations.

NOTES

1 A.H. Robertson, *European Institutions: Co-operation: Integration: Unification* (London: Steven & Sons Ltd, 1973), pp.33–60.
2 R. Dahrendorf, 'A Third Europe', Monnet Lecture, Florence, EUI, 1979, p.11.
3 C. Pentland, 'Political theories of European integration: between science and ideology', in D. Lasok and P. Soldatos (eds), *The European Communities in Action* (Brussels: Bruylant, 1981), p.553.
4 Council of Europe, *Chart showing signature and ratifications of Council of Europe Conventions and Agreements, 1972–1987*, vol.1, Strasbourg, 1987. Details of agreements since 1987 received from the Council of Europe.
5 Council of Europe, *25th Anniversary of the European Social Charter: Origins, Operation and Results of the Charter* (Strasbourg, 1986).
6 Council of Europe, *Chart showing signatures and ratifications of Council of Europe Conventions and Agreements,* op. cit.
7 Ibid.
8 G. Kelly, 'The Council of Europe and local government', *Local Government Studies*, 1980, vol.6, pp.63–70.
9 Exchange of letters between the Council of Europe and the European Community, *EC Official Journal*, L 273/35–37, 26 September 1989.
10 Quoted in Robertson, op. cit., p.45.
11 Council of Europe, Report to the Council of Europe, Colombo Commission, Strasbourg, 1986, p.12.
12 Ibid.
13 Ibid.
14 Council of Europe, Declaration of the Committee of Ministers on the 'Future role of the Council of Europe in European construction', Strasbourg, 84th Session of the Committee of Ministers, 5 May 1989.
15 R.C. Hine, *The Political Economy of European Trade* (Brighton: Wheatsheaf Books, 1985), p.49.
16 H. von der Groeben, *The European Community: the Formative Years* (Brussels: EC Official Publications, 1987), pp.119–89.

17 E.C. Hallett, 'Economic convergence and divergence in the European Community: a survey of the evidence', in M. Hodges and W. Wallace (eds), *Economic Divergence in the European Community* (London: Allen & Unwin, 1981), pp.16–31.

18 EC, *Social Europe*, September 1983, p.106.

19 L. Tsoukalis, *The Politics and Economics of European Monetary Integration* (London: Allen & Unwin, 1977), p.125.

20 L. Tsoukalis, 'Looking into the Crystal Ball', *Journal of Common Market Studies*, 1982, vol.21, pp.229–44.

21 K. Kaiser, C. Kerlini, T. de Montbrial, E. Wellerstein, W. Wallace, *The European Community: Progress or Decline?* (London: Chatham House, 1983), p.1.

22 J. Lodge (ed.), *European Union: the European Community in Search of a Future* (London: Macmillan, 1986).

23 EC Bulletin, Supplement 5/1984, 3.4.1.

24 P. Keatinge and A. Murphy, 'The European Council's *ad hoc* Committee on Institutional Affairs', R. Pryce (ed.), *The Dynamics of European Integration* (London: Croom Helm, 1987), pp.217–37.

25 L.N. Lindberg and S.A. Scheingold, *Europe's Would-be Polity* (Englewood Cliffs, N.J.: Prentice-Hall, 1970), p.137.

26 R.O. Keohane and S. Hoffman, 'Institutional change in Europe in the 1980s', in R.O. Keohane and S. Hoffman (eds), *Decision-making and Institutional Change in the European Community* (Boulder Colorado: Westview, 1991).

27 E. Noel, 'The Single European Act', *Government and Opposition*, 1984, vol.24, pp.3–14.

28 EC Commission, 'Making a success of the single European act – a new frontier for Europe', Brussels, Bulletin Supplement 1/87.

29 H. Wallace, *Widening and Deepening: the EC and the New European Agenda*, discussion paper, no.23., London, RIIA, 1989.

30 V.Curzon, *Essentials of Economic Integration: Lessons of the EFTA Experience* (London: Macmillan, 1974), chapter 6.

31 C. Archer, 'EFTA and the Nordic Council' in K.J. Twitchett (ed.), *European Co-operation Today* (London: Europa Publications, 1980), pp.91–2.

32 Ibid., p.97.

33 Ibid., p.95.

34 Luxemburg Declaration, ministerial meeting between the EC and its member states and the states of EFTA, Luxemburg, 1984.

35 For a detailed analysis of EC/EFTA multilateral relations see P.G. Nell, 'EFTA in the 1990s: the search for a new identity', *Journal of Common Market Studies*, 1990, vol.28, pp.327–58.

36 B. Sundelius, 'Coping with transnationalism in northern Europe' *West European Politics*, 1980, vol.3, pp.219–29.

37 B. Sundelius and C. Wiklund, 'Regional Co-operation', *Journal of Common Market Studies*, 1979, vol.18, p.71.

38 For an extensive analysis of Nordic co-operation see F. Wendt, *Co-operation in the Nordic Countries* (Stockholm: Almqvist and Wiksell International, 1982).

39 Ibid., p.237.

40 C.-E. Stalvant, 'The Nordic countries and the European Community: dual integration paths to European partnership or acquiescent adaptation?', paper presented to the ECPR Joint Sessions, Amsterdam, 11–15 April 1987.

41 Sundelius and Wiklund, op. cit., 1979, pp.59–75.

42 The three reports are 'The Nordic Council and international co-operation', Stockholm, 1989; 'Nordic Council of Ministers, NORDEN in Europe, 1989–1992', Copenhagen 1989; 'Nordic Council of Ministers, NORDEN in Europe 11', Copenhagen 1989.

43 Address by Commission President Jacques Delors to the Parliamentary Assembly of the Council of Europe, 26 September 1989.

44 Case 26/62 Van Gend en Loos, 1963.

45 For an analysis of the role of law in EC integration see J. Weiler, 'Community, member states and European integration: is the law relevant?', *Journal of Common Market Studies*, 1982, vol.21, pp.39–55.

46 The figures for the Commission are taken from European Documentation, *The European Commission and the Administration of the Community*, Luxemburg, EC Official Publications, 1989, p.23, and for the other European organizations, Nordic Council and International Co-operation, op. cit.

47 Figures contained in P.C. Schmitter and W. Streeck, 'Organized Interests and the Europe of 1992', paper presented to a conference at the American Enterprise Institute, Washington, D.C., 6–8 March 1990.

48 Ibid., p.11.

TOPICS FOR DISCUSSION

1 Why did the Council of Europe fail to live up to the ideals of the Hague Congress?

2 Why was there a resurgence of formal integration in the EC in 1985?

3 Why and how did the EC emerge as the core organization in Western Europe?

4 What are the main differences between Nordic co-operation and EC integration?

5 What is the main challenge facing EFTA in the 1990s?

FURTHER READING

Archer, C. *Organising Western Europe*, Sevenoaks, Kent: Edward Arnold, 1990. This volume covers all the main West European and Atlantic organizations. Each organization is examined from the perspective of its establishment, institutional structure, achievements and contribution to the management of inter-state relations in Western Europe.

Twitchett, K.J. (ed.), *European Co-operation Today*, London: Europa Publications, 1980. This book provides a useful overview of all of the organizations designed to foster co-operation and integration in Europe, but it is somewhat out-of-date.

The European Community

George, S. *Politics and Policy in the European Community* Oxford: Clarendon Press, 1985. Although somewhat dated, this book provides an overview of the EC in the 1970s and early 1980s. A second edition is due to be published in autumn 1991.

Nicoll, W. and Salmon, T.C. *Understanding the European Communities*, London: Philip Allen, 1990. This volume provides a detailed analysis of the development of the EC, its institutional framework, and Britain's membership of it. The chapter on EPC treats an increasingly important aspect of the Community.

Nugent, N. *The Government and Politics of the European Community*, London: Macmillan, 1989. This volume treats thoroughly the institutions of the EC, the varying effectiveness of the EC's policy process and its 'supranational' and 'intergovernmental' features.

Taylor, P.G. *The Limits of European Integration*, London: Croom Helm, 1983. Taylor presents a critique of neo-functionalism and portrays the EC as an intergovernmental forum.

Tsoukalis, L. (ed.), *The European Community: Past, Present and Future*, Oxford: Blackwell, 1983. This volume brings together the papers presented in 1982 at a *Journal of Common Market Studies* conference. The papers provide a useful insight into academic analysis of the EC at the height of the budgetary crisis and draw attention to the apparent inabilty of the EC to adapt its policies and institutions to new challenges.

Articles on the European Community

Hoffman, S. 'The European Community and 1992', *Foreign Affairs*, 1989, vol.64, pp.27–47. This article is essential reading for a student wishing to trace the resurgence of formal integration in the EC in the latter half of the 1980s.

Sandholtz, W. and Zysman, J. (1989) '1992: recasting the European bargain', *World Politics*, vol.XLII, pp.1–30. This article examines both the domestic and international pressures that led to the SEA and the new dynamism in the EC.

Wallace, H. *Widening and Deepening: the European Community and the new European agenda*', discussion paper 23, London: RIIA, 1989. This monograph assesses the challenges facing the EC in the light of the East European revolutions, 1992 and relations with EFTA.

Publications on other organizations

A special edition of the *Journal of Common Market Studies* (28 June 1990) gives the most up-to-date assessment of the challenges facing EFTA. There are articles on EC/EFTA relations, EFTA's search for a new identity, EFTA and the Nordic countries, Austria and the EC, and the potential for EFTA to play a role in developing relations with the countries of Eastern and Central Europe.

Sundelius, B. and Wiklund, C. 'Regional Co-operation', *Journal of Common Market Studies*, 1979, vol.18, pp.59–75. This article assesses Nordic integration in the light of integration in Western Europe. It is useful as an introduction to the essential characteristics of Nordic integration but also because it helps to illuminate EC integration.

Wendt, F. *Co-operation in the Nordic Countries*, Stockholm: Almqvist and Wiksell, 1981. A comprehensive overview of the policy scope and institutions of Nordic co-operation.

Chapter 3

Economic integration
The home market

The decision to complete the home market by 1992 placed the Community's economic order high on the EC agenda. During the stagnation and low growth of the 1970s, foreign policy co-operation (EPC) was regarded as the model for future European co-operation. The resurgence of formal integration in Western Europe by the mid-1980s owes much to what is known in popular parlance as the '1992 programme'. An ambitious legislative programme, it aims to abolish the remaining barriers to economic exchange among the member states of the European Community by the end of 1992. Flanked by EC policies on research and development, the completion of the internal market is central to the achievement of sustained economic recovery in Europe. The apparent dynamism of the programme has contributed to renewed confidence in the EC and has fuelled demands for further economic integration in the form of economic and monetary union. A genuine internal market requires such a development. This chapter analyses the changes in the international political economy and in domestic economic policies in the member states that moulded the internal market programme. Attention then turns to the issue of the 'non-Europe', the Single European Act and the Cecchini Report. The internal market programme itself is examined from the perspective both of the White Paper and of its dynamic effects on the private sector. The wider dimension of the 1992 programme is addressed in the final section of the chapter.

A CHANGING GLOBAL POLITICAL ECONOMY

The 1992 programme must be seen in the context of a global economy that is growing ever more interdependent. Technological developments and related change in business strategy and corporate structure are now international in character. European industry finds itself in a global market, faced with intense competition from the US, Japan and the newly industrializing states. Changing patterns of production and trade have altered economic relations within Western capitalism. The hegemonic position of the US after World War II gave way progressively to a more pluralistic system. The Japanese economy underwent a profound transformation. Japan's industrial strategy of achieving a high market share in selected sectors proved very successful. In the 1980s a strong export performance in colour television sets, videos, photocopying machines and integrated circuits saw the Japanese penetrating the US and Western European markets. The low propensity of the Japanese to import creates tensions in its relations with the US and Western Europe.[1]

Technology is the key to this third industrial revolution. The development, acquisition and application of new technologies is a critical factor in Europe's search for renewed competitiveness.[2] European firms, research institutes and universities must not only innovate but also translate new technologies into marketable products, and must apply them in industry, in services and throughout the economy. Although European industry is relatively strong in a number of sectors – notably chemicals, pharmaceuticals and electrical equipment – it is weak in electronics. By 1986 Japan dominated the world market for memory chips, an essential product in the manufacture of computers. Between 1978 and 1988, the US share of the world market for semi-conductors fell from 56 per cent to 32 per cent, with a corresponding rise in the Japanese share from 18 per cent to 45 per cent. The EC's fall in market share in this period was of the order of 8 per cent, from a relatively modest share of 22 per cent to 14 per cent.[3] However, the challenge of international competition could not have been addressed without significant changes in economic policy in key member states.

CHANGING DOMESTIC POLITICS

Economic turbulence in the 1970s upset the post-war consensus on economic management, which looked to governments to provide full or near full employment by using Keynesian-type demand management. This order was challenged in the 1970s by growing inflation, unemployment and a fiscal crisis. At first, Europe responded by 'sacrificing the future for the present', according to the Albert and Ball report submitted to the EP in 1983, Entitled '*Towards European Economic Recovery in the 1980s*, the report emphasized that Europe was 'caught up in the web of its past, adopting what the psychologists might call an "escapist posture"'.[4] Wages were boosted at the expense of profits, and consumption was favoured more than investment. The European labour market was highly structured and offered extensive protection to those in jobs but little opportunity for employment to marginalized groups in the labour market.

Traditional strategies of economic management were challenged with ideological fervour by the British Prime Minister, Margaret Thatcher, from 1979 onwards. More significantly, in France and Spain, socialist governments embraced a market-oriented approach. On assuming power in 1981, President Mitterrand attempted to achieve high growth rates and job creation by expansionist economic policies. The ensuing fiscal crisis, trade deficit and a weakened franc had led, by March 1983, to a major reassessment of economic strategy. Within the French cabinet, a battle was waged between ministers favouring a policy of autarky and those who were convinced of the need for retrenchment. The decision to maintain the franc in the EMS marked a turning point for President Mitterrand. Thereafter, he pursued French economic goals in an EC context. Liberalization and deregulation became the hallmarks of economic and industrial policy as the 1980s progressed.[5] A consensus developed around the issue of the 'non-Europe'.

The non-Europe

Faced with increasing global competition, hampered by rigidities in industrial structure and labour market policies, Europe's future economic prosperity seemed endangered. Pessimism about Western Europe was rife. The Albert and Ball report spoke of the 'European malady'.[6] Economists, business leaders, politicians and officials diagnosed and prescribed for the patient. 'Non-Europe' was identified as a major component of Europe's problems. What is meant by 'non-Europe'? Although the Rome Treaty (EEC) set out to establish a common market, a host of non-tariff barriers to trade remained, and the free movement of capital and services was far from achieved. Europe's highly fragmented market could appropriately be called an 'uncommon market'. The following examples highlight the 'non-Europe':

- The specification for colour television sets is not the same in France (SECAM) as it is in Germany (PAL), with the result that a French television set is not suitable in Cologne, nor a German one in Strasbourg.
- Delays at border crossings and the myriad forms required to pass through the member states borders meant that a 1,200 km (750 mile) round trip from London to Milan (excluding the ferry crossing) took 58 hours, whereas a journey of equivalent length from London to Edinburgh took 36 hours.
- A consumer organization estimated that a person travelling through ten member states without spending any money would return to the starting country with only 53 per cent of his or her money, because of the cost of currency exchange.

The establishment of a separate Internal Market Council in 1982 demonstrated, albeit in a limited way, the growing importance of this policy domain for the Community's future. The 1983 Albert and Ball report was instrumental in placing the notion of the 'non-Europe' on the Community's political agenda. Its message was clear: public procurement policies, delays at borders, lack of co-ordination in research and development – all were costing a large amount of money, to the detriment of Europe's economic well-being.

Europe's industrialists entered the fray. In 1983 the head of AB Volvo, the Swedish car producers, founded the Roundtable of European industrialists to build bridges between EC and EFTA industry. The Roundtable, consisting initially of the presidents of seventeen of Europe's leading companies, moved its headquarters from Paris to Brussels to be near EC institutions.[7] Early in 1985 Philips, the Dutch multinational, published a paper entitled 'Europe 1990: an Agenda for action', endorsing the Commission's approach.[8] Meetings between the captains of Europe's largest firms, national politicians and Commission officials proliferated. Although it is difficult to assess the impact of European business élites on the evolution of the internal market programme, the views of Europe's top businessmen encouraged national politicians to consider reforming the EC's institutions and decision-making processes.

THE PATH TO REFORM

Pressures from the world economy and changing domestic priorities facilitated a convergence of views around a new strategy for Europe among key individuals in the national capitals, the Commission and European industry. The kernel of this strategy is found in the June 1985 Commission White Paper *Completing the Internal Market*.[9] The White Paper, known as the Cockfield Document after the Commissioner responsible for the Internal Market portfolio in the first Delors Commission (1985–1989), when endorsed by the 1985 Milan European Council assumed a central role in the development of the EC. It was accepted in the majority of member states that an intergovernmental bargain, embracing a new package of policies, had to be fashioned before the Cockfield White Paper could enter the realm of practical politics.

The aspirations of the White Paper could not be achieved without reform of the Community's decision-making process. Successive enlargements, the legacy of de Gaulle and timidity on the part of the Commission engendered a slow, frequently tortuous process of decision-making which resulted in no agreements, or agreements based on the lowest common denominator. It took ten years for the Community to agree on standards for fork-lift trucks; the appropriate pedal system was the major bone of contention. Without institutional change, the Cockfield White Paper would have gathered dust as the 300 proposals wound their way through the Council's labyrinth.

The Single European Act provided the political cement for the 1992 programme. Articles 13–15 of the Act provide for the inclusion of three new articles (8A, 8B and 8C) in the EEC Treaty. Article 8A contains the commitment of 'progressively establishing the internal market over a period expiring on 31 December 1992'. It defines the internal market as an 'area without internal frontiers in which the free movement of goods, persons, services and capital is ensured in accordance with the provisions of this Treaty'.[10] The 1992 deadline is merely a political aspiration, because a declaration annexed to the Act specifies that the deadline does not have an automatic legal effect.

The SEA's provisions on majority voting are the most striking manifestation of the member states' commitment to the 1992 programme. Qualified majority voting becomes the norm for most aspects of the internal market. A new article, 100A, is the most important Treaty amendment, as it makes provision for the Council to 'adopt the measures for the approximation of the provisions laid down by law, regulation or administrative action in Member States which have as their object the establishment and functioning of the internal market' by qualified majority voting.[11] Although fiscal harmonization, the free movement of people and the rights of employed persons are excluded from the remit of Article 100A, it has very wide application.

The notion of differentiation (see p.13) is present in the SEA. Within narrow limits, the Act stipulates that the Commission, when drawing up its proposals, must take into account the requirements of economies 'showing differences in development' and may propose appropriate provisions, including derogations.[12] This provision (Article 8C) recognizes the increasing heterogeneity of the Community of Twelve. With respect to the application of Article 100A, countries may 'apply national provisions on grounds of major needs referred to in Article 36 or relating to protection of the environment or the working environment'.[13] Article 36 of the original Treaty (EEC) specified that national measures could be applied for a long list of reasons, notably public morality, public policy and public security. Thus, states that are outvoted in the Council could continue to apply national measures. However, there are strict limits to the possibility of 'opting out'. This clause has not in fact been used by any member state since the ratification of the SEA.

As a consequence of the commitment of the member states to the completion of the internal market, attitudes towards majority voting were transformed even before the full ratification of the Act. In July 1987, the formal rules of the Council were amended to provide for the greater use of weighted voting. The 'rules of the game' in the Internal Market Council have altered significantly, since decisions are no longer blocked at working party level. The Commission and the presidency need only forge an agreement that is acceptable to the majority. The threat of a vote is often sufficient to get a recalcitrant state to agree. National policy-makers are working out their positions on Commission proposals with greater speed and establishing coalitions with partners in order to construct a qualified majority or a blocking minority. The dramatic impact of the SEA on decision-making may be gleaned from the following examples. Before the SEA, a directive creating technical norms or standards required thirty-one months in the Council, but it took a mere thirteen months after the passing of the SEA. Likewise, Directive 84/538 on lawn mowers took sixty-nine months, but a related Directive 88/181 was passed in fourteen months.[14]

The Cecchini Report: an economic rationale?

As part of its strategy to create and maintain momentum towards the completion of the market, the Commission established in 1986 a research forum, directed by Paolo Cecchini, to study the costs of the non-Europe and the benefits that would accrue after the abolition of non-tariff barriers. The research was a major undertaking in economic analysis; twenty-four studies were commissioned, covering different barriers and industrial sectors in addition to analyses of the methodological problems associated with research of this kind. The results of the Cecchini Report, setting out the microeconomic and macroeconomic effects of the 1992 programme, were published in two volumes in 1988. The main argument of the report is that

> the completion of the internal market could, if strongly reinforced by the competition policies of both the Community and Member States have a deep and extensive impact on economic structures and performance. The size of this impact, in terms of the potential for increased non-inflationary growth, could be sufficient to transform the Community's macroeconomic performance from a mediocre to a very satisfactory one.[15]

The report estimated the costs to Europe's consumers and businesses of the fragmented market. According to the report, manufacturing industry is worst hit by customs formalities, technical regulations and disparate tax treatment, whereas in fields such as telecommunications, energy and transport, protectionist public procurement policies lead to inefficient companies. The extensive regulation of the services sector impedes competition, thereby contributing to costs.[16]

The authors of the report established an estimate of the microeconomic effects of the single market. Table 3.1 presents an overview of their main findings.

The report went on to examine the macroeconomic effects of the programme. It estimated that market integration, in the medium term, could trigger a major relaunch of economic activity by adding, on average, 4.5 per cent to EC GDP; it would also lead to a reduction in consumer prices because of increased competition and greater efficiency, and would improve the balance of public finances by an average equivalent to 2.2 per cent of GDP. Cecchini also found that employment would increase by 1.8 million jobs after five to six years of adjustment.[17]

Table 3.1 Potential gains from the completion of the internal market:
The Cecchini Report

Barriers	% GDP
Removal of barriers (frontiers)	0.2–0.3
Removal of barriers (public procurement)	2.0–2.4
Immediate benefits	2.2–2.7
Economies of scale	2.1
Reducing inefficiency	1.6
Longer-term gains	3.7
TOTAL 12 Member states at 1988 prices	4.3–6.4

Source: Cecchini (1988), p.84.

The Cecchini conclusions support the economic rationale behind
the Commission's White Paper, but its authors emphasize that for
the potential gains to accrue, the legislative programme must be
completed, transposed into national law and enforced. European
industry must rationalize and restructure, and the 1992 programme
must be accompanied by appropriate economic policies. The Padoa-
Schioppa Report of 1987 concluded that, although the internal
market programme was important in improving the efficiency of
resource allocation in the EC, complementary policies were needed
to foster monetary stability, the equitable distribution of the gains
of economic welfare and a strategy for growth.[18]

Some economists have criticized the Cecchini Report for its mode
of analysis and findings. A number of them conclude that the
anticipated benefits are greatly exaggerated and that the regional
impact of the 1992 programme does not get sufficient attention in the
mammoth output of the Cecchini research forum.[19] Notwithstanding
the inevitable debate about the likely impact of the 1992 programme,
it provided a powerful catalyst for a resurgence in formal integration.
Even if its benefits prove to be exaggerated, the public and media
attention it receives have forced companies to look beyond their
limited national borders to think in continent-wide terms.

The White Paper – How fares it?

The Cockfield White Paper set out 300 internal market directives
under three general headings physical barriers, technical barriers
and fiscal barriers. The original proposals have been whittled down

to 282 by the elimination of some and the grouping of others. The listing of concrete proposals and a target date (calendar technique) was astute. It put pressure on the Council to achieve the targets, captured the imagination of élites and the wider public, and provided a global picture of the programme.

According to two analysts:

> The difficult political questions could be obscured by focusing on the mission and by reducing the issues to a series of apparently technical steps. In a sense the tactic is to move above and below the level of controversy.[20]

The White Paper was presented as the execution of already agreed policy. The politicians, having declared themselves to be in favour of a large home market of 320 million consumers, were now being asked to bring their political will and capacity to bear on its successful completion.

By April 1990, the pre-legislative phase of the internal market programme was complete when the Commission submitted its last proposal to the Council.[21] By December 1990 a decision had been taken or a common position arrived at in the Council on 200 of the proposals.[22] The pace of decision-making owes much to the institutional changes already referred to, but also to the adoption of an approach known as the 'the new citizenship of mutual recognition'.[23] For years the Community's attempts at harmonization were stymied by the density of national regulations. An over-zealous Commission, in its search for the 'Euro-beer' and 'Euro-bread' in the early 1970s, damaged the credibility of its work among the wider public.

Physical barriers: border controls

Customs barriers at seaports, airports and the roadside are a very visible symbol of the 'uncommon market'. They are there to control the movement of goods and people. The aim of the programme is to abolish internal borders in the Community by 1993. Up to January 1988, when a standardized customs form was introduced, there were no fewer than seventy-eight different customs forms in use, at a high cost to industry. The strategy is to simplify and then to abolish border checks on goods. So far, directives have been passed that will abolish vehicle checks at borders; veterinary checks have been reorganized, and the obligation to supply a transit note at borders has been abolished. Substantial progress, however, depends on developments on indirect taxation (see p.86).[24]

The dismantling of border checks for people is proving to be very problematic. Fears of drug trafficking, terrorism, the treatment of third country nationals and refugees raise difficult issues for national justice ministries and police forces. In June 1989 a Co-ordinator's Group of national officials, responsible for outlining proposals in this field, submitted the Palma Report, which advocates extensive intergovernmental co-operation, to the Madrid European Council. The resort to intergovernmental co-operation, rather than Treaty-based procedures, testifies to the political nature of this field. The signing of the first intergovernmental convention on asylum-seekers in June 1990 suggests that the member states are determined to put the necessary legislative framework in place. A second convention on external borders and visa policy is at the negotiating stage. The right of third country nationals legally resident in one member state to move within the internal market is a major issue. It appears that they will have the right to move freely within the EC but not to seek employment or residence, because migration policy remains a national policy competence. This could well raise difficulties for companies with a substantial migrant work-force who wish to take up public procurement contracts in another member state.

The Schengen process, launched in 1985 by France, Belgium, The Netherlands, Germany and Luxemburg, introduces an element of 'variable geometry' to the debate on the free movement of people. These five core EC countries signed the Schengen Agreement in June 1990 with the purpose of abolishing border formalities for their nationals on their common borders ahead of 1992. Italy joined the group in December 1990, and the countries of the Iberian Peninsula have observer status in the group.[25] The breaching of the Berlin Wall in November 1989 delayed the signing of the actual Treaty because of fears concerning the intra-German border and the potential influx of refugees from Eastern Europe. The agreement provides for the 'Schengen Information System', or SIS, to allow the exchange of information about suspects and stolen goods among the national police forces and administrations. Co-operation on law enforcement and on visa policy form a central part of the agreement.

Technical barriers

Technical barriers include a wide array of impediments to free trade in goods and services. They are among the most effective non-tariff barriers available to the member states in their attempts to protect the domestic market. The White Paper identifies six different areas for action under the general rubric of technical barriers. These are technical standards, public procurement, free movement of labour, services, capital movements and legislation affecting the operation of businesses. Considerable progress has been made in the legislative programme. (See Table 3.2.) The main provisions on technical standards and public procurement are in place. A significant number of directives that will liberalize the services sector have now been passed. Progress is slower with regard to company law because of continuing conflict about proposals on worker participation.

The progress of the legislative programme through the Council owes much to the Commission's new approach, which manifests itself in technical standards, and the free movement of labour and services. The 'new approach' owes much to a number of key judgements by the European Court of Justice, notably the *cassis de Dijon* case of 1979. This judgment established the principle that a product legally produced in one country must move freely throughout the Community unless a member state can prove that its exclusion was necessary for reasons of public health and safety. The case was taken by the French Government when *cassis de Dijon* was barred from the German market on the grounds that it was not a liqueur since its alcohol content was below that of its German equivalent.[26]

The principle of 'mutual recognition' spilled over into the free movement of workers. A directive passed in June 1988 established the principle that qualifications gained in universities or their equivalent in any member state had to be recognized throughout the Community, provided that the course pursued involved a minimum of three years' study. The desire to avoid too much EC legislation is also found in the services area. The 'second banking' directive establishes the principle that a bank licenced to trade in any one member state can set up in another subject to the control of the 'home country' authorities.[27]

Fiscal barriers

Different rates of VAT and excise duties persist in the EC, despite an 1977 agreement on a common basis for assessing VAT. Disparities in VAT rates applied in the member states and their coverage in addition to widely differing rates of excise distort consumption patterns. The fact that VAT is not paid on exports is one more reason for border controls. The approximation of indirect taxation has proved to be one of the most intractable and contentious issues facing the Council because of the impact of approximation on national systems of taxation and on the revenue-generating capacity of national exchequers. The first proposals on indirect taxation were placed before the Economic and Finance Ministers' Council in September 1987 by the Internal Market Commissioner,

Table 3.2 Summary of progress on technical barriers

Technical standards: Legislative programme complete
       *Prior notification to Commission of new standards
       *Principle of mutual recognition
       *Commission green book on standards – CEN and CENELEC

Public procurement: Legislative programme complete except for directive on contracts dealing with services
       *Improved directive on supplies and public works
       *Utilities directive: transport, energy, water and telecommunications included
       *Improved enforcement and remedies

Free movement of labour
       *Directive on mutual recognition of professional qualifications
       *Negotiations still continuing on complementary directive on qualifications of less than three years

Capital movements
       *Directive on full liberalization on a phased basis
       *Failure to adopt a directive on withholding tax

Services
       *Agreement on a number of directives dealing with banking, insurance, transport and the audio-visual sector

Company law and industrial property – slower progress
       *European economic interest grouping directive 1989
       *Agreement on European patent convention but dispute about the location of the EC trade mark office.
       *Directive on mergers delayed because of conflict with regard to worker participation provisions

Lord Cockfield, but later they were substantially modified by his successor, Mme Scrivener. The Council delegated responsibility for analysing the proposals to an *ad hoc* working party of national experts, with the result that the matter did not come before the Council until the autumn of 1989.[28] The Council did not have much time to work out a compromise in time for the 1992 deadline.

The Council deferred the difficult decisions by agreeing to a transitional phase until December 1996. During this transition, border controls will be eliminated as of the first of January 1993, but intra-Community exports will continue to be zero-rated for VAT. In other words, VAT will be paid in the country where goods are purchased rather than produced. Yet there will be no border checks to ensure that goods actually leave a country. During the transitional phase, an alternative to border checks will have to be found. The decision opens the way for considerable fraud. The Commission has proposed a transitional arrangement requesting companies to supply national authorities with details of all exports to regulate the VAT situation. The 1992 programme, which aims to reduce red tape for industry and enterprise, may in fact contribute an additional burden if this system is put in place.[29] The Council has not yet reached agreement on the approximation of VAT rates and excise duties. The requirement of unanimity on indirect taxation demonstrates the difficulties that will have to be faced if consensus is required.

Implementation: the missing link

Implementation is a key element in the successful operation of the internal market. Unless the member states transpose and enforce EC law, the home market will not become a reality.
According to Pelkmans and Winters:

> Legislation may be agreed, but unless vigorously implemented the economic objectives behind the internal market will remain a pious wish.[30]

The European Parliament and the Commission have been concerned for a number of years about the uneven performance of the member states in implementing EC law. A major study of implementation concluded that there were major differences among the EC member states concerning their capacity to implement and enforce EC law.[31] Table 3.3 gives details of the number of infringements by different member states taken up by the Commission in 1987.[32]

The picture emerging in Table 3.3 is of three countries with serious difficulties with implementation. For years, Italy has been identified as the state with most difficulty in implementing EC law. Greece and Belgium also have a weak record of implementation. Ireland, France and Germany are found in the second grouping of states with over 50 infringements each. Denmark, The Netherlands, Luxemburg and Britain have a good record of implementation. The figures for Spain and Portugal are not that revealing because they are still relatively new member states.

Table 3.3 Number of infringements of directives, 1987

Country	Cases	%
Belgium	75	12
Germany	57	9
Denmark	37	6
Greece	76	13
Spain	35	6
France	56	9
Ireland	59	10
Italy	89	15
Luxemburg	33	5
Netherlands	36	6
Portugal	8	1
UK	42	7

Source: EC Commission, Com (88) 425 final, 3 October 1988, Table 6. Figures rounded.

The Commission raised the issue of implementation in the Council in September 1989 because of its concern about the transposition of internal market directives into national law. Although some eighty-eight texts resulting from the SEA should have been implemented by December 1989, only fourteen were in place in all member states. By March 1990, this had risen to twenty-one because of improvements in Spain and Portugal. Italy remains the country with the gravest problems in implementing EC law.[33] It could well be that the present volume of EC legislation exceeds the administrative and parliamentary capacity of some member states.

THE DYNAMIC EFFECTS OF 1992

The response of corporate Europe to the programme is vital. Unless European firms adopt Continent-wide strategies, the European market will continue to be fragmented. Once the credibility of the

1992 idea was established with the SEA and the successful German presidency of the Council in 1988, business began to accept it as part of their business environment. National media campaigns financed by governments exhorted companies to examine their corporate strategies with a view to ensuring success in the post-1992 Europe. Some companies began to concentrate their production facilities. For example, the Swiss company Jacob Suchard reduced its number of production facilities from seventeen to just six. Distribution and marketing is another area where companies have sought to anticipate the home market. Colgate-Palmolive, a US multinational, created a board of management in Brussels for all its European operations and reduced the number of its storage depots from ten to five.

A significant increase in merger and take-over activity among European firms is apparent as they seek to consolidate in the run-up to 1992. According to the Commission, the total number of mergers or take-overs undertaken by the top thousand firms rose from 227 in 1985/86 to 383 in 1987/88 and 492 in 1988/89.[34] In January 1988, Carlo de Benedetti, the President of Olivetti, launched a take-over bid for one of the core Belgian companies, Société Générale de Belgique. Although de Benedetti did not succeed in taking a controlling share in the company, the debate in Belgium and the rest of Europe about the need to consolidate to create pan-European companies highlights the link between the 1992 programme and business strategies for the 1990s.[35]

In addition to mergers and take-overs, there is a significant increase in joint ventures between two or more companies. The German electronics group AEG formed a consortium with Nokia, a Finnish electronics group, and Alcatel, the largest telecommunications group in France, to enter the market for mobile telephones. A common Europe-wide agreement on standards for new mobile phones made this possible. In other industries a similar pattern is emerging; in banking, Barclays, Deutsche Bank and Commerzbank have joined forces, and in management consultancy Ernst and Whinney and Arthur Young and Company have merged. The defence industry, which is exempt under Article 223 of the Rome Treaty from EC competition rules, has not escaped the merger and take-over phenomenon. Inter-corporate networks are becoming the business dynamic of the 1990s.[36]

The Western European economy is performing with renewed vigour. Production has risen by some 20 per cent, and 8.5 million jobs have been created in the Community since 1984. Trade between EC states is recovering from a decline in the early 1980s. Intra-Community trade as a share of exports rose from 55 per cent in 1982 to 62 per cent in 1988. US investment in the Community rose from $83,900 million US in 1985 to $126,500 million in 1988, while the flow of Japanese investment has risen from $2,000 million in 1985 to $8,300 million in 1988.[37] Mergers, joint ventures and corporate networks draw attention to the need to strengthen the capacity of the EC to control the creation of European wide monopolies through an effective competition policy.

Competition policy

Two main dispositions in the Rome Treaty (EEC) deal with competition policy: Article 86 on the abuse of a dominant position and Articles 92–4 on state aid. Commissioner Peter Sutherland, in the first Delors Commission (1985–9), adopted a very active approach to competition policy as a major component of the internal market. In September 1990 a new system of merger control was put in place. The purpose of the new procedures is to ensure that large-scale mergers do not become Europe-wide monopolies. Only mergers that amount to 5,000 million ECUs in global turnover are covered by the new procedures. The member states continue to have exclusive jurisdiction under this threshold. The current Competition Commissioner, Sir Leon Brittain, has also turned his attention to excessive state aid.[38]

Trans-European networks

As the legislative phase of the 1992 programme draws to a close, the member states and the Commission are looking at industrial policy and infrastructural policy in the barrier-free Europe. EC industrial policy, long associated with declining industry in the Community, is again on the agenda. A Commission working paper of September 1990 is designed to promote debate about an industrial policy concept for the Community.[39] Commission attention is increasingly turning to trans-European networks (TEN). The Commission portrays the internal market as a living organism with a circulation system (transport), a nervous system (telecommunications), a muscular system (energy) and a brain (training). The concept of trans-European networks is designed to overcome the widespread fragmentation of infrastructure in Europe.[40]

THE WIDER DIMENSION

Although the impulse for the creation of a single European market came from within Western Europe, especially from the poor performance of the West European economies, it has attracted considerable attention in the US, Japan and the EFTA states. The EC's trading partners are busily assessing the likely impact of 1992 on their access to the Community market and on direct investment. Their major priority is to ensure, both in bilateral negotiations and through the GATT, that the internal market will not resemble a 'Fortress Europe'. As the world's largest trading bloc, a protectionist Community would have serious consequences for the world economy. The EFTA states, in particular, must adapt their traditional integration policies to the new realities of Western Europe.[41]

The notion of a European Economic Area or 'Space' (a phrase coined at a joint EC–EFTA ministerial meeting in 1984) becomes a compelling goal for the EFTA states as the EC intensifies its efforts to achieve a barrier-free Europe. Continuing access to the Community market is vital because the EC is EFTA's major trading partner. In 1988, 56 per cent of EFTA exports went to the EC, which was, in turn, the source of 60 per cent of imports. Although EFTA is also the Community's largest trading partner, the level of dependency is much lower; in 1987, it accounted for 26.5 per cent of EC exports and 23.6 per cent of imports.[42] Heretofore the joint EC–EFTA free trade area afforded companies in the EFTA states access to the market without the political costs and obligations of membership. However, continued privileged access requires either active adaptation to EC norms on a unilateral basis or an accommodation with the Community concerning the joint management of economic exchange in Western Europe.

The political impulse for the creation of the EEA was given by President Jacques Delors when he presented the programme for his second term of office to the European Parliament in January 1989. The EFTA heads of government accepted the Delors offer at a summit in Oslo in the same year. In a wide-ranging communiqué, the EFTA countries acknowledged that EC-EFTA relations had intensified following 1984 but that 'this broadened co-operation had not quite matched our ambitions and expectations'.[43] Formal EC-EFTA negotiations on the EEA opened in June 1990. The aim of the talks is to agree to a treaty with the following characteristics.

First, the treaty will be a multilateral one between the Community and EFTA. As a consequence of this, EFTA has had to speak with one voice in the negotiations. Second, the agreement will be broad in scope, as all four freedoms (goods, capital, services and people) are included. Third, the treaty will provide for a 'structured' relationship between the two parties. In his EP speech, Delors implied that there would be 'joint decision-making and administrative procedures' to govern the EEA.[44]

The EEA negotiations touch on many sensitive issues for both sides, and these must be resolved before agreement is reached. In 1987, the EC Commissioner for External Relations, Willy de Clercq, set out three principles that govern the Community's approach to its relations with EFTA:

1 The completion of the internal market has priority.
2 The Community's autonomy in decision-making must be respected.
3 There must be a balance between rights and obligations.[45]

From the outset, the Commission and an increasingly vocal European Parliament stressed the autonomy of the Community's law-making processes. The EFTA states, on the other hand, seek genuine joint decision-making and common institutions. For its part, the Commission distinguishes between decision-making and decision-shaping. During the policy preparation stage, the Commission envisages an exchange of views between a joint body of EC and EFTA representatives leading to agreement on the best way to proceed. Presumably, in the absence of agreement the Commission would proceed to table proposals. The implementation of EEA-related decisions also gives rise to difficulties. The EFTA states have expressed their unwillingness to accept laws that have not been jointly decided on.

EFTA's adaptation to the existing *acquis communautaire* is not without difficulty. The Commission forsees a speedy transition, with limited derogations for fundamental national interests. On the other hand, the EFTA list of proposed derogations is lengthy, which suggests that individual EFTA countries still have a hankering for an á la carte approach, whereas for the Community the *acquis* is a totality and must be taken as such. Each EFTA state brings with it its own particular interests: fishing for Iceland, transit traffic and free movement of people for Switzerland, forests for Finland and restrictive laws concerning foreign investment for Norway.

The development of the European Economic Area implies a major evolution in EFTA as an organization, given its weak tradition of collective endeavour. To date, the EFTA states have pursued disparate individual interests in their relations with the Community, rather than collective ones. Package deals and trade-offs are an essential characteristic of any international regime. Individual EFTA countries will have to sacrifice some national interests in their search for a global agreement and in the ongoing management of the EEA. The size of the EFTA secretariat has grown in response to the EEA talks. It is forseen that it will have a staff of 120, which represents a strengthening of its resources, although it will continue to be small in relation to the Commission.[46] There would be deep resistance within EFTA to endowing it with supranational decision-making powers. It was in order to avoid participation in such institutions that many EFTA states opted for the EFTA model of integration in the first place.

The extent of economic ties between the Community and EFTA is a powerful incentive to resolve the sensitive and difficult issues that confront the negotiators. The experience of negotiating on the EEA may well lead a number of EFTA countries to opt for the certainties of full membership, leaving the remaining countries to work out bilateral arrangements with the enlarged Community. Austria made its membership application in 1989, Sweden in 1991, and the debate on membership is now part of the political agenda in Norway, Finland and even Switzerland.

CONCLUSIONS

Agreement on the '1992 programme' has served as the catalyst for renewed dynamism in the European Community. The completion of the internal market was endorsed by all member states, encouraging institutional change and more efficient decision-making. As the consequences of the legislative programme for companies work their way through the economic system, the EC will become even more interdependent. Companies are adapting corporate strategies to take account of the changing business environment with an increase in merger activity and joint ventures. From 1988 onwards, the international consequences of the policy has assumed a central place on the agenda. The European Economic Area negotiations represent an effort to establish an international regime for Western Europe as a whole, covering nineteen countries. Although 1992 has taken-over the headlines, there is a wider economic agenda which forms the subject of the next chapter.

NOTES

1 G. Daniels, 'EC–Japan: past, present and future', in J. Lodge (ed.), *The European Community and the Challenge of the Future* (London: Frances Pinter, 1989), pp.279–84.
2 S. Woods, *Technology and the Future*, Atlantic Paper, no.63, Paris, Atlantic Institute for International Affairs, 1987. See also M. Richonner, 'Europe's decline is not irreversible', *Journal of Common Market Studies*, 1984, vol.22, pp.227–43.
3 W. Sandholtz and J. Zysman, '1992: Recasting the European bargain' *World Politics*, 1989, vol.XLII, p.104 and C. Farrands, 'EC chip manufacturers struggle to compete', *European Trends*, (London: Economist Intelligence Unit, 1990), no.3, p.71.
4 M. Albert and R.J. Ball, *Towards European Economic Recovery in the 1980s* (Luxemburg: EP, 1983), p.11.
5 A. Moravcsik, 'Negotiating the single act: national interests and Conventional Statecraft in the European Community', Working Paper Series, Paper no.21, Harvard Center for European Studies, 1990, pp.13–15.
6 Albert and Ball, op. cit.
7 A. Krause, 'After European economic integration, what next?, *European Affairs*, 1988. vol.3, p.50.
8 C. Van der Klugt, 'An Agenda for immediate action', *European Affairs*, 1988, vol.3, p.57.
9 EC Commission, *Completing the Internal Market: White Paper from the Commission to the European Council* (Brussels, 1985).
10 Single European Act, EC Bulletin Supplement 2/86, Article 8A.
11 Ibid, Article 100A.
12 Ibid, Article 8C.
13 Ibid, Article 100A.4.
14 C.-D. Ehlerman, 'The Institutional development of the EC under the Single European Act', *Aussenpolitik*, 1990, vol.41., pp.135–46.
15 EC Commission, *The Economics of 1992*, European Economy Series, 1988, no.35, p.21.
16 P. Cecchini, *1992: the Benefits of a Single Market* (Aldershot: Gower), 1988.
17 Ibid., pp.91–102.
18 T. Padoa-Schioppa, *Efficiency, Stability and Equity: a Strategy for the Evolution of the Economic System of the EC* (London: Oxford University Press, 1987).
19 T. Cutler, C. Haslam, John Williams, Karel Williams, *1992: the Struggle for Europe* (New York: Berg, 1989), pp.54–75.
20 W. Sandholtz and J. Zysman op. cit., p.115.
21 EC Commission, *Fifth Report of the Commission to the Council and the European Parliament Concerning the Implementation of the White Paper on*

the Completion of the Internal Market, Com (90) 90 final, 28 March 1990.

22 Figures taken from address by Michael Ayrl, EC Commission Seminar, Team 92, 29 November 1990.

23 A. Bressand, 'Beyond Interdependence: 1992 as a global challenge', *World Politics*, 1989, vol.XLII, p.60.

24 EC Commission Fifth Report, op. cit., pp.12–14.

25 Agence Europe, no.5379, 28 November 1990.

26 J. Pinder, 'The Single Market: a step towards European union', in J. Lodge, op. cit., p.97.

27 J. Dermine, 'The Specialization of financial institutions: the EC model', *Journal of Common Market Studies*, 1990, vol.28, pp.222–33.

28 EC Commission *Fifth Report*, op. cit., pp.26–7.

29 EC Commission, Information Memo, *Abolition of Tax Frontiers: Achievements to Date and Prospects for Work in Hand*, (Brussels, 18 January 1991).

30 J. Pelkmans and A. Winters, *Europe's Domestic Market*, (London: Routledge, 1988), p.80.

31 H. Siedentopf and J. Ziller (eds), *The Implementation of Community Legislation in the Member States* (London: Sage, 1988), vol.1.

32 EC Commission, *Fifth Annual Report on the Application of Community Law: 1987*, Com (88), 425 final, 3 October 1988.

33 EC Commission *Fifth Report concerning the implementation of the White Paper on the completion of the internal market*, op. cit., p.4.

34 EC Commission, *Three Years to the Completion of the Internal Market: A First Assessment of its Impact*, Sec (90) 494 final, 28 March 1990.

35 A. Krause, op. cit., p.46.

36 Ibid., pp.46–54.

37 *Three Years to the Completion of the Internal Market*, op. cit.

38 Address by Sir Leon Brittain, commissioner responsible for competition, to CEPS seminar, Brussels, 24 September 1990.

39 EC Commission, working paper on *Industrial Policy in an Open and Competitive Environment*, 14 September 1990.

40 EC Commission Communication to the Council and Parliament, *Towards Trans-European Networks*, draft, November 1990.

41 P.G. Nell, 'EFTA in the 1990s: the search for a new identity', *Journal of Common Market Studies*, 1990, vol.28, pp.327–58.

42 Ibid., p.332.

43 Oslo Declaration, text appended to EP research paper, *EFTA and the Community's Internal Market*, External Economic Series, no.1, October 1989, pp.18–20.

44 Quoted by Ambassador B. von Tscharner, head of Swiss mission to the EC, CEPS seminar, Brussels, 26 November 1990.

45 EC Commission, Bulletin 5/1987, point 65.

46 C. Church, 'The Politics of change: EFTA and the Nordic countries' responses to the EC in the early 1990s', *Journal of Common Market Studies*, 1990, vol.28, pp.400–11.

TOPICS FOR DISCUSSION

1 How did the 1992 programme emerge as the key political goal for the EC from 1985 onwards?
2 What was the strategy behind and the main elements of the Commission's White Paper on the completion of the internal market?
3 How has corporate Europe responded to the 1992 programme?
4 Analyse the main issues in the EC/EFTA negotiations on a European Economic Area.

FURTHER READING

The 1992 programme has led to a proliferation of books on the White Paper and its implications for economic exchange.

Calingaert, M. *The 1992 Challenge from Europe: Development of the European Community's Internal Market*, Washington: National Planning Association, 1988. This volume provides an excellent overview of the purpose and scope of the Commission's White Paper. It combines a political and an economic analysis.

Cecchini, P. *1992: The Benefits of a Single Market*, Aldershot: Gower, 1988. This volume gives a summary of the main findings of the Cecchini Report. It is intended for popular consumption.

Cutler, T., Haslam, C., Williams, J. and Williams, K. *1992 – 1 The Struggle for Europe*, New York: Berg, 1989. The authors of this book seek to identify the economic and political assumptions underlying the 1992 programme. They then provide a critique of these assumptions, arguing that the official claims for the programme are greatly exaggerated.

Mottola, K. and Patomaki, H. (eds) *Facing the Change in Europe: EFTA Countries' Integration Strategies*, Helsinki: Finnish Institute for International Affairs, 1989. This volume provides an overview of the attitudes towards integration of individual EFTA states and analyses EC/EFTA relations.

Pelkmans, J. and Winters, A. *Europe's Domestic Market*, London, Routledge, 1988. This volume offers an excellent overview of the strategy behind the 1992 programme, with a chapter on its implications for Britain.

Articles

Agnelli, G. 'The Europe of 1992', *Foreign Affairs*, 1989 vol.68, pp.61–70. This article by the chairman of Fiat provides a useful insight into the attitude of Europe's industrialists to 1992.

Bressand, A. Beyond interdependence: 1992 as a global challenge', *International Affairs*, 1990, vol.66, pp.47–65. This is a very important article on the dynamic environment of 1992. Its main emphasis is on the importance of inter-corporate networks and the impact of 'mutual recognition'.

Hoffman, S. 'The European Community and 1992', *Foreign Affairs*, 1989, vol.68, pp.27–47. This article, from one of the main proponents of an intergovernmental approach to the study of the EC, is significant because it attempts to grapple with the renewed dynamism in the EC.

Wallace, H. and Wessels, W. 'Towards a new partnership: the EC and EFTA in the wider Western Europe', EFTA, Occasional Paper no.28, March 1989. This paper offers a number of scenarios for EC/EFTA relations.

A special edition of the *Journal of Common Market Studies*, 1990, vol.28, has a series of articles that explore EFTA's future, its relations with the EC and the attitude of Austria, Switzerland and the Nordic countries.

Chapter 4

Economic integration
The wider agenda

Although the single market was the catalyst for a resurgence in formal integration, the agenda of economic integration goes beyond the internal market. Collaboration on research and development is a necessary complement to market liberalization. Europe's ability to maintain its industrial position depends on overcoming the technological gap between itself and the other industrial powers. The creation of a large internal market raises questions about the distribution of economic welfare in the EC. The politics of redistribution are an intrinsic part of the debate on economic integration. The size and nature of the EC budget comes into prominence in any debate about the role of public finance in integration. Economic and monetary union, again part of the agenda, represents a 'quantum leap forward' in the Community's aspirations towards the creation of an advanced level of economic integration. The purpose of this chapter is to address the issues arising from the wider agenda of economic integration. There are four sections in this chapter dealing with research and development, the politics of redistribution, the Community budget, and economic and monetary union.

INDUSTRIAL POLICY AND R. & D.

At the 1972 Paris Summit, deep-rooted differences concerning industrial policy between the French, who favoured widespread *dirigisme* characterized by a emphasis on medium-term planning, on the one hand, and the Germans, who subscribe to a liberal market philosophy, made it difficult to translate into reality the call for a single industrial base. During the 1970s the Community's industrial policy was devoted in large measure to the 'losers' of the industrial game. The problems of Europe's traditional industries: textiles, clothing, steel and shipbuilding, presented the member states and the Community with major problems. In a context of massive job losses, obsolete industrial structures and declining markets, extensive restructuring was needed. Government subsidies proliferated as each member state sought to minimize job losses. By the mid-1970s, the Commission, with a new Commissioner, Etienne Davignon, began to develop a strategy for the crisis sectors, aimed at reducing capacity and reintroducing competition by curbing state aid.

In the 1980s the 'winners' in the industrial game, high technology industries, impinged more and more on the EC agenda. Earlier attempts to develop a technological community faltered, with individual governments favouring their national champions. Gradually an awareness of Europe's weak performance in high-technology industries filtered through to discussions on the future of European industry. In 1978 M. Davignon commissioned the FAST (Forecasting and Assessment in Science and Technology) programme, which highlighted Europe's weakness in translating research into commercial products. Subsequently the Commissioner, together with the captains of European industry, established a detailed research programme for the 1980s. The ESPRIT programme grew out of a number of round-table discussions between the Commission and the heads of Europe's leading electronic firms. Since then a plethora of programmes, notably RACE, BRITE and JET, all aimed at overcoming Europe's 'technological deficit', have been established by the EC. The EUREKA programme, established in 1985, with its own secretariat, involves the EC member states, EFTA states and Turkey, thus adding an element of 'variable geometry' to this policy arena. Table 4.1 gives a list of the programmes and their scope.

In 1984 a full ten-year ESPRIT programme was launched, promoting research in micro-electronics, softwear development, office systems, computer-aided manufacturing and advanced information processing. The main features of the ESPRIT programme are worth noting because it became the model for the other programmes. ESPRIT:

- is restricted to pre-competitive research
- is based on co-funding by the Community and industry
- involves firms, research institutes and universities in more than one EC country

- provides the participants in any project with freedom to apply the results of the project on a commercial basis
- permits access at this point to other ESPRIT participants
- has a light and speedy grant-awarding process.[1]

Some 227 research programmes, involving 3,000 researchers from 536 organizations, were selected as part of ESPRIT I.[2] An early assessment of ESPRIT in October 1985 was generally favourable, although suggestions were made about management procedures and possible links with other collaborative research initiatives, EUREKA and RACE.[3] ESPRIT II was negotiated to run from 1987 to 1991 but has been overtaken by the third framework programme which began in 1990 and is scheduled to last until 1994.

The development of an EC role in R. & D. highlights the capacity

Table 4.1 The main EC programmes in research and development

Programme	Area	Budget
Information and Communication		
ESPRIT II	Micro-electronics	1,600 M ECU
RACE	Telecommunications	550 M ECU
DELTA	New technology and learning	20 M ECU
AIM	IT and Medical science	20 M ECU
Industrial Sectors		
BRITE	Application of new technologies	499 M ECU
BCR	Chemical analysis	59 M ECU
Raw Materials	-	45 M ECU
Biological Resources		
BRIDGE	Biotechnology	100 M ECU
ECLAIR	Agriculture and biotechnology	80 M ECU
FLAIR	Agro-industrial research	25 M ECU
Energy		
Radioactive waste	Disposal	62 M ECU
Decommissioning nuclear	installations	31 M ECU
TELEMAN	Nuclear waste	19 M ECU
Fusion	Research	60M ECU
Joule	Alternative energy	122 M ECU

Source: EC Commission Booklet, EC Research Programmes, September 1989

of the Community to expand its policy scope into new fields, albeit in a halting and tardy manner. The SEA finally gave the EC a substantial mandate in this policy domain. The new Article 130.1 provides for a multiannual framework programme, setting out the objectives and priorities of R. & D. and the financial contribution of the EC. Decisions relating to the multiannual programme require unanimity, but other decisions relating to new technology can be taken by a qualified majority.[4]

The financing of the Community's programmes has not been free from contention. Efforts to increase the budgetary resources devoted to research did not have immediate success. In 1986, Commissioner Narjes put forward a plan to treble the budget over the five-year period 1987–92. His plan met with considerable opposition within the Council, especially from Britain, whose government was determined to place controls on EC spending. The British finally agreed to a figure of 5.3 million ECUs, which represented an increase on the 3.7 million of the first framework programme (1984–7) but which fell well short of the 10 million ECUs that the Commission had requested. Within one year of the adoption of the framework programme, over 90 per cent of the total budget had been allocated.[5] Conflict about the budget reappeared in 1989–90 concerning expenditure for the third programme. The final allocation of 5,700 million ECUs again fell short of the Commission's request.

The Community is not the only site of research collaboration. In 1985 the European Research Co-ordination Agency (EUREKA) plan was announced by President Mitterrand. Initially it was portrayed as France's response to 'Star Wars' or the Strategic Defence Initiative (SDI). It was clearly intended to stem the flow of European scientists to the United States and to ensure that Europe had its own research agenda. The EUREKA charter was adopted by an intergovernmental conference of foreign ministers and research ministers in Hanover in November 1985. A small EUREKA secretariat is located in Brussels. Research on lasers, robotics, information and telecommunications, marine technology, transport technologies and biotechnology fall within the EUREKA framework. An example of the impact of EUREKA research on product development in Europe is its funding of research on high-definition television. The HDTV standard that emerged from this project has been adopted by the EC.

EUREKA differs from EC-based research collaboration in a number of important respects. First, it is not confined to the countries of the European Community. It involves nineteen countries: the EC Twelve, the EFTA Six and Turkey. Second, although the EC and the Commission may contribute funds for EUREKA research programmes, it has no direct responsibility for the scheme. The Community is part-financing JESSI, a project designed to improve Europe's competitiveness in semi-conductors. Third, the emphasis in EUREKA is less on pre-competitive research and more on product development for the market. Fourth, the emphasis in EUREKA is on flexibility. The form of co-operation is determined by the parties involved, provided that projects include trans-border collaboration, involve high technology and qualified personnel, and will achieve a significant advance in product and process technology. It is up to individual firms to take the initiative.[6]

A EUROPEAN TECHNOLOGICAL COMMUNITY?

The launch of the ESPRIT programme, followed by a host of other programmes, carved out a Community role in R. & D. designed to substitute 'Euro' champions in high technology for national champions. Assessment of the EC's achievements is difficult because of its short timeframe. However, a number of observations can be made. It took the EC Commission a considerable length of time to get acceptance of the worth of transnational collaboration and to establish the means of implementing cross-national programmes involving research institutes, universities and companies. Networks of this kind are costly in terms of time and human resources. The benefits may take a long time to materialize. It is difficult to translate the particular interests of individual companies into shared objectives. A considerable amount of time is taken up with establishing who pays for what and who does the work. The politics of grantsmanship lead to the financing of some dead-weight projects, as the Commission seeks to ensure that there is a spread of collaboration across firms and countries.

The focus in ESPRIT on pre-competitive research does not tackle directly the main problem of European industry in this area, namely the difficulties it faces in translating research into marketable products. Most analysts agree that Europe's problems are not confined to technology alone but are embedded in an industrial and entrepreneurial environment that inhibits innovation. A 'management gap', no less than a 'technology gap' characterizes Europe's lack of adaptation to new technology. In a study of innovation in six industrial sectors, Sharp concluded that Europe lagged in the commercialization and use of new technologies because of a lack of flexibility in management and the absence of sufficiently long-term goals.[7] Transnational collaboration alone will not alter corporate attitudes and traditional ways of doing things.

It is unclear whether or not European collaboration will leave the major European companies sufficiently strong to compete in the rapidly changing high-cost electronics industry. The cycle of innovation, development and application of semi-conductors is becoming ever shorter. The cost of establishing new manufacturing facilities for the most advanced memory chips is getting prohibitive at a time when the price of chips is falling.[8] The large European electronics companies – Siemens, SGS Thompson and Philips – may not be capable of funding the investment required for the latest developments in memory chips. Philips's weak performance in 1990, with extensive losses, undermines one of Europe's leading champions in electronics; it may have to seek partners outside Europe if it is to survive. The take-over of ICL, Britain's largest computer manufacturer, by the Japanese company Fujitsu in 1990 does not augur well for European electronics. Siemens' technology agreements with IBM and Toshiba underline the global character of innovation. European consortia, the hallmark of EC policy, may not be adequate for the future. EC protection for native producers through tariffs and 'rules of origin' has led to considerable inward investment as Intel, Sony, Fujitsu and Hitachi seek market access. Thus domestic European companies are facing increased competition, not only on the world markets but in their own markets as well.

The EC's policies on R. & D. and EUREKA projects have fostered an embryonic technological community as companies, research institutes and universities are tied into a dense cross-national network of collaboration. Once established, networks tend to survive. As companies collaborate on research and development, the possibility of product development is opened up, and such collaboration provides an important constituency in favour of the 1992 programme. However, the policy of the 1980s based on European champions and European consortia, is not appropriate in the 1990s, when global alliances will prove decisive.

THE POLITICS OF REDISTRIBUTION

The founding fathers of the European Community did not pay adequate attention to the question of regional disparities among the member states and regions of the Community. There was no provision for an active instrument of regional policy in the Rome Treaty (EEC). A commitment to 'harmonious development by diminishing both the disparities between the various regions and the backwardness of the less favoured regions' is found in the Preamble to the Treaty of Rome. Article 92 of the Treaty, which specifies that state aid in general is not compatible with the Treaty did, however, permit regional aid. And the European Social Fund (ESF) was included in the Treaty to provide financial aid for retraining Italian agricultural workers on their way to the factories of the North. The 1972 Paris Summit took a decision in principle to establish a regional development fund. Since then the regional dimension of all EC policies has come under scrutiny, and the question of economic disparities occupies an important place on the EC agenda.[9]

Regional disparities in the Community

Regional disparities are a much more striking element of the Community of Twelve than of the original Community of Six. The first enlargement, in 1973, involved Ireland, whose level of economic development was well below the EC average, and Britain, a country with significant problems of industrial adjustment. The southern enlargements, to include Greece (1981) and Spain and Portugal (1986), have further exacerbated regional problems in the Community. Successive enlargements mean that the population living in regions whose GDP per capita is 25 per cent below the Community average has risen from 24 million (10 per cent) to 62 million (20 per cent), according to the Padoa-Schioppa Report. Unemployment rates range from 3 per cent in Luxemburg to 30 per cent in Andalusia, Spain. The ratio of GDP per capita in purchasing power parity terms (PPP) is 1 to 5 between Thrace, in Greece, and Hamburg, in Germany.[10]

There are essentially two kinds of problem region in the Community:

• less-favoured regions located at the periphery of the Community, with deficient infrastructure, low productivity and a sizeable agricultural work-force. Greece, Portugal, Ireland (North and South), the Italian Mezzogiorno, and half of Spain are regions with a per capita income that is less than 75 per cent of the EC average.

• areas of industrial decline that have a predominance of ailing industries such as coal mining, iron and steel, shipbuilding and textiles. Parts of all Community countries are experiencing industrial decline, but especially the United Kingdom, Belgium, The Netherlands and northern France. High unemployment is the main problem in these regions.[11]

The recessions of the 1970s exacerbated the problems of economic divergence in the EC. (See Table 4.2.)

Regional disparities: a Community role?

The extent and nature of the Community's role in alleviating economic disparities has been the subject of much debate in the Community. The Commission's May 1980 mandate, reported in June 1981, advocated the use of the structural funds as an expression of Community 'solidarity' and stressed that 'the reduction of regional imbalances remains a priority Community objective'.[12] At a minimum, there is agreement among the member states that if the workings of the common market serve to exacerbate

Table 4.2 Regional disparities in the European Community

Region	Country	GDP/capita current PPP 1985 EUR 12=100	Unemployment
Thrakis	Greece	43.2	3.6
Portugal	–	54.6	8.7
Andalucía	Spain	58.3	30.2
Puglia	Italy	64.7	13.3
Ireland	–	69.5	18.7
Aragón	Spain	81.8	16.7
Toscana	Italy	103.1	8.6
Brabant	Belgium	121.3	9.2
Hamburg	Germany	195.5	11.4
Groningen	NL	237.4	13.2

Source: Padoa-Schioppa Report (1987) pp.172–7

regional disparities, corrective measures must be taken. Proponents of an active Community role – the lesser-developed member states – constantly urged a Community commitment that would go beyond corrective policies, citing the pledge in the Preamble to the Treaty to maintain 'harmonious development'. During the intergovernmental conference on the reform of the Treaties, the issue of convergence was to the fore. A commitment on convergence was seen as an essential trade-off by the peripheral regions for the internal market programme. The negotiations on the Single European Act (SEA) afforded the peripheral countries an opportunity to extract concessions from the richer countries on the regional dimension of the Community's development. The lesser-developed countries argued that the liberalization of the market inherent in the 1992 programme would accentuate regional imbalances, a conclusion substantiated by the Padoa-Schioppa Report.[13] The inclusion of a section on economic and social cohesion in the SEA Treaty, including a commitment to reform the structural funds, was the outcome of the SEA package deal.

Policy instruments

The Community has a range of policy instruments at its disposal which have a bearing on regional policy in the widest sense. Although the establishment of a regional fund was extremely difficult, the birth of the European Regional Development Fund (ERDF) in 1975 strengthened the commitment of the Community to tackle economic divergence. It added a new policy instrument to the Treaty-based ones, the European Social Fund (ESF), the guidance section of the European Agricultural Guidance and Guarantee Fund (EAGGF) and European Investment Bank Loans. These funds have a number of characteristics in common. First, they are all financed from the Community budget and are considered as part of the 'non-compulsory' or optional component of that budget. Second, they part-finance activities at national level. The ESF covers vocational training and direct job creation, the ERDF finances infrastructure and industrial development, and the guidance section of the EAGGF contributes to farm modernization, marketing of agricultural products and rural development.

The structural funds suffer from a number of well-documented limitations. First, they are relatively meagre, because of the small size of the EC budget and the dominance of that budget by the CAP. Second, because the funds developed at different times under varying legislative regimes, there has been a marked lack of co-ordination even within the Commission. Third, additionality and conditionality, the two main principles of EC financing, are difficult to implement. At its simplest, additionality means that EC expenditure should be additional to, and not a substitute for, national expenditure. Conditionality refers to the impact of the funds nationally. The Commission argues that the funds must be used to support 'objectives defined by the Community itself' and must not be confined to a marginal role of participating in financing national policies. The Commission traditionally has looked to increase its control over EC structural expenditure.[14]

The distance from Brussels to the member states adds to the complications of managing and evaluating the use of structural fund monies. It is not easy to design policy instruments that are sensitive to the needs of twelve member states, especially when the regulations are the result of intensive bargaining in the Council. There are always problems of interpreting the law and applying it to the practical realities at national level. The politics of grantsmanship ensure that the funds have not necessarily been concentrated in areas of greatest need.

The SEA provided an opportunity to reform the management and operation of the structural funds.[15] Legislative change and an increase in the size of the financial resources devoted to cohesion formed the core of the Commission's paper 'A New Frontier for Europe'.[16] The European Council of February 1988 agreed that the resources of the funds should double for priority regions by 1992, with an effort to achieve a total doubling by 1993. According to the conclusions of the European Council, commitment appropriations are set to increase by 1,300 million ECU from 1989 to 1992, reaching a total of 13,000 MECU at 1988 prices by 1992.[17] Not only are the resources of the funds increasing, but the rate of subvention for the priority regions in the Community may now reach 75 per cent of the cost of an eligible programme, in contrast to the previous figure of 55 per cent.[18]

Increased financial resources was accompanied by a major change in the grant-awarding procedures, and the objectives of the funds were clarified. Five main objectives were established for the various funds:

1 promoting the development and structural adjustment of the regions that are lagging behind
2 converting the regions, frontier regions or parts of regions seriously affected by industrial decline
3 combating long-term unemployment
4 facilitating the occupational integration of young people
5 in order to reform the CAP:

   (a) speeding up the adjustment of agricultural structures;
   (b) promoting the development of rural areas.[19]

The ERDF has the task of supporting objectives 1, 2 and 5. The Social Fund will contribute primarily to objectives 2 and 3 but can also participate in measures under the other three objectives. Measures under objective 5 will be financed primarily by the EAGGF, although the other two funds can be called upon. The regions covered by objective 1 must have a per capita income below 75 per cent of the EC average. Ireland, Greece and Portugal, together with parts of Spain and Italy and the French overseas territories, are eligible for finance according to this criterion.[20]

A number of central issues dominated the negotiations on the latest reform of the structural funds, notably, programmes and partnership. A consistent theme in Commission thinking for over a decade has been the need to move away from financing individual projects to financing programmes. The bureaucratic nightmare of processing more than 14,000 individual applications each year underlines the Commission's need to alter the grant-awarding procedures to help overcome the implementation difficulties that have beset the funds over the years. A programme approach makes EC grants more akin to 'block' grants, rather than 'categorical' grants for specific projects. Under the new procedures, each objective 1 region must submit an overall plan setting out its priorities, the measures it proposes to adopt to redress particular problems and the use that would be made of Brussels money. Within six months of the submission of a regional plan the Commission adopts a Community Support Framework (CSF), the Community's response to the needs expressed in the plan and the proposed measures. The CSF is at the heart of the grant-awarding system because it sets out an agreed framework for assistance over a four-year period. Provision is made in the CSF for monitoring and evaluation. Each region then submits 'operational programmes' to the Commission to put flesh on the original plan. The process of drawing up an overall plan, operational programmes and the Community Support Framework involves dialogue between the Commission and national agencies.[21]

By adopting a programme approach, the Commission is seeking a greater say over the use of structural fund monies at national level. The new grant-awarding procedures bring it into partnership with agencies at national level. The principle of partnership is included in Article 4 of the framework regulation, which states that Community operations

> shall be established through close consultations between the Commission, the Member State concerned and the competent authorities designated by the latter at national regional, local or other level, with each party acting as a partner in pursuit of a common goal. . . . The partnership shall cover the preparation, financing, monitoring and assessment of operations.[22]

Each operational programme is monitored by review committees that includes Commission officials.

The SEA enshrined the principle of solidarity in the Treaties and strengthened the Community basis for a policy of economic and social cohesion. Nonetheless, economic divergence is likely to remain a hotly debated issue on the EC agenda into the 1990s. When the budgetary agreement runs out in 1993, it will have to be renegotiated at a time when the main contributor to the EC budget, Germany, is faced with the costs of unification. Economic reform in Eastern and Central Europe add an extra-EC dimension to the politics of redistribution. The role of public finance in European integration is part and parcel of the debate on the future of the EC budget in the context of EMU.

THE COMMUNITY BUDGET

Budgets, according to Wildavsky, lie at the heart of the political process and are statements of political intent.[23] The EC budget should not be compared to national budgets because it is not an instrument of economic policy in the way that national budgets are. Yet its structure and scope go beyond those of international organizations. The EC budget has a separate source of revenue, and its resources are dispersed independently by EC institutions. Since 1958 there has been a significant increase in the range of financial instruments available to the Community. See Table 4.3 for an overview of the 1989 budget.

The Brussels European Council of February 1988 closed a particularly difficult phase of budgetary politics in the Community. During the 1980s the budget was bedevilled by a problem of resources and the dominance of agriculture in EC expenditure and an inability to fund new policy initiatives adequately. The nub of all these problems was the size of the British contribution to the budget, a contribution that Britain was refusing to accept. Agreement on the British problem at Fontainebleau in June 1984 opened the way for constitutional reform in the Community and released energies to concentrate on the completion of the internal market. A successful transition to the post-SEA world rested on agreement about the financial resources of the EC budget over a five-year period, achieved at the European Council meeting of February 1988.

The main elements of the new budgetary package included an increase in the resources of the EC budget by the creation of an additional source of revenue known as the 'fourth resource'; a ceiling on agricultural expenditure; a doubling of the resources of the structural funds by 1993 and a continuation of the 1984 Fountainebleau Agreement until 1991, involving a reduction in British contribution to the EC budget. The budget was set to increase from 44,000 M ECUs (1988 prices) in 1988 to 52,800 M ECUs by 1992, with provision for annual up-dating.[24] Events in Eastern/Central Europe and the Gulf and the re-emergence of problems with agricultural expenditure have created strains in the budget before the 1992 deadline for the present projections.

A new budgetary deal to coincide with the completion of the

Table 4.3 EC Budget 1989 by main areas of expenditure

Area	Amount M ECU	%
Agriculture	29,293.35	65.3
Fisheries	389.24	0.9
Regional/Transport	4,330.92	9.7
Employment	3,269.36	7.3
Energy/Research	1,461.20	3.2
Development Co-operation	1,031.63	2.3
Rebates Member States	2,912.07	6.5
Institutions	2,150.03	4.8
Total	44,837.80	100.0

Source: EC Documentation 3/1989, p.9.

internal market and developments in EMU will have to be negotiated. If the gains from market integration are distributed unevenly
in the Community, as is likely, the peripheral countries will press for
additional resource transfers. This will relaunch the debate on the
role of public finance in integration, first raised by the MacDougall
Report in 1977. The team of researchers who contributed to the
MacDougall Report adopted an approach called fiscal federalism
in their attempt to establish criteria and standards that should
govern the granting of financial functions to the Community.
Having examined the finances and financial functions of a number of
different federal systems, the report strongly argued for a 'pre-federal'
EC budget with resources equivalent to between 2 per cent and
$2^1/2$ per cent of Community GNP and advocated the extension
of the Community's policy scope to include direct inter-regional
and inter-personal transfers.[25] In 1989 the EC budget amounted
to just over 1 per cent of the Community's gross national product
and 4 per cent of the combined national budgets of the member
states. Its resources, despite the significant increases after February
1988, remain very limited.[26] The predominance of agriculture is still
marked, with just over 65 per cent of the budget devoted to the CAP
in 1989.[27]

ECONOMIC AND MONETARY UNION

Economic and monetary union is considered by proponents of
deeper integration in the EC as the penultimate step on the
road to full political union. Following the apparent success of the
1992 programme, EMU is firmly on the agenda for the 1990s.
Co-operation on monetary and economic matters has a chequered
history in the Community. Assessment of current attempts must be
made in the light of the experience of the early 1970s and the later
successful launch of the European Monetary System in 1979.

Early attempts

The Rome Treaty paid little attention to the monetary dimension of
integration, as the stability of the Bretton Woods system, dominated
by the US dollar, enabled the EC states to ignore monetary
matters. However, a series of currency crises in the late 1960s
which culminated in the breakdown of the Bretton Woods system
in 1971, brought monetary policy to the top of the international

economic agenda. The two leading EC states, France and the Federal Republic of Germany began to reconsider the question of monetary co-operation in 1969. Both felt that the existing policies, notably the Common Agricultural Policy, would come under severe pressure in a situation of floating currencies. However, the French and Germans soon had differences about the best route to closer economic and monetary co-operation. The Germans considered that economic co-operation was a prerequisite for monetary co-operation, whereas the French wanted to move on the monetary front immediately. The ensuing debate between the 'monetarists' and the 'economists' is a recurring theme in discussions of EMU.[28]

The Werner Report set out a phased plan for EMU that advocated a step-by-step approach, to culminate in the establishment of an EMU by 1980. The core of the plan was the total and irreversible convertibility of currencies within the ten-year period and the establishment of a centre of decision-making for economic policy and a Community system of central banks. During the first phase of the plan, which was adopted by the Council of Ministers in March 1971, there was to be a gradual narrowing of the margins within which exchange rates of the member states' currencies would be permitted to fluctuate. In April 1972, the 'snake in the tunnel' arrangement was launched whereby the EC states agreed to restrict fluctuations to $2^{1}/4$ per cent on either side of existing intra-EC parity rates. Britain, Ireland, Denmark, Sweden and Norway joined the 'inner Six' in the 'snake'. When the dollar floated in 1973, the 'snake' came under considerable pressure; the pound sterling, lira, krone and franc made their exit. The franc and krone re-entered the system, but the franc again was forced to leave in 1976. This left a small DM area functioning outside the Community.[29] The recession of 1973–4 made the goal of economic and monetary union unrealistic, as increasing divergence of economic performance and policies manifested themselves in the Community.

The EMS – the beginning of a regional currency bloc

In 1978 the prospect of renewed progress in monetary co-operation emerged when the German Chancellor, Helmut Schmidt, launched his EMS proposal. This was turned into a Franco-German plan when the French President, Valéry Giscard d'Estaing, endorsed the relaunch of monetary co-operation. A variety of factors converged to make this an opportune time for renewed monetary co-operation.

First, the European states did not favour the excessive fluctuations that characterized this period of floating exchange rates. Second, high levels of inflation in a number of European countries undermined business confidence. Third, the Germans, in particular, were disenchanted with US leadership, or its absence, in the monetary field. The smaller continental EC states favoured monetary co-operation because they had formed part of the DM zone since the time of the original snake. Italy and Ireland were willing to join the EMS in return for side-payments to help with the process of adjustment. Britain alone opted to remain outside the exchange rate mechanism of the EMS. Greece, Portugal and Spain also remained outside after accession, although the last-named joined in June 1989, just before the Madrid Summit, and Britain opted for membership in October 1990. The EMS remains one of the main examples of 'variable geometry' at work in the Community.

The purpose of the EMS was to create a 'zone of monetary stability' in the Community; the fluctuation rate was set at 2.25 per cent, within a wider band of 6 per cent. With the introduction of the EMS, the European Unit of Account, which had been used to express the different monetary values of national currencies, was replaced by the European Currency Unit (ECU) to be used for the settlement of debts between monetary authorities. It was anticipated that the EMS should lead to common institutions, notably a European Monetary Fund, within two years. Rules were laid down concerning interventions by monetary authorities if currencies crossed a 'threshold of divergence'. Facilities for short-term and medium-term credit were put in place.[30]

The EMS has been in operation for just over ten years, and there are numerous assessments by economists concerning its operation. A number of achievements have been highlighted by analysts. First, the EMS has in fact created the 'zone of monetary stability' anticipated by its proponents. Second, a gradual alignment of inflation rates has evolved in the participating countries. The external discipline of the Deutschmark proved significant for countries experiencing high rates of inflation. Third, the EMS is a major and successful step towards the creation of a regional currency bloc and a system of joint policy-making in monetary matters. Fourth, the ECU lays the foundations for the emergence of a single European currency. However, there are also problems with the operation of the EMS. The dominance of the Deutschmark determines the operation of the system. It is an asymmetrical system in which the Bundesbank sets the monetary policies of the other countries. Because combating inflation is such an important part of German monetary policy, the EMS has an inbuilt anti-inflation bias, which may have contributed to low growth rates and high unemployment in Europe during the early 1980s.[31]

EMU revisited

The dynamism created by the SEA and the internal market programme focused attention on a deepening of integration via the creation of EMU. As is usual in the EC, consideration of the political and economic issues involved began with a report, in this case the Delors Report on EMU. In June 1988 at the Hanover European Council, the President of the Commission, Jacques Delors, was asked to chair a committee of the governors of the national central banks on economic and monetary union. The Delors Report, published in April 1989, regards moves towards EMU as a 'natural consequence of the commitment to create a market without internal frontiers' and as a 'quantum jump' in the development of the Community.[32] Undoubtedly the creation of EMU would signal a quantum leap forward in the development of the EC, as it would extend the competence of the Community into core areas of economic policy. States could no longer exercise independent monetary policies, and budgetary policies would have to come within the ambit of EMU. EMU thus entails a significant reduction in formal sovereignty for the participating states.

The Delors Report began with a definition of the components of monetary union and economic union. (See Table 4.4). The Report advocates a three-stage approach to the achievement of EMU, but emphasizes that 'the decision to enter upon the first stage should be a decision to embark on the entire process'.[33] The report sees a parallelism between economic and monetary union. Furthermore, 'monetary union constitutes a currency area in which policies are jointly managed'.[34] In other words, common institutions are necessary. However, to assuage fears of a centralizing Community, the report argues that the principle of subsidiarity should govern the allocation of responsibility for economic policies in the union. Thus, the 'attribution of competences to the Community would have to be confined specifically to those areas in which collective decision-making was necessary'.[35] Translating the principle into reality in the negotiations is frought with difficulties. The Delors

Report was considered by the Madrid European Council in June 1989, and a decision was taken at the subsequent Strasbourg Council in December 1989 to convene an intergovernmental conference to negotiate an EMU treaty. The conference began its deliberations in December 1990.

Preparatory work on the IGC gathered momentum during 1990, as the EC institutions and the member states began to work out their response to the Delors Report. The final stage of EMU, according to the Delors Report, is the 'irrecoverable locking of exchange rate parities'. Since then, the notion of replacing existing currencies with a single currency has gained widespread support. The communiqué of the Rome Council (October 1990) favoured a single currency – a strong and stable ECU for the final phase of EMU. Britain is the only member state unwilling to accept this long-term aim.[36] The Delors Report sets out two intervening stages. The first stage, which began in July 1990, merely strengthens existing economic co-ordination and envisages the inclusion of all currencies in the exchange mechanism of the EMS. Stages 2 and 3 can come into force only as the result of a new EMU treaty. Stage 2 has been described as the 'soft' stage involving monetary union with a European System of Central Banks but no locking parities.[37] The Rome European Council set 1 January 1994 as the date for the beginning of stage 2 and consideration of stage 3 not more than three years from that date.

Table 4.4 The main components of economic and monetary union: the Delors report

Monetary Union
- total and irreversible convertibility of currencies
- the complete liberalization of capital transactions and full integration of banking and other financial markets
- the elimination of margins of fluctuation and the irrevocable locking of exchange rate parities

Economic Union
- single market
- competition policy
- common policies aimed at structural change and regional development
- macroeconomic policy co-ordination, including binding rules for budgetary policies

Source: Delors Committee Report on EMU, April 1989, pp.10–12.

The Design of the system

The groundwork for the intergovernmental conference was laid by a series of reports from a 'High Level Group' set up by the Economic and Finance Council, the Commission, the European Parliament, the Monetary Committee and the Committee of European Central Banks. Work is advanced on the design of the system, especially with regard to monetary union. The Rome European Council (December 1990) endorsed the following principles:

- A new monetary institution comprising member states central banks and a central bank (Eurofed)
- The task of the monetary institution is to maintain price stability (counteract inflation)
- The members of the monetary institution will be 'independent of instructions'.[38]

The Committee of EC Central Banks has agreed on the statutes for the new monetary institution ahead of the IGC. There is also agreement that the member states in an EMU could not finance budget deficits by printing money, nor will the Community take on any responsibility for the debts of any member state.

There is less agreement about the economic conditions that would allow a move to the second and, more importantly, the third stages of EMU. The importance of convergence of economic performance, notably, inflation levels and sound public finances is emphasized in the various reports. Those countries whose economic performance is already convergent favour a rapid transition to EMU. Germany, France, the Benelux countries and Denmark could cope with a rapid transition. The Italian debt is considered to be a problem. The attitude of Germany to the negotiations is critical. A Bundesbank paper issued in September 1990 places considerable emphasis on convergent economic policies, whereas the Chancellor's office and the Foreign Ministry are politically committed to EMU. According to Karl Otto Pohl, the former president of the Bundesbank, 'It is conceivable that the treaty will be ratified by all members but also that some who are unable to or do not want to participate straightaway are invited to take part at a later stage'.[39] This raises the spectre of a two-speed EMU or perhaps a 'multispeed' EMU, with the core countries taking the lead.

Britain, opposed to the imposition of a single currency, offers the concept of a 'hard ECU' as a parallel currency, which could circulate and be used in financial transactions throughout the Community. This proffers an evolutionary approach to EMU. The proposal has met with little outright support from the other member states, although Spain accepts that it may have a useful role in the second stage. Germany, and particularly the Bundesbank, is opposed to the proposal. The peripheral member states all support the goal of EMU but do not want to find themselves in the lower tier of a two-tier Europe. For Greece and Portugal, it will be very difficult to participate in monetary union in the short term. Spain favours a long transitional period, and Ireland wishes to participate in stages 2 and 3 from the outset. A priority for the lesser-developed countries is to ensure that the role of public finance and the Community budget in an economic union is adequately investigated and dealt with.

CONCLUSIONS

The EC's economic agenda is a mixture of old policy issues, such as the CAP, and new policy goals, notably the creation of EMU. The focus so far in the EMU debate on the design of monetary institutions relegates the more important question of the allocation of policy responsibility in an economic union to the margins. The potential adverse effects of EMU on the lesser-developed parts of the Community has not found its way to the top of the agenda. If, in the absence of countervailing policies, EMU exacerbates regional disparities within the Community, monetary union may prove shaky indeed. Existing EC structural policies, based on a plethora of financial instruments, will not prove sufficiently strong to tackle the problems of redistribution in the EC. Only a larger and more developed Community budget could perform the functions usually associated with macroeconomic management in existing economic and monetary unions. Questions about the role of public finance in integration and the meaning of cohesion in the context of EMU will not disappear. Economic and monetary union spills over into political union as well. Central monetary institutions must be politically accountable in a democratic system of government, and the policies of a EUROFED must be developed in the context of wider macroeconomic considerations, the responsibility of democratically elected politicians.

NOTES

1 M. Sharp, 'The Community and new technologies' in J. Lodge (ed.), *The European Community and the Challenge of the Future* (London; Frances Pinter, 1989), pp.202–20.
2 EC Commission, *Second Framework Programme for R. & D. Activities*, summary of ESPRIT programme, sheet 2.
3 EC Commission, *The Mid-Term Review of* ESPRIT, Executive Summary 1985.
4 SEA Article 130 F-Q, EC Bulletin, supplement 2/86.
5 Sharp, op. cit., p.215.
6 S. Woods, *Western Europe: Technology and the Future*, Atlantic Paper no.63, Paris, Atlantic Institute for International Affairs, 1987, pp.88–92.
7 M. Sharp (ed.), *Europe and the New Technologies* (London: Frances Pinter, 1983), p.291.
8 M. Smith, 'Changing forces and strategies in world semi-conductor trade: can the Community meet the challenge?, EUI, *European Trends*, no.3, 1990, pp.79–92.
9 M. Keating and B. Jones (eds), *Regions in the European Community* (Oxford: Clarendon Press, 1985).
10 T. Padoa-Schioppa, *Efficiency, Stability and Equity: Strategy for the Evolution of the Economic System of the European Community* (Oxford, Oxford University Press, 1987), pp.89–108.
11 Ibid., pp.162–3.
12 EC Commission, *Report to the European Council Pursuant to the Mandate of the 30th May 1980*, EC Bulletin, Supplement 1/81.
13 Padoa-Schioppa, op. cit., p.5.
14 EC Commission, *Increasing the Effectiveness of the Community's Structural Funds*, EC Bulletin, Supplement 3/83, p.8.
15 SEA Article 130A.
16 EC Commission, *A New Frontier for Europe*, EC Bulletin, Supplement 1/87.
17 M. Shackleton, *Financing the European Community* (London: Francis Pinter, 1990), p.17.
18 B. Laffan, 'While you're over there in Brussels, "get us a grant": the management of the structural funds in Ireland', *Irish Political Studies*, 1989, vol.4, p.49.
19 EC, 'Council Regulation on the Tasks of the Structural Funds', no.2052/88, *Official Journal*, L185/9, 15 July 1988.
20 Ibid.
21 B. Laffan, op. cit., pp.45–8.
22 Council Regulation 2052/88, op. cit.
23 A.W. Wildavsky, *Budgeting: Comparative Theory of Budgetary Processes* (Boston: Little, Brown, 1975), p.4.
24 M. Shackleton, op. cit., p.17.

25 *Report of the Study Group on the Role of Public Finance in European Integration*, The MacDougall Report, April 1977.
26 M. Shackleton, op. cit., p.5.
27 Table on the budget in EC Commission, *The European Commission and the Administration of the Community*, European Documentation, 3/1989, p.9.
28 J. Statler, 'EMS: cul-de-sac or signpost on the road to EMU', in M. Hodges and W. Wallace (eds), *Economic Divergence in the European Community* (London: Allen of Unwin, 1981), pp.101–7.
29 Ibid., pp.107–13.
30 Ibid., pp.113–23.
31 L. Tsoukalis, 'The Political economy of the EMS' in P. Guerrieri and P. Padoan (eds), *The Political Economy of European Integration* (London: Harvester Wheatsheaf, 1989), pp.58–84.
32 *Delors Committee Report on Economic and Monetary Union*, April 1989, p.6.
33 Ibid., p.24.
34 Ibid., p.10
35 Ibid., p.9.
36 Communiqué of the Rome European Council, *Agence Europe*, no.5360, 29/30 October 1990.
37 N. Thygesen, 'The Delors Report and European economic and monetary union', *International Affairs*, 1989, vol.65, pp.637–52.
38 Communiqué of the Rome European Council, op. cit.
39 Quoted in S. Collignon, 'The EMU debate: a common or a single currency?, EUI, *Economic Trends*, 1990, no.3, p.65.

TOPICS FOR DISCUSSION

1 In what way do the EC's R. & D. programmes complement the 1992 programme?
2 Assess the interaction between budgetary politics in the EC and the politics of redistribution.
3 Why has EMU re-emerged on the EC agenda?
4 What were the main issues for debate at the EMU IGC?

FURTHER READING

Guerrieri, P. and Padoan, P. (eds) *The Political Economy of European Integration*, London: Harvester Wheatsheaf, 1989. This volume contains many useful articles on macroeconomic policy in Europe, and on the EMS.

Harrop, J. *The Political Economy of Integration in the European Community*, Aldershot: Edward Elgar, 1989. This volume is best for students of economics but is relatively accessible to a non-specialist reader.

Padoa-Schioppa, T. *Efficiency, Stability and Equity: Strategy for the Evolution of the Economic System of the European Community*, Oxford: Oxford University Press, 1987. The Padoa-Schioppa report was produced by a committee established by the EC Commission on the future economic order of the EC. It is an excellent report that covers all the main policy issues within the context of an economic order. It is suitable for non-economists.

Shackleton, M. *Financing the European Community*, London: Frances Pinter, 1990. This Chatham House paper provides an excellent overview of the 1988 budgetary agreement and its implementation.

Sharp, M. and Sherman, C. *European Technological Collaboration*, London: Routledge and Kegan Paul, 1987. This book gives a current review of the Community's R. & D. policies.

Woods, S. *Western Europe: Technology and the Future*, Paris: Atlantic Institute for International Affairs, 1987. Another review of technological collaboration in Europe.

Articles

Lord Cockfield 'Beyond 1992 – the single European economy', *European Affairs*, 1988, vol.4, pp.76–4.

Dowd, K. 'The Case against a European central bank', *The World Economy*, 1989, vol.12, pp.361–72.

Grewlich, K.W. 'The Struggle for global telepresence', *Aussenpolitik*, 1989, vol.40, pp.160–72.

Reinz, K. 'EUREKA: 3 years already! Results so far and future outlook', *European Affairs*, 1989, vol.3, pp.112–14.

Thygesen, N. 'The Delors Report and European economic and monetary union', *International Affairs*, 1989 vol.65, pp.637–52.

Williams, R. 'The EC's technology policy as an engine for integration', *Government and Opposition*, 1989, vol.24, pp.158–76.

Chapter 5

A people's Europe

The revolutions in Eastern Europe and the magnetic attraction of the Western European model for the nascent democracies serve to underline the relative success of Western Europe in re-establishing economic prosperity and a social equilibrium after the war. Remarkable economic prosperity during the first two decades after the war and the development of strong, albeit diverse, welfare states, have engendered considerable political stability. The Western European welfare state revolves around the notion that all citizens have a right to benefit from the material wealth created by economic growth, and that those who fail to benefit must be protected by redistributive social welfare policies.

This chapter addresses the notion of a 'people's Europe' by examining the participation of EC citizens in the Community's policy process and the role of public opinion in integration. The chapter also charts the emergence of a consensus on what constitutes basic political and judicial rights for citizens. Community policies in the social domain, in education, in vocational training and on the environment that set out to enlarge the concept of a 'people's Europe' are addressed in turn. Increased mobility of people inevitably brings with it the need to ensure that such mobility does not endanger law and order in the participating states. Thus police co-operation also is treated in this chapter.

Links between Western European societies are more varied and deeper than ever. Accessible and cheap transport fosters the movement of people across borders as tourists, consumers or workers. Cultural exchange schemes, joint research and development initiatives at a university or company level, schemes to foster student mobility, cross-national professional organizations, and town-twinning all serve to break down the barriers between peoples and make national borders lose some of their significance. Extensive collaboration arising from formal integration and informal networks flourishes in Western Europe, despite the fact that strong national and regional identities remain.

Extra-national organizations play an important role in fostering the development of multiple ties between peoples and in protecting civil liberties and social rights. The Council of Europe provides the strongest mechanism for the protection of fundamental freedoms by means of its Charter. The 1950 Social Charter and the 1978 Convention on the legal status of migrant workers carry on the Council's work in establishing legal principles for the protection of citizens' rights. The boundaries of EC social policy have gradually expanded beyond the narrow confines of the Rome Treaty. Workers, women, young people, the handicapped, and migrant workers are all affected by the Community's social role. The completion of the internal market adds a new impetus to the social dimension of integration. The search for policy responses to the growing problems of drug abuse, illness and international terrorism expands the agenda of the EC and international politics more generally. Environmental issues assumed a major place on the agenda of world politics in the 1980s.

Yet the increasing level of cross-national collaboration reduces the autonomy of national governments and creates a widening gap between the governed and those who govern. The authority of government in liberal democracies is founded on legitimacy accorded by citizens through democratic elections. Major decisions affecting the lives of individual citizens are now taken in forums far removed from 'the man on the street'. A striking feature of the 1980s resurgence of formal integration in the EC was the key role exercised by national governmental élites, EC commissioners and the captains of European industry. The mass public was largely absent. Political accountability is a key issue to be resolved in the next phase of integration.

SUPPORT FOR EUROPEAN INTEGRATION

Public opinion

There is much debate about the significance of public opinion, especially mass public opinion, for European integration. For some

writers, notably Deutsch, integration is synonymous with the creation of a 'sense of community', of 'mutual sympathy and loyalties;
of "we-feelings", trust, and mutual consideration'.[1] Lindberg and
Scheingold, two neo-functionalist writers, consider on the other
hand, that no massive shift in loyalties is required. Rather, a
'permissive consensus' based on a mixture of utilitarian and affective
support is sufficient to maintain integration. Utilitarian support is
derived from perceived gains and losses, whereas affective support
depends on an emotional attachment to the notion of co-operation
and integration.[2] The Preamble to the Rome Treaty sought 'ever
closer union among the peoples of Europe', not just a transformation
of relations between states and governments.

Democratic theory suggests that viable central institutions need
popular legitimacy, and that such legitimacy depends in the long-
term on the consent of the people. Two principal views about the
role of public opinion in integration are discernible. According to
one approach, governments and political élites set the agenda, take
the major decisions and rely on persuading and converting the mass
public. Public opinion, in this view, lags behind political decisions.
Put simply, mass attitudes are led by élite attitudes. The other view
of public opinion is that a supportive public will push national élites
towards greater integration.[3]

Public attitudes towards the EC and integration are well docu-
mented because the Commission conducts extensive public opinion
surveys, known as 'Eurobarometers' in all the member states
to monitor attitudes towards the EC. Analysis of the survey
data has produced a sizeable literature on mass attitudes towards
integration. Although it is not possible to summarize this literature
here, a number of observations are appropriate. Most studies
agree that there is a high degree of support for the notion of
European unification and the 'idea of Europe', that attitudes
towards membership of the EC vary across the member states and
that support tends to be utilitarian. In other words, support for the
EC does not translate into a willingness to make sacrifices for other
member states in economic difficulties. Nor are large sections of the
Western European population very interested in the Community.[4]
The literature on public opinion suggests that there is a 'permissive
consensus' in favour of the 'idea of Europe', but that support for
integration is not a deeply held emotion capable of translating itself
into pressure on governments towards further integration. National
élites have a relatively free hand in determining their integration

policies, provided that they maintain the passive support of the mass public.

Support for membership of the Community is measured by asking people if membership of the EC is a good or bad thing for their country. Here there are large variations across the member states.(See Table 5.1)

The most positive attitudes towards membership of the EC are found in the original six member states. Particularly high percentages of positive responses towards membership are obtained in The Netherlands, Italy and Luxemburg, with support in the 1980s running at over 70 and 80 per cent. Support in the Federal Republic dipped somewhat to 54 per cent in 1985, perhaps as a result of the constant wrangles about the EC budget, which heightened Germany's sense of being the paymasters of the Community. Support in France dipped to 51 per cent in 1980. A striking feature of this table is the fact that the percentage saying that EC membership is a 'bad' thing never reaches 10 per cent in the inner 'Six'. Not so, in the countries that joined the Community in 1973, although a distinction must be drawn here between Ireland, on the one hand,

Table 5.1 Attitudes to membership of the European Community

Country	1975 G %	1975 B %	1980 G %	1980 B %	1985 G %	1985 B %	1990 G %	1990 B %
Belgium	57	3	57	2	64	6	69	5
FRG	56	8	65	6	54	7	62	7
NL	64	3	75	3	77	3	82	3
Luxemburg	65	7	84	3	84	2	72	8
France	64	4	51	9	68	6	63	7
Italy	71	3	74	3	72	4	75	3
EC SIX	63	5	64	5	65	6	68	6
UK	47	21	21	55	32	40	52	19
Ireland	50	20	52	19	53	20	74	8
Denmark	36	25	33	29	29	31	49	25
Greece	–	–	–	–	45	17	70	5
Spain	–	–	–	–	62	6	65	8
Portugal	–	–	–	–	28	10	62	4
EC 10/12	59	9	55	15	60	11	65	8

Source: Eurobarometer Trends, 1974–90, no.33, June 1990
Figures taken from first Eurobarometer survey each year.
Respondents were asked, 'Generally speaking, do you think that your country's membership of the common market is a good thing, a bad thing, or neither good nor bad? Answers to the first two categories are included in this table.

and Britain and Denmark, on the other. Ireland is consistently more positive about EC membership than the other two states, although the proportion of respondents saying that EC membership is a 'good thing' does not reach the levels of the 'inner Six' until the late 1980s. The percentages saying that EC membership is a 'bad thing' are very high in the UK and Denmark, although the proportion of Danish respondents saying that EC membership is a 'good thing' rises to 49 per cent in 1990 from 35 per cent in 1985. The value of the EC as a framework for German unification is the most likely explanation in the sudden increase in support for EC membership in Denmark. The attitude of the two Iberian states is generally more positive than the countries of the first enlargement.[5]

In an attempt to translate the 'permissive consensus' on European unification into affective support, EC institutions began to address the meaning of a 'People's Europe' in the 1980s. The Adonnino Committee was established by the Fontainebleau European Council in 1984 to outline a series of measures to strengthen and promote the identity of the EC for its citizens.[6] The Committee put forward proposals on the rights of citizens, culture, youth exchanges, health, social security, town twinning and symbols of EC identity. The Community now boasts a European flag (twelve gold stars on a blue background), which was adapted from the Council of Europe's original flag and which adorns many public buildings side by side with the national flags. The flag appears in the most unlikely places – on beaches that conform to EC standards, at festivals and at sporting events. Beethoven's 'Ode to Joy' has been adopted as the Community anthem, and citizens of the member states carry a common passport that indicates their country of origin and their status as citizens of the EC. A standard driving licence is the latest symbol that seeks to give the peoples of the Community a sense of common identity. Symbols have long played an important role in promoting the authority and legitimacy of individual nation-states.[7]

Over many years such symbols, if reinforced with tangible political and social rights, can contribute to the creation of a sense of unity among the peoples of the Community. The notion of parallel citizenship – citizenship of a member state and citizenship of the Union – is mooted for discussion at the Political Union Intergovernmental Conference. A Spanish government paper submitted for consideration at the IGC seeks to transform the status of non-nationals in any member state from that of 'privileged alien' into EC citizen. Citizenship of the Union will be based on the rights already established by the Treaties, political participation in the country of residence and consular assistance to Community citizens outside EC frontiers.[8] Given the strength of national loyalties, shared loyalty, rather than an all-or-nothing shift of loyalty, is more likely than any radical transformation of identity.

Direct political representation

Citizens play a pivotal role in major political decisions when referenda are held concerning membership of the EC or its development. During the 1970s referenda were held in Ireland, Norway, Denmark, Switzerland, France and Britain on the issue of EC membership. A negative vote in the Norwegian referendum kept that country out of the Community despite the completion of accession negotiations. In the 1980s, the ratification of the SEA led to referenda in both Denmark and Ireland.

Since 1979, direct elections to the European Parliament have afforded the citizens of the member states direct participation in the Community's political system every five years. The periodic elections are now an integral part of the national political calendar and an additional focus for party competition. Direct elections fuelled demands from the European Parliament for a greater say in the Community's policy process, particularly in relation to legislation. European parliamentarians are critical of the weakness of political accountability in the Community. The EP cites the existence of a 'democratic deficit' in its search for increased powers. The widespread use of majority voting in the Council, as a consequence of the SEA, leads to a situation in which laws passed there are directly applicable in all member states, even if the representatives of individual member states voted against the said laws. And national parliaments are finding it increasingly difficult to monitor policy developments in the EC so as to ensure executive accountability.[9]

The SEA strengthened the role of the European Parliament in the policy process by giving it the right to a second reading of the Council's 'common position' and by its stipulation that the consent of the Parliament is necessary for membership and association agreements. The new co-operation procedure works well and has resulted in an enhancement of the Parliament's institutional standing. The dominant role of two political groupings, the Socialists and the Christian Democrats, who since the 1989 elections together have 301 deputies out of 518, facilitates the attainment of the necessary majorities for the amendment of proposals, if these two groups can achieve agreement. (See Table 5.2.) Majority voting in the Council enables the EP to seek support from individual member states. The Council requires unanimity to alter the amendments of the EP at the second reading so that support from one member state lends weight to the EP's proposals.

The relative effectiveness of the EP in using its powers under the SEA strengthens its hand in looking for an increased legislative role. There is, however, the question of the dual democratic imperative. The EP, on the one hand, argues for a greater say in the making of EC legislation, based on its direct democratic mandate following from direct elections. Yet direct elections to the EP are not core political events in the member states. Political scientists have categorized EP elections as 'second order' elections, more akin to local and regional elections than to 'first order' national elections.[10] Turn-out in EP elections is consistently below 'first order' national elections; in 1979, 63 per cent of those entitled to vote participated in the election. This figure fell to 61 per cent in 1984 and to 58 per cent in 1989.[11] These figures conceal considerable differences across the member states, from a high of 90 per cent in Belgium, where non-voters are fined, to 46 per cent in Denmark and a mere 36 per cent in the UK. Turn-out was less than 60 per cent in six member states.[12] Low turn-out weakens the EP's case for increased legislative powers when

Table 5.2 1989 European Parliament election results

Party Grouping	B	D	G	Gr	S	F	Irl	I	L	NI	P	UK	12
Socialists	8	4	31	9	27	22	1	14	2	8	8	46	180
EPP	7	2	32	10	16	6	4	27	3	10	3	1	121
LDR	4	3	4	–	6	13	2	3	1	4	9	–	50
ED	–	2	–	–	–	–	–	–	–	–	–	32	34
Greens	3	–	8	–	1	8	–	7	–	2	1	–	30
EUL	–	1	–	1	4	–	–	22	–	–	–	–	28
EDA	–	–	–	1	–	13	6	–	–	–	–	–	20
ER	1	–	6	–	–	10	–	–	–	–	–	–	17
CL	–	–	–	3	–	7	1	–	–	–	3	–	14
RBW	1	4	–	–	2	1	1	3	–	–	–	1	13
Independents	–	–	–	–	4	1	–	5	–	1	–	1	11
Totals	24	16	81	24	60	81	15	81	6	25	24	81	518

Source: EP Official Election Results
Key: EPP – European People's Party, LDR – Liberal Democratic and Reformist Group, ED – European Democratic Group, EUL – European United Left, EDA – European Democratic Alliance, ER – European Right, CL – Coalition of the Left, RBW – Rainbow Group

ministers and heads of government sitting in the Council can call on their governmental mandate derived from 'first order' national elections. The 'democratic deficit' is a key issue on the agenda of the Political Union Intergovernmental Conference. The Council of Europe's work in the field of human rights has contributed greatly to the concept of a 'people's Europe'.

THE PROTECTION OF INDIVIDUAL RIGHTS

The protection of human rights and fundamental freedoms assumed a central place in the post-war reconstruction of Western Europe. Respect for human rights was made a condition of membership of the Council of Europe under Article 3 of its statute. The Council went on to champion the Charter of Human Rights. The emphasis in the Convention is more on traditional legal and political rights than on economic and social rights. The drafters of the Convention relied on the Universal Declaration of the UN for a catalogue of fundamental rights. (See Table 5.3.) Not content with a simple listing of rights, the Convention makes provision for an elaborate machinery consisting of the Commission of Human Rights, the Court of Human Rights and the Council of Europe's Committee of Ministers. (See Table 5.3.)

One of the most significant innovations in the Convention was the provision made for individuals to petition the Commission to seek redress for violations of their rights. Without this provision, the Convention would lack teeth. In addition, the Convention allows for 'inter-state' cases, whereby one or more signatories may issue proceedings against another. There are thus two types of case dealt with in Strasbourg: 'individual' cases and 'inter-state' cases. The right of individual petition must be granted by individual states under the first protocol to the Convention. It was a slow process to get countries to accept that its citizens should have access to a judicial process outside their own jurisdiction. By the end of the 1950s only nine countries had ratified the necessary instruments. By 1974, however, only five members of the Council of Europe – France, Cyprus, Greece, Malta and Turkey – failed to allow individual petition. By 1990, Cyprus, Lichtenstein and San Marino were the only member states not to allow individual petition.[13]

The Convention in action

How does one assess the effectivness of the Convention? There were just seventeen inter-state cases between 1956 and 1989, because fellow signatories of the Convention would consider taking a case only in the event of suspected far-reaching violations. One of the most important cases was taken by a number of countries, notably Denmark, Norway, Sweden and The Netherlands against Greece in 1967 following the April *coup d'état*. The four governments alleged that Greece had violated numerous articles of the Convention and that inhuman and degrading treatment had been inflicted on political prisoners by the Athens security police. The Greek government responded by saying that it had the right under Article 15 of the Convention to take exceptional measures because of political instability in Greece. The Commission of Human Rights carried out an exhaustive investigation of the allegations of ill-treatment. It found that torture had been inflicted in a number of cases and that there was an established practice of ill-treatment by the Athens Security Police of people arrested for political reasons. This case was not forwarded to the Court of Human Rights because Greece did not recognize its jurisdiction, so it was left to the Committee of Ministers to rule on the report of the Commission. The Committee found that Greece had violated nine articles of the Convention, including Article 3, which deals with torture and inhuman and degrading treatment. The Greek government decided to withdraw from the Council of Europe and denounce the Convention of Human Rights when it was faced with likely suspension by the Committee of

Table 5.3 Fundamental rights enshrined in the Charter of Human Rights

- Right to life
- Freedom from inhuman or degrading treatment
- Freedom from slavery, servitude, forced or compulsory labour
- Right to liberty and security of person
- Right to a fair and public hearing
- Right to respect for private and family life
- Freedom of thought, conscience and religion
- Freedom of expression
- Freedom of peaceful assembly and freedom of association
- Right to marry and to found a family

Source: Articles 1–12, European Convention of Human Rights and Fundamental Freedoms

Ministers. The actions of the member states of the Council and the Commission of Human Rights in the Greek case served further to undermine the legitimacy of the Greek regime internationally and at home. Greece ratified the Convention again in 1974 when democracy was re-established.[14]

The right of individual petition is the cornerstone of the system, because it allows individual citizens to seek redress against their national authorities outside the confines of their national jurisdiction. No government likes to face examination by an outside body such as the Commission of Human Rights. In fact, on numerous occasions, a letter from the Commission to the national authorities has been sufficient to get a friendly settlement of a matter in dispute. Only a small proportion of applications to the Commission are admissible; of the 14,466 applications made up until the end of 1988, 90 per cent were deemed inadmissible. Notwithstanding this figure, the issues raised in the cases that were allowed led in many instances to legislative change in the member countries. The abolition of corporal punishment in the United Kingdom, the introduction of female suffrage in Switzerland, new remand provisions in Austria and the Federal Republic of Germany, the introduction of a system of free legal aid in Ireland, and the revision of the Belgian constitution with respect to the rights of linguistic minorities all took account of proceedings in Strasbourg.[15] The absence, in the UK, of a written constitution and a bill of rights leads to more complaints from Britain (768 in 1988) than from any other country.[16]

Links between the Convention and the law of the European Community

Although the European Community has created its own body of law and a new legal order, its Treaties do not contain a detailed catalogue of freedoms that must be observed in the application of EC law. Yet from an early stage, the Court of Justice has had to consider cases in which it was alleged that EC law violated a fundamental right guaranteed by national constitutions. In a number of judgments, the Court of Justice declared that it could not 'accept measures incompatible with fundamental rights recognized and protected by the constitutions of member states' and that international treaties for the protection of human rights on which the Member States have collaborated or of which they are signatories, can supply guidelines which should be followed within the framework of Community law.[17]

Since 1974, when all member states of the Community had ratified the Convention on Human Rights, the Court of Justice began to use the ECHR as an important source for deriving guidelines about the constitutional traditions of the member states. A Commission White Paper of 1979 argued in favour of the Community's adherence to the Convention, although this has not progressed.[18]

THE EUROPEAN COMMUNITY'S HUMAN FACE

Social policy

Although the Rome Treaty contained a chapter on social policy, it was not central to the *raison d'être* of the Community. Given the emphasis in Article 3 of the Rome Treaty on the customs union and the common market, it is not surprising that most of the provisions on social policy were linked to the creation of the common market and the equalization of competition among the member states. The Treaty endowed the Community with a number of different powers in the social field, notably regulatory or legislative powers, financial powers and the power to consult with the social partners (i.e. trade unions and employers' organizations). The Treaty also included social aspirations, highlighted in the Preamble, on improving the living and working conditions of workers. The inclusion of a chapter on social policy, dealing largely with employment and working conditions, demonstrated a degree of awareness among the founding fathers of the need to deal with the social consequences of economic integration.

Between 1958 and 1968 the Community's activities in the social domain related largely to the establishment of the rights of workers to move freely within the Community and to enjoy the same advantages as nationals regarding employment, remuneration and working conditions. Ex-farm workers or 'green labour' from Italy and workers in the Federal Republic were the major beneficiaries of the Social Fund. A reappraisal of the Community's role in social policy began in 1969, when Chancellor Willy Brandt submitted a memorandum on social policy to the Hague Summit, in which he argued that progress in the economic field necessitated parallel progress in the social field. This view was reiterated in the early 1970s by the Commission, which concluded that a European Human Union must have the consent of the 'man in the field or factory and the housewife in the home'.[19]

The Paris Summit of 1972 endorsed the idea of a European Social Action Programme. This was launched by the Community in 1974 and was described by the Commission as the first attempt 'by the Community to draw up a coherent social policy setting out in a purposeful way the initial practical steps on the road towards the ultimate social goal of a European Social Union'.[20] The Council of Ministers had a much more restricted view of the programme and stressed that there was no question of 'seeking a standard solution to all social problems or attempting to transfer to Community level any responsibilities which are assumed more effectively at other levels'.[21] This tension between the Commission's vision of social solidarity and the more cautious approach of the Council remains.

The programme's objective of full and better employment quickly gave way to a concern with rising levels of unemployment in the member states. The activities of the Social Fund were greatly expanded in the 1970s to cover workers in declining industries, women, migrant workers, young people and the handicapped. The regulatory powers of the EC were used to pass laws protecting workers' rights concerning mass redundancies, company mergers, insolvent employers and health and safety in the work-place. The Community developed an extensive policy on equality issues, beginning in 1975 with the directive on equal pay for men and women. This was followed by legislation on access to jobs, training and social security. The appearence of a strong body of law protecting women's rights reflected the changing socio-economic position of women and the politicization of women's issues on the political agenda in the 1970s.

By the end of the social action programme, when many of the legislative proposals were on the statute books, the Commission began to consider the broad outlines of a second programme. This never materialized because of the adverse economic conditions of the 1970s. François Mitterrand's call for 'l'espace social Européenne' fell on deaf ears in 1981. Nevertheless, the Commission continued with its work in this domain by launching 'second generation' programmes on health and safety, women's rights, migrant workers and other aspects of social policy. Difficulties arose in the attempt to get agreement on a number of directives dealing with part-time workers and employee participation. The latter directive, known as the Vredeling Directive, on procedures for informing and consulting employees in multinational companies, aroused deep controversy between the social partners.

The influence of the Community's social legislation makes itself felt through a growing body of cases taken by individuals to the European Court of Justice. The judgments of the Court have pushed the boundaries of EC social protection way beyond the narrow protection of workers in employment. For example, an Italian couple working in Germany were refused a low-interest loan by a Land bank in Baden-Württemberg because they were not German nationals. The Court of Justice ruled that the loans were a form of social benefit because they were available only to low-income couples and that therefore any employee from any member state working in Germany was entitled to one. Likewise, a case taken by the family of a severely handicapped twenty-year-old man in France had a major impact on social legislation. The French authorities refused the handicapped person a disability allowance on the grounds that he had never worked in France and that his parents were Italian. The Court accepted that, as a non-worker, the young man could not be given the same entitlement as a worker, but it found that because his parents were employed in France, a denial of benefit might cause his parents to return to their country of origin. Thus, on the principle of free movement, the French authorities had to award the disability allowance.[22] Citizens of the EC member states have rights under both the Convention of Human Rights and the EC Treaties. The two European courts in Strasbourg and Luxemburg empower individuals to seek redress of grievance outside the narrow confines of any one state.

The Politics of the Social Charter

In 1985, Jacques Delors, as the new President of the Commission, decided to relaunch the 'social dialogue' by setting up a meeting with the social partners in Val Duchesse, a chateau in the south of Belgium. This gave rise to the 'Val Duchesse' dialogue. Community social policy received a further impetus with the signing of the SEA and the reform of the structural funds. The SEA revises the social provisions of the Rome Treaty in two respects. First, a new Article 118 A strengthens the Community's legal competence with regard to the 'working environment' and the 'health and safety of workers' and stipulates that 'qualified majority voting' should apply to legislation in this field. Second, Article 118 B endorses the importance of 'dialogue between management and labour at European level' and allows for Europe-wide agreements between the social partners. The social, as well as the economic, aspects of cohesion are enshrined as part of the 'harmonious development' of the Community in the SEA.[23]

Following the adoption of the internal market programme as the major Community priority for the end of the 1980s, attention was drawn to the social aspects of the 1992 programme by the German and Greek presidencies of the Council in 1988. The Commission – particularly Jacques Delors – was keen to establish a linkage between the social and economic aspects of integration. The Marin Report of September 1988 set out the Commission's thinking about future social policy. Its call for a Social Charter was a major innovation.

After lengthy negotiation and much dissension, a Social Charter was signed by eleven of the twelve heads of government at the Strasbourg European Council in December 1989. The British Prime Minister, Margaret Thatcher, refused to sign the document. The main components of the Charter are a reaffirmation of the rights to the free movement of workers; the right to an 'equitable wage', defined as a wage to enable workers to have a decent standard of living (an earlier version of the Charter used the term 'minimum wage'); the right to adequate social protection and an adequate level of social security benefits; the right to form and join a trade union; the right to vocational training and equal treatment of men and women; health and safety in the work-place; and the right of worker participation. Although the main thrust of the Charter relates to those in employment, a number of general statements about the young, the elderly and the disabled are included. The Commission is now entrusted with the task of implementing the Charter by means of a new social action programme. The programme can cover only those areas for which the Community has policy responsibility under the Rome Treaty. EC policy must thus complement national policies or the member states retain primary responsibility for promoting the rights enumerated in the Charter.[24]

The drafting of the Social Charter led to considerable conflict between the member states, the social partners and Community institutions. The debate ranged from questions of principle to the wording of the document. Margaret Thatcher claimed that it was inspired 'by the values of Marxism and the class struggle'.[25] Because of her attachment to economic liberalism, Mrs Thatcher wanted to restrict EC social policy to health and safety in the work-place. British objections to the Charter are shared by UNICE, the transnational interest organization representing European industry.

The Secretary-General of UNICE objects to the Social Charter on the grounds that it seeks to centralize and regulate social policy matters at EC level and that it concerns itself with matters that are unsuitable for EC action.[26] The employers' representatives want to limit EC social policy to health and safety, mobility, education and equal opportunities. Not unexpectedly, the European Trade Union Confederation (ETUC) takes a rather different view. At the outset, the trade union movement was critical of the absence of any concern with the social dimension of the internal market. The ETUC favoured a legally binding Social Charter and criticized the 'weakness, the fragility and uncertainty of the commitment' to workers' rights contained in the Charter.[27]

Support for the Charter came from the Commission, particularly from its President, Jacques Delors, from those member states with high standards of social protection and high wage costs, from the trade union movement and from the socialists, the largest grouping in the European Parliament. These forces see the need for upgrading social standards in the EC so that there is a minimum level of Community-wide protection. The Delors view of Europe includes a strong social component. The Federal Republic was one of the main proponents of a Social Charter because it feared that without minimum standards for employees' rights throughout the Community, social dumping might become commonplace in post-1992 Europe. In other words, industry would move from countries with high standards of protection and high wages to lower-cost countries. The DGB, the German trade union confederation, was particularly worried about the possible consequences of 'social dumping' for its members. The Federal Republic would have supported the imposition of minimum wage levels on a Europe-wide basis. However, the peripheral countries with high levels of unemployment opposed any such imposition because of its implications for costs to industry and their attractiveness as locations for foreign investment.

The Social Charter was a much weaker document than the first Commission draft. Even the name of the Charter changed, from the Charter of Basic Social Rights to the Community Charter of the Fundamental Social Rights of Workers, thereby underlining the special relationship between Community social policy and working people. Forty-seven initiatives are contained in the Commission's proposals for the implementation of the Charter; they deal with such matters as free movement, health and safety, social security for migrant workers, vocational training and employment conditions.[28]

Legislative proposals on part-time and contract work, protection for pregnant women and access to information for employees form the core of the Commission's immediate programme. The proposed directives are likely to be hotly debated in the Council as British opposition continues and as employers' organizations and the representatives of small businesses seek to highlight the impact of the proposed laws on their costs. The legal basis for the proposals is an issue of major contention. The Commission is basing its proposals on Article 100 of the Treaty, which deals with the internal market on the grounds that different regimes for atypical work in the member states affect competition. The use of Article 100, which allows for qualified majority voting (see p.79), would overcome the problem of British opposition.[29] A number of member states are uneasy with the Commission's use of Article 100 in this case. The scope and implementation of the Community's role in the social domain is likely to remain a contentious issue in the 1990s.

Education

The Council of Europe has fostered limited co-operation on educational matters by acting as an umbrella for the Conference of Ministers of Education and by promoting debate on higher education and language learning for many years. The European Community, on the other hand, had no mandate to develop policies with a bearing on the national educational systems. The member states were reluctant to see the Community play a role in an area that impinged on core national values. Since 1970, however, there has been a slow but steady build-up of measures in areas that fall within the general ambit of education. Policies on the free movement of people impinged on educational policy by requiring the mutual recognition of diplomas and language skills. The European Social Fund, although a training fund, began to treat such matters as the education of migrant workers' children and of the handicapped, equal opportunities for the sexes and the transition from school to working life. A concern to promote teaching about the EC and Europe more generally in schools was the focus of a Council of Ministers of Education resolution of 1985.

In the latter half of the 1980s a series of EC programmes heralded a more active involvement by the Community in educational policy. COMETT, aimed at facilitating co-operation between universities and industry for training young technologists, was launched in 1987.

The number of universities and companies involved in the COMETT programme has doubled since 1987. In 1990, 2,000 universities, 2,500 companies and 3,000 professional bodies were participating in the programme, including 155 projects with participants from EFTA.[30] Likewise in the university sector, the ERASMUS programme was launched in 1987; this is designed to promote greater mobility of university staff and students. The number of students involved in the exchange component of the programme increased from 4,000 in 1987 to 15,000 in 1988–9 and to 28,000 in 1989–90. The goal of the programme is to ensure that from 1992 onwards 10 per cent of students in the EC spend a period of study abroad. The EFTA states have now joined the ERASMUS network.

ERASMUS has experienced a number of problems in the early days of its operation. In 1987, 62 per cent of all student exchanges stayed within a triangle involving the three most populous EC countries (France, Germany and Britain). By 1990 this had fallen to 42 per cent. The ERASMUS budget is insufficient to finance all eligible applications, and the level of grant awarded to individual students differs from one EC country to another. Individual academics attempting to establish ERASMUS networks experience considerable difficulties in working out examination procedures, course development and language requirements.[31] The concept of 'Jean Monnet chairs' – academic posts partially funded by the EC – was launched in 1990 to promote teaching on the European Community in third-level institutions.

Attempts by the EC to get involved in educational policy at school level has proved more difficult. The launch, in 1989, of the Lingua programme, a programme to promote language teaching, met with some resistance from Britain and the German *Länder*, notably Bavaria. It was argued that the EC had no mandate to get involved in the national curricula or in student exchanges at secondary level. In the ensuing debate, subsidiarity was invoked to restrict EC involvement to the co-ordination, technical support and provision of language teaching for the employed.[32]

There has been a gradual development of a Community interest in educational policy in response to the dynamics of integration, notably the free movement of people, and as part of a deliberate attempt at social engineering by fostering ties among second- and third-level students and by promoting teaching on European integration. The gradual spread of a web of contacts among educational establishments and students in the member states will lead to a diffusion of ideas about educational matters among the member states. ERASMUS and COMETT promote the free movement of labour and intensify social integration by creating a growing nucleus of people who have lived in another member state.

CO-OPERATION ON POLICING MATTERS

Police co-operation on a European and international scale is nothing new, but the prospect of a barrier-free Europe by 1992 raises important problems about the management of police co-operation. Drug trafficking, terrorism and fraud increasingly require cross-national co-operation. The Trevi Group, founded in 1976 as an intergovernmental forum for examining ways of combating serious crime, consists of the EC member states, organized parallel to the Community itself. The group meets at ministerial, senior-official and working-group levels. A working group, Trevi 92, was set up to examine the police and security aspects of the internal market programme. The Trevi ministerial meeting held in Dublin in June 1990 proposed an ambitious programme for co-operation on crime. However, the efficacy of the Trevi Group is questioned on the grounds that it does not have a permanent headquarters or adequate staffing.[33]

Co-operation on legal matters is fostered by the Council of Europe. It produces a large number of resolutions and recommendations on such diverse matters as the treatment of foreign prisoners, prison rules, the international validity of legal judgments and the harmonization of national laws in relation to asylum. Three of its conventions provide the legal framework for co-operation on criminal matters; these are the 1957 Convention on Extradition, the 1959 Convention on Mutual Assistance in Criminal Matters and the 1977 Convention on the Suppression of Terrorism. With the spread of IRA activity from Northern Ireland to the British mainland and to continental Europe, the need for co-operation on extradition is likely to become more pressing. The intensification of police co-operation, which is characterized by a strengthening of its legal framework, by the creation of European intelligence units and by increased placement of officers in the forces of other countries, may lead in the longer term to demands for a European police force and a Europe-wide court system. The idea of a 'Euro-FBI' has already been mooted by the German government.[34] Heretofore, because co-operation in the Trevi Group is outside the ambit of formal EC activity, the group has escaped democratic scrutiny and is a rather secretive body.

ENVIRONMENTAL POLITICS

Environmental politics are part of the 'new politics' of Western Europe. Although concern with the adverse effects of industrialization is not new, the 1980s have seen the growing political salience of environmental issues. The success of the Green Party in the Federal Republic demonstrated that green parties were capable of breaking into national and European politics. Traditional political parties, in turn, had to adapt their party programmes to the growing concern for the environment. In the 1989 European elections, the green vote rose to 7.7 per cent, in contrast to a mere 2.7 per cent in the 1984 election.[35] Consequently, the 'greens were in a position to establish their own grouping of 30 MEPs drawn from seven countries.

Why the increased concern for the environment? Part of the explanation lies in the deterioration of the global environment as a consequence of high levels of air and water pollution since World War II. The 'ozone layer', the 'greenhouse effect' and the depletion of the rain forests are testimony to man's abuse of the earth's natural resources. Health problems caused by emissions from factories and power stations serve to increase people's consciousness of environmental issues. Communities are increasingly alert to the environmental consequences of road -building, chemical factories, the quality of drinking water, the cleanliness of beaches and bathing water, and the quality of the air they breathe and the food they eat. The nuclear disaster at Chernobyl and the discharge of toxic chemicals into the Rhine from a Swiss factory in 1986 highlighted the cross-national aspect of environmental problems. Green issues are part of the local, regional, national, European and international political agendas. Underlying the relative success of green parties is a change of values among a segment of the electorate, who are now more concerned with collective non-economic issues than with traditional socio-economic conflicts.[36]

The role of the European Community

Environmental issues are yet another example of the expansion of the EC's agenda since its inception. At the Paris Summit of 1972, the participants called for an EC policy on the environment despite a weak treaty basis for such a policy. Until the SEA formally added environmental issues to the policy scope of the Community, EC action relied on the use of Article 100, which deals with the common market, and Article 235, which allows for EC measures to fulfil goals of the treaties where adequate legal provisions were not included in the initial treaties.

Three principles of environmental policy are outlined in Article 130R:

> Action by the Community relating to the environment should be based on the principles that preventative action should be taken, that environmental damage should as a priority be rectified at source, and that the polluter should pay.

Moreover, the Community should adopt EC measures only to the extent that environmental objectives can be attained better at Community level than at the level of the individual member states. In other words, subsidiarity governs EC action in this field. The link between environmental policy and other EC policies is established in the SEA. Article 100a on the internal market stipulates that Commission proposals must begin from a high level of environmental protection.[37] Article 130t stipulates that member states in fact may maintain or adopt more stringent measures, provided that these measures are compatible with the Treaty.[38]

The Council adopted the first EC action programme on the environment in 1973 and it has been followed by three others. The fourth action programme, set to run until 1992, builds on the work of past policy but is considerably more ambitious because of the SEA mandate. EC action includes measures to combat air and water pollution, waste disposal, the movement of dangerous substances, the protection of nature and the extension of international co-operation. In 1985 the Environmental Impact Assessment Directive was passed. This directive establishes the principle that all major development projects must be subjected to an environmental assessment based on Community-wide standards and criteria at an early stage in the development process.[39] A regulation establishing an Environmental Protection Agency was passed in May 1990. The agency is responsible for collecting comparable data on the environment and for developing environmental forecasting techniques.[40]

The Community's environmental policy has achieved mixed results. The Community is capable of passing legally binding directives that must be enforced by the member states. The Council of Europe, on the other hand, relies on 'well meant self-commitments with limited direct impact'.[41] The standards imposed by EC directives are limited to the level of agreement that can be forged by the member states and EC institutions. Among the member states there are varying levels of concern for the environment and varying capacities to shoulder the costs of preventing pollution. The Federal Republic, Denmark and The Netherlands seek high standards of environmental protection, whereas other member states are content with minimum standards. The Nordic states in general adopt much more stringent environmental protection measures. The European Parliament, which has a strong 'green' lobby, insisted on higher standards limiting emissions from cars than was envisaged by the Council in its original deliberations of a proposed directive dealing with fuel emissions from small cans. The EP was successful in its attempt to strengthen the directive because it was supported by Denmark, Germany and The Netherlands. The implementation of environmantal directives leaves much to be desired. In a February 1990 report, the Commission listed 362 infringements of EC directives on the environment. (See Table 5.4.) The improper application of the law is the most frequent problem; however, it can be corrected if the Commission takes infraction proceedings against the member states.

EC action on environmental issues acts as a resource for national ecology groups. There is an increasing tendency for individuals to complain to the Commission if national authorities are failing to apply the law; the number of complaints rose from a low of 11 in 1984 to 460 in 1989. Moreover, local and national environmental groups exchange information about environmental issues and use the Environmental Impact Assessment Directive as a lever in the planning process.

CONCLUSIONS

Policy-making in the EC, with its myriad committees and incessant meetings conducted in arcane language, remains remote from the mass public. National political, administrative and economic élites have always been the major participants in the development of the Community. Yet their activities in Brussels are buttressed by public opinion, which is generally in favour of European unification and the European Community. The level and nature of support for integration may not, however, be sufficient to support the development of stronger central institutions in the Community. With this in mind, Community institutions have embarked on a deliberate policy of creating a 'People's Europe'. The EC flag, anthem, and sports teams are attempts to create an emotional attachment to the notion of Europe among the citizens of the member states. Debate about the 'democratic deficit' and the need to strengthen democratic accountability derives from a continuing concern about the kind of polity required for a European Union. The notion of dual citizenship is likely to extend to the EC in the 1990s. Some fusion of the rights elaborated in the Convention of Human Rights and EC citizenship may well occur.

For a long time the human face of the EC was based on a narrow interpretation of the social policy articles contained in the Treaties. A focus on workers' rights still characterizes the Community's social policy, although there is an attempt to accord the right of free movement to all EC citizens, regardless of occupational status. The implementation of the Social Charter is riven with conflict because employers' organizations and Britain are fundamentally opposed to the Commission's approach. Differing capacities to fund social protection among the member states also poses problems, as the lesser-developed parts of the Community do not want to increase the costs to industry.

Increasing co-operation on policing, education and environmental matters reflects the dynamics of integration among industrialized adjacent countries. Police co-operation must intensify in response to the reduction of barriers among the member states and the

Table 5.4 Infringements of environmental directives, 1990

Country	Number of infringements
Spain	57
Belgium	47
Greece	45
France	41
Italy	40
UK	31
FRG	29
NL	24
Ireland	21
Portugal	14
Luxemburg	12
Denmark	5
Total	366

Source: Commission Report on the Implementation of Environmental Directives, February 1990

international character of some criminal activities. The Community's policies on education complement the internal market programme by increasing student mobility. They are also part of a deliberate attempt by the Commission and the Council to influence curriculum development in universities and schools. The arrival of green politics on the EC agenda reflects the transnational nature of much pollution and the growing salience of green issues in the political context.

NOTES

1 K.W. Deutsch *et al.*, *Political Community in the North Atlantic Area* (Princeton, N. J.: Princeton University Press, 1957), p.36.
2 L.N. Lindberg and S.A. Scheingold, *Europe's Would-be Polity* (Englewood Cliffs., N. J.: Prentice-Hall, 1970), pp.45–63.
3 M. Hewstone, *Understanding Attitudes to the European Community a Socio-psychological Study in Four Member States* (Cambridge: Cambridge University Press, 1986), p.18.
4 D. Handley, 'Public opinion and European integration: the crisis of the 1970s', *European Journal of Political Research*, 1981, vol.9, pp.335–64, and M.Slater, 'Political élites, popular indifference and community building', *Journal of Common Market Studies*, 1982, vol.21, pp.69–87.
5 *Eurobarometer*, vol.2, no.33, June 1990, Appendix, p.59.
6 EC Bulletin, *Report on A People's Europe*, Supplement 7/85.
7 W. Wallace, *The Transformation of Western Europe* (London: Frances Pinter, 1990), p.104.
8 Spanish submission to the preparatory committee for the intergovernmental conference on political union, 'The Road to European Citizenship', 24 September 1990.
9 For a discussion of the democratic deficit see V. Bogdanor, 'The June 1989 European elections and the institutions of the Community', *Government and Opposition*, 1989, vol.24, pp.199–214.
10 K. Reif and H. Schmitt, 'Nine second-order national elections – a conceptual framework for the analysis of European election results', *European Journal of Political Research*, 1980, vol.8, pp.3–44.
11 E. Lakeman, The European Elections, 1989, *Parliamentary Affairs*, 1990, vol.43, p.87.
12 Ibid., p.86.
13 C. Archer, *Organising Western Europe* (Seven oaks, Kent: Edward Arnold, 1990), p.48.
14 A.H. Robertson, *Human Rights in Europe* (Manchester: Manchester University Press, 1977), pp.39–42 and 176–8.
15 Council of Europe, *Stock-taking on the Convention*, yearly supplements.
16 Ibid., supplement 1988, p.115.
17 Quoted in EC Bulletin *Accession of the Communities to the Convention of Human Rights*, Supplement 2/79, p.7.
18 Ibid.
19 M. Schanks, 'European social policy: the next stage', in B. Burrows, G.

Denton and G. Edwards (eds), *Federal Solution to European Issues* (London: Macmillan, 1978), p.137.

20 EC Bulletin *Social Action Programme*, Supplement 2/74.
21 EC Council Resolution of 21 January 1974, *Official Journal*, 13, 12 February 1974, p.1–4.
22 EC, *European, You have Rights*, Commission booklet, June 1986.
23 EC, SEA Article 118A–B, EC Bulletin, Supplement 2/86.
24 *Agence Europe Documents*, Charter on the Fundamental Social Rights of Workers, 8 November 1989.
25 Quoted in R. Morgan, 'A View from continental Europe', *Policy Studies*, 1989, vol.10, p.58.
26 Secretary-General, UNICE in *Social Europe*, 1/1990, pp.22–4.
27 Secretary-General, ETUC, Ibid., pp.25–7.
28 *Agence Europe Documents*, First Proposals by the European Commission for Implementing the Charter of Basic Social Rights, no.1634.
29 Memorandum of the Italian Presidency of the Council, *Agence Europe*, no.5304, 27 July 1990, p.11.
30 EC Commission, COMETT *Information Note*, 23 July 1990.
31 EC Commission, *Erasmus Report*, Sec(89), 2051 final, 13 December 1989.
32 M. Wilke and H. Wallace, *Subsidiarity*, RIIA Discussion Papers, no.27, 1990, p.34.
33 For a detailed overview of the pattern of police co-operation at European and international levels, see UK House of Commons, Home Affairs Committee, *Report on Practical Police Co-operation in the EC*, 20 July 1990, no.363–1, pp.20–4.
34 Ibid., p.34.
35 J.G. Anderson, 'Environmentalism', 'New politics' and 'Industrialism: some theoretical perspectives', *Scandinavian Political Studies*, 1990, vol.13, p.101.
36 R. Eckersley, 'Green politics and the new class: selfishness or virtue?', *Political Studies*, 1989, vol.27 pp.205–23 and J. Hofrichter and K. Reif, 'Evolution of environmental attitudes in the European Community', *Scandinavian Political Studies*, 1990, vol.13, pp.119–46.
37 EC, SEA, op. cit., Article 100a.
38 EC, SEA, op. cit., Article 130t.
39 E. Gouge, 'The UK implementation of environmental assessment (EA): organisational and political implications', *Local Government Policy Making*, 1989, vol.15., pp.55–63.
40 EC, Council Regulation (EEC) no.1210/90, *Official Journal* L 120/1, 11 May 1990.
41 W. Weidenfield, *European Deficits European Perspectives – Taking Stock for Tomorrow* (Bertelsman Foundation, Guterslok, 1989), p.115.

TOPICS FOR DISCUSSION

1 What is the role of public opinion in European integration?
2 Have economic imperatives, rather than social imperatives, been the motor force in integration?

3 How real is the notion of a 'people's Europe'?
4 Why has the Social Charter been so controversial in the EC?

FURTHER READING

Lodge, J. 'Social Europe: Fostering a People's Europe' in J. Lodge (ed.), *The European Community and the Challenge of the Future*, London: Frances Pinter, 1989, pp.303–18. This chapter provides an overview of the main issues on the social policy agenda for the 1990s.

Venturini, P. *1992: The European Social Dimension*, Luxemburg: Official EC Publications, 1989. This volume, part of the EC's Documentation series, examines the social dimension of the internal market.

Wallace, W., *The Transformation of Western Europe*, London: Frances Pinter, 1990. This Chatham House paper provides a useful insight into the development of informal integration in the social domain.

Articles

Glenn Mower, A. 'Human rights in Western Europe: progress and problems', *International Affairs*, 1976, vol.52, pp.235–51.

Gouge, E. 'The UK implementation of environmental assessment (EA): organisational and political implications', *Local Government Policy Making*, 1989, vol.15, pp.55–63.

Handley, D.H. 'Public opinion and European integration: the crisis of the 1970s', *European Journal of Political Research*, 1981, vol.9, pp.335–64.

Hofrichter, J. and Reif, R. 'Evolution of environmental attitudes in the European Community', *Scandinavian Political Studies*, 1990, vol.13, pp.119–46.

Jachtenfuchs, M. 'The European Community and the protection of the ozone layer', *Journal of Common Market Studies*, 1990, vol.28, pp.261–77.

Jones, G.W. 'The British Bill of Rights', *Parliamentary Affairs*, 1990, vol.43, pp.27–40.

Mazey, S. 'European Community action on behalf of women: the limits of integration', *Journal of Common Market Studies*, 1988, vol.27, pp.63–84.

Teague, P. 'European Community Labour Market Harmonisation', *Journal of Public Policy*, 1989, vol.9, pp.1–33.

Slater, M. 'Political élites, popular indifference and community building', *Journal of Common Market Studies*, 1982, vol.21, pp.69–87.

Chapter 6

Western Europe in world politics

With the division of the Continent into two camps, following World War II, Western Europe formed a distinct regional system in world politics. Over time, the EC became the focus of collective diplomacy by the member states and other actors in the international system. One hundred and forty countries have diplomatic missions in Brussels and are accredited to the Community. The EC's diplomatic identity is moulded by the external competences of the Rome Treaty, on the one hand, and the system of foreign policy co-operation (EPC), on the other. These form the twin pillars of the EC's role in the world. At the outset, the member states were loath to give the EC a competence with regard to traditional foreign policy, an area of 'high politics', but granted the EC powers in relation to 'low policy' issues in the economic sphere. Even then, the member states transferred competence in an niggardly manner by establishing numerous committees to oversee the Commission in its conduct of the EC's external relations.

The desire to speak with one voice and the perceived benefits of a collective diplomatic personality led to the development of European Political Co-operation (EPC) in 1970. EPC evolved as an intergovernmental forum outside the boundaries of the Treaties – again testimony to the member states' desire to control foreign policy co-operation themselves and to their continuing ambivalence about the transfer or sharing of competence in this sensitive area of policy.

The Single European Act, by codifying European political Co-operation, brings the two parallel strands of the Community's foreign policy role within a common constitutional framework. However, Western Europe's security policy is elaborated outside the EC framework in NATO and the Western European Union.

The purpose of this chapter is to identify the powers, procedures and competences that constitute the Community's international role and to outline in some detail how the EC acts in its relations with different parts of the world.

First, let us identify the main changes in the international system during the second half of the 1980s that challenge the notion of Western Europe as a defined region in world politics.

A CHANGING AND TURBULENT EXTERNAL ENVIRONMENT

The latter half of the 1980s saw complex changes in the global political and economic system, highlighted by the breakdown of the bi-polar world and the post-war European order. The following factors must be emphasized:

1 When Mikhail Gorbachev assumed the post of General Secretary of the Communist Party of the Soviet Union (CPSU) in 1985, he set in train a reform process that has had profound consequences for the USSR, Eastern Europe and the world. Gorbachev took power at a time when the Soviet economy was in severe difficulty, with the annual growth rate approaching zero. Without fundamental economic reform, the USSR was set to lose its superpower status by the twenty-first century. Gorbachev embarked on a policy of economic restructuring known as *perestroika*. The new economic philosophy began with reform of state enterprises, but it became apparent that profound changes in property relationships and in the monetary, financial and prices systems could not be avoided. To date, *perestroika* has been singularly unsuccessful in transforming the command economy. Shortages of food and consumer goods, a perennial feature of the Soviet economy, have become, if anything, more acute.

Glasnost, or 'openness', was seen by Gorbachev as a necessary complement to *perestroika*. It has certainly led to very open criticism of the performance of the Soviet political and bureaucratic system and to demands for fundamental political reform. Economic turmoil and a weakening of communist control of the media unleashed hidden ethnic and national conflicts. Nationalist movements are flourishing in many Soviet republics. The breakup of the CPSU is in train, with a severe weakening of its control over the Soviet political system. The failure of a *coup* by hardline Communists in August 1991 speeded up the disintegration of the USSR, as many Soviet republics asserted their independence and as the Baltic states had their independence recognized internationally. A loose confederation of independent states is likely to replace this confederation; Russia, led by Boris Yeltsin, will be the predominant political and military power. Thus the Soviet Union's retreat from empire is being accompanied by the breakup of the multinational Soviet state.[1]

2 As part of the reform process, Gorbachev sought to improve relations with the outside world, leading to 'new thinking' about Soviet foreign policy. [2] Co-operation, rather than confrontation, became the hallmark of Soviet foreign policy. There was a disavowal of the 'Brezhnev Doctrine', which justified the use of force by the USSR against any socialist country straying from the orthodoxies of Marxist-Leninism. At the Council of Europe in 1989, President Gorbachev stated:

> The philosophy of the concept of a 'common European home' rules out the probability of an armed clash and the very possibility of the use of threat of force, above all military force, by an alliance against another alliance, inside alliances or wherever it may be.[3]

Events in Eastern Europe in the latter half of 1989 bear this out.

3 The changes in Soviet foreign policy go far beyond declaratory statements. Soviet forces left Afghanistan, and a new period of East–West *détente* began. After 1986–7, a remarkable improvement in superpower relations became apparent. The 'new cold war' (1979 onwards), characterized by increasing regional tensions and an arms build-up, was replaced by a series of superpower summits, culminating in the December 1989 Malta Summit which announced the end of the cold war. The 1987 Intermediate Nuclear Forces (INF) Treaty on intermediate nuclear weapons put arms control and disarmament back on the agenda of superpower relations.[4]

4 The Gorbachev revolution gave the countries of Eastern Europe, under Soviet tutelage since the war, a 'window of opportunity'. Poor economic performances in the 1980s, leading to shortages of basic foodstuffs, heavy borrowing from the West (especially by Poland and Hungary) and a worsening ecological crisis undermined the authority of the governing Communist Parties. The fragility and lack of legitimacy apparent in the Eastern European political systems was exposed with breathtaking speed in 1989. The first critical changes were launched in Poland, where a Solidarity prime minister took power in the summer of 1989. Change in Hungary come from within

the Communist Party itself. As it became apparent that the USSR was withdrawing from empire, street protests in one East European country after another led to the replacement of the communist leaderships. The countries of the Eastern bloc are now embarking on the difficult transition from command economies and totalitarian political systems to market-led economies and democratic systems based on the rule of law. The depth of the economic problems differs from one country to the other, as does their level of indebtedness. The fragile democratic traditions of these countries do not give grounds for optimism. The social cost of transforming inefficient economic structures will place a severe strain on the legitimacy of these nascent democracies.[5]

5 The German Democratic Republic (GDR) could not survive as an independent entity after the collapse of communism. Once the Berlin Wall was pulled down, the GDR lost its *raison d'être*. German unification, for so long part of ritual Western declarations on the 'Iron Curtain', became inevitable. The speed with which the unification of the two Germanies was accomplished has taken analysts by surprise. Monetary union in July 1990 was followed by full political union in October and all-German elections in December.

6 The collapse of communism in Eastern Europe and Gorbachev's desire to withdraw from empire calls into question the post-war European security order. The Warsaw Pact, once the cornerstone of Soviet security policy, ceased as a security organization in summer 1991. The elected governments in Hungary, Poland and Czechoslovakia negotiated the phased withdrawal of all Red Army troops. The withdrawal of Soviet forces from the former GDR is part of the arrangements on German unification agreed by the Federal Republic and the USSR. The disintegration of the Warsaw Pact raises questions about NATO's future role.

7 The future of NATO is bound up with the continuing role of the United States as a guarantor of Western European security and as the linchpin of the Atlantic Alliance. The Bush administration is in the process of working out its role in the new 'European architecture', a term coined by the US Secretary of State, James Baker. West-West relations, no less than East–West relations, are in a period of flux.

8 Iraq's invasion and annexation of Kuwait in August 1990 brought the euphoria following the ending of the cold war to a speedy and abrupt end. Saddam Hussain's use of force in this most unstable part of the globe highlighted the dangers of non-European

conflicts, or an 'out of area' threat to Western and West European interests.

For the member states of the European Community, the comfortable certainties of a divided continent are gone. Europe is in a period of transition, as the old order crumbles and existing institutions are adapted to meet the challenge of the 1990s. The EC will need all its new-found confidence if it is to ensure that the emerging order is peaceful and prosperous. German unification, enlargement, economic aid for the East, and security all add to the complexity of the tasks facing the Community.

A PATCHWORK OF POWERS, PROCEDURES AND COMPETENCES

External relations

The term 'external relations' is used to describe the foreign policy competences exercised by the EC arising from the foundation treaties. A key feature of the customs union was the transfer of responsibility for foreign trade policy from the member states to the Community under Articles 110–116 of the Rome Treaty. Article 113, the most important provision in the Treaty concerning trade policy, states that 'after the transitional period has ended, the common commercial policy shall be based on uniform principles'.[6] A series of additional articles make provision for EC accords with individual countries and groups of countries. (See Table 6.1.)

The Community's external relations have fostered association agreements and accords with individual countries, groups of countries and international organizations. Responsibility for trade policy endows the Community with a formidable role in the General Agreement on Tariffs and Trade (GATT). Accords with Third World states makes the EC an important element of North–South relations. A landmark judgment of the Court of Justice strengthened the Community's external competence by establishing the right of 'implied powers'.[7] Put simply, the Court ruled that there was a direct connection between the Community's internal and external competences. If external agreements are necessary for the attainment of internal policy objectives, the EC has an implied external power in that field.

European political co-operation

EPC dates from the Hague Summit in 1969, when the heads of government asked their foreign ministers to examine and report on the best way of achieving progress towards political union. The first attempt to give the Community a role in 'high politics' foundered in the early 1960s, when the smaller member states rejected President de Gaulle's efforts to promote foreign policy co-operation by means of the Fouchet plan. The foreign ministers, in what is known as the Luxemburg Report (1970), advocated the development of foreign policy co-operation among the member states in an intergovernmental format. Further reports, notably, Copenhagen (1973) and London (1981), assessed progress in EPC and made recommendations concerning its scope and working methods. The SEA formalizes and institutionalizes the practices of EPC.

Political Co-operation deals with the ways and means by which the member states harmonize their views on world politics and speak with one voice in the international arena and on major world issues. The Luxemburg Report (1970) envisaged that all major questions of world politics would fall within the ambit of EPC, with the exception of bilateral relations between the member states and defence policy, a major component of foreign policy. As the process of EPC broadened and intensified, agreement was reached in the London Report (1981) that issues 'bearing on the political aspects of security' could be discussed.[8]

Title 111 of the Single European Act codifies EPC and gives it a

Table 6.1 EC external relations: Rome Treaty

Article	Area
113	Common commercial policy
131	Association with non-European states
228	Power to negotiate accords
229	Relations with UN, GATT
230	Co-operation with Council of Europe
231	Co-operation with OECD
237	Membership applications
238	Accords with third parties–EFTA/ASEAN

Source: EEC Treaty 1957

treaty basis for the first time. The member states pledge themselves to endeavour jointly to formulate and implement a European foreign policy (Article 30.1). The word 'endeavour' conveys the limits of the process as it exists. A European foreign policy would require a convergence of interests on foreign policy matters among the member states. Much of the language used in Title 111 is non-binding. For example, the participants in EPC 'shall endeavour to avoid any action or position which impairs their effectiveness as a cohesive force in international relations or within international organisations' (Article 30.2 (d)) or 'shall, as far as possible, refrain from impeding the formation of a consensus and the joint action which this could produce' (Article 30.3(c)).

The key feature of EPC is set out in Article 30.2, which states that the participants shall undertake 'to inform and consult each other on any foreign policy matters of general interest' and to consult before taking final positions. In order to increase their capacity for joint action in foreign policy, the article defines 'common principles and objectives' which form a 'point of reference' for the participants (Article 30.2). This reconciles the goal of a European foreign policy with national foreign policies.

The SEA breaks down the distinction between EPC and the Community's external relations by stating that 'the external policies of the European Community and the policies agreed in European Political Co-operation must be consistent' (Article 30.4.). Both the presidency and the Commission must ensure this consistency within their spheres of competence. The issue of security is dealt with in Article 30.6, which suggests that closer co-operation on questions of European security would contribute to the development of a 'European identity' in external policy matters, and to this end the participants in EPC will co-ordinate their positions more closely 'on the political and economic aspects of security' and will 'maintain the technological and industrial conditions necessary for their security' (Article 30.6). Defence policy lies outside the scope of the SEA.[9]

EPC machinery has evolved in a pragmatic and piecemeal manner and is characterized by a vertical expansion of levels within the process and more frequent meetings at all levels. The presidency plays a pivotal role in the operation of EPC; it has responsibility for the EPC agenda, EPC procedures and meetings, relations with third countries and international organizations, and political dialogue with the European Parliament.[10] The London Report (1981) made a series of practical recommendations for improving EPC and for overcoming some of its procedural inadequacies. Provision was made for intensifying the 'Troika' procedure, whereby the current holders of the chair and the preceding and succeeding presidencies consult to ensure coherence and continuity in the process. A crisis procedure was developed to allow for meetings at ministerial level or of the political directors within forty-eight hours, at the behest of any three countries. The major institutional innovation in the SEA was the establishment of a small EPC secretariat in Brussels. The Treaty gave formal recognition to the Commission's right to be 'fully associated with the proceedings of Political Co-operation' (Article 30.3 [b]). The SEA also provides for discussions of foreign policy matters on the 'occasion of meetings of the Council', which take place at least monthly, thereby allowing an intensification of EPC.[11]

The Characteristics of EPC

EPC, which began with limited goals in 1970, has evolved into a sophisticated system of collective diplomacy among a diverse group of countries. Because EPC has been in operation for some twenty years, it has a well-established 'policy style' and ingrained respect for the 'rules of the game'. A strong commitment to exchanging information among the national foreign ministries and to consulting with one's partners before adopting a foreign policy position is evident in EPC most of the time. The so-called 'co-ordination reflex' leads the member states to respond jointly to many international issues. EPC relies on the traditional instruments of diplomacy – joint declarations, *démarches* and joint action in international organizations. The rhythem of activity in EPC depends very much on the state of the international system and on the capacity of the member states to reach a consensus, the predominant 'rule of the game' in EPC. Growing change in world politics during the latter half of the 1980s has led to greatly increased activity in EPC. The number of statements emanating from EPC increased from twenty-five in 1983 to eighty-one in 1988 and to ninety-nine in 1989.[12]

EPC has extensive policy instruments if there is a willingness to use the provisions of the Treaties in foreign policy. During the 1980s, sanctions were used against Iran, Poland, the USSR, Argentina and South Africa. For example, in 1982 the Community suspended imports from Argentina after that country's invasion of the Falklands. The relevant regulation read as follows:

> The invasion of the Falklands Islands ... has given rise to discussions in the context of European political co-operation which have led in particular to the decision that economic measures will be taken with regard to Argentina in accordance with the relevant provisions of the Community Treaties.[13]

Denmark insisted on implementing this regulation by means of national law in order to give the veneer of national control in this sensitive area of policy. Ireland and Italy failed to re-impose sanctions after the initial three weeks.

The failure to maintain consensus on the question of sanctions against Argentina underlines a key feature of EPC, namely its non-binding nature. EPC rests on the foreign policies of twelve different states which have varying foreign policy traditions arising from differences of history, geography and economic development. Greece found it particularly difficult to adjust to participation in EPC in the early 1980s because of a significant divergence between its foreign policy traditions and those of its partners. Ireland's non-membership of NATO makes it hesitant about the development of a Western European security policy. Denmark is sometimes torn between foreign policy co-operation in EPC and Nordic co-operation.

A distinction must be drawn between the large states in EPC, on the one hand, and the small states, on the other. The large member states – France, the UK and the Federal Republic – consider themselves the 'serious countries' in EPC. Italy is sometimes but not always considered to be a 'serious country'. Undoubtedly, the larger states, by virtue of size, economic power and military capability, form an 'inner core' whose agreement must be forthcoming for any major EPC initiative. The larger states sometimes feel constrained, because EPC has been likened to a convoy that moves at the pace of the slowest ship.[14]

The larger states have a tendency to 'go it alone' when it suits them. For all member states there is a tension between the advantages of collective diplomacy and the maintenance of divergent foreign policy styles and dearly held traditions.

Notwithstanding the diversity of national foreign policies among the member states, EPC has built up an extensive *acquis politique* since its inception; common positions have been arrived at on many international issues, and as we shall see below, positions are refined as the scope of agreement widens. EPC goes beyond gestures of co-ordination to involve habits of working together, a mutual sensitivity, an air of familiarity, and a new *esprit de corps*.[15] EPC provides the member states with foreign policy actions without the straitjacket of a common foreign policy. Yet the time may have come when the member states can no longer eat their cake and have it. The goal of a common foreign and security policy is firmly on the agenda of the Political Union Intergovernmental Conference.

THE EC IN ACTION: SOME EXAMPLES

The following examples were chosen to highlight the possibilities and limits of the EC as an international actor using the Community's external competences and EPC.

Lomé and Southern Africa

The Lomé Convention stands at the pinnacle of the Community's development co-operation effort. It was heralded in 1975 as a harbinger of new relations between a group of industrialized and less developed countries. The preamble to the first Convention spoke of a relationship based on 'complete equality between partners'.[16] The first Lomé Convention, signed by forty-six African, Caribbean and Pacific (ACP) states, was part of an anticipated new era in North–South relations. The fourth Lomé Convention, signed by sixty-seven ACP states, entered into force in January 1990.

An important aspect of the Lomé Convention is the global nature of the Conventions; the ACP states have maintained an impressive record of speaking with one voice in Lomé negotiations. The main components of the Conventions are:

- trade co-operation
- development aid
- Stabex and Sysmin for the stabilization of export earnings
- industrial and agricultural co-operation
- consultative institutions.[17]

The Community's attitude towards the Lomé process is to consolidate and improve the workings of the Conventions at each revision, whereas the Lomé states look for substantial further development in the scope and nature of co-operation.

Although the Lomé Conventions are unique instruments of development co-operation, they have singularly failed to redress the balance in the nature of the relationship between the developed economies of the Community and the ACP states. Although trade co-operation in Lomé is based on non-reciprocity and access for industrial and some agricultural products to the Community market, the ACP share of EC imports fell from an average of 8 per cent between 1970 and 1974 to 6 1/2 per cent between 1975 and 1984.[18] Despite the fact that some ACP states have increased their exports to the Community of textiles, clothing, leather goods, meat, fish and processed food, the ACP share of the EC's total imports of industrial goods in 1987 was a mere 2.4 per cent.[19]

The provision of development co-operation monies through the European Development Fund (EDF) is one of the main features of the Lomé system. EDF aid is granted on favourable terms, as it is untied aid. ACP criticisms of the EDF relate to the amount of money available and the manner of its distribution. Between 1976 and 1985 per capita transfers fell in real terms by 40 per cent.[20] Excessive red tape has characterized the EDF, especially during the first two conventions. A new and relatively successful system of dialogue on development co-operation priorities was instituted during the third convention, although there are still sizeable delays in the disbursement of EDF monies. Stabex and Sysmin are designed to protect the ACP states from fluctuations in their export earnings. Stabex covers so-called 'soft commodities' or agricultural produce, and Sysmin deals with mining. During the life of the third convention, demands for finance from the schemes outstripped available resources. Consequently, there is a two-thirds increase in the Stabex fund in the fourth convention.[21]

The severe economic crisis that hit black Africa in the 1980s, marked by a high level of indebtedness, hampered the African states' ability to foster economic development and to increase their exports to the Community. The Community's commitment to supporting the transition to democracy in Eastern and Central Europe, together with the demands of the EC's own periphery, does not augur well for ACP-EC relations in the 1990s. The demands on the Community's budgetary resources are ever-increasing.

EPC and Southern Africa

ACP-EC relations have invariably become entangled in political issues. The ACP-EC institutional machinery, which meets at ministerial, official and parliamentary levels, gave the African states ample opportunity to influence the EC's policy towards developments in Southern Africa. The achievement of independence by Mozambique and Angola in 1976 brought Southern Africa onto the EPC agenda. The Community issued its first declaration on Southern Africa in February of that year. This was followed by a long line of *démarches*, seeking Namibian and Rhodesian independence and the end of apartheid in South Africa. In September 1977 the member states introduced a code of conduct for Community firms operating in South Africa, a policy instrument intended to give teeth to the Community's oft-repeated condemnation of apartheid and designed to ward off criticism from the African states about the extent of economic ties between the larger Community states, especially the United Kingdom and the Federal Republic of Germany, and South Africa.[22]

From 1984 onwards, the deteriorating situation within South Africa led the industrialized countries to consider policy options that went beyond cool diplomacy; the debate shifted to sanctions, despite the instincts and official line of many of the major governments concerned. A mini-sanctions package was agreed upon in 1985. A combination of pressure from the ACP states, the Commonwealth, the Nordic states and internally from the smaller EC partners led to demands for stronger sanctions.

The Dutch presidency of the Council presented a sanctions package to a foreign ministers meeting in June 1986. Its rejection by Britain, the Federal Republic and Portugal made South Africa the major item on the agenda at the subsequent Hague Summit. The absence of consensus at this summit led to a further foreign ministers meeting in September, when, after a thirty-six-hour debate, sanctions were agreed. The package consisted of a ban on new investments and on the importation of iron, steel and gold coins. Coal, which represented 15 per cent of South Africa's exports to the Community, was missing from the final package. Although the agreement represented the lowest common denominator, two of the largest member states, Germany and the UK, were forced to adopt a position on sanctions at variance with their policy preferences.[23]

The achievement of independence in Namibia in 1989 and the

release of Nelson Mandela in South Africa in 1990 signalled the beginning of post-apartheid South Africa. The member states are finding it difficult to maintain the *acquis* in light of these changes, despite establishing a set of guiding principles at the Strasbourg European Council in December 1989. Following the release of Mandela, the British government indicated its intention to authorize new investments in South Africa, even before the issue was debated in EPC. While the British Foreign Minister was discussing the issue with his partners, the British prime minister announced in the House of Commons that her government would authorize new investments. The other member states have agreed to a gradual relaxation of pressure on South Africa when it becomes apparent that the process of change is 'profound and irreversible'.[24] In December 1990 the Rome European Council agreed to lift the ban on new investments and to begin dismantling the 1986 sanctions when the South African government repealed the Group Areas Act and the Land Acts. The subsequent announcement by South African President de Klerk of his government's decision to abolish all the remaining pillars of apartheid means that EC sanctions are set to end. A post-apartheid South Africa would probably become a member of the Lomé Convention.

The Mediterranean and the Middle East

The Gulf crisis served to underline Europe's vulnerability to events in the Mediterranean, the Middle East and the Gulf. For reasons of history and geographical proximity, the Mediterranean region is of special interest to the countries of the Community. The crisis-prone Middle East is of vital importance as a source of oil. Instability in the Middle East and the Gulf directly threatens Western European security, either through terrorist attacks in Europe or through the consequences of war in the Middle East. Yet the results of an extensive range of EC foreign policy actions, based both on the treaties and on EPC, is mixed.

Since 1972 the EC has operated what is known as a 'global approach' in its dealings with the countries on the southern shores of the Mediterranean. This 'global' policy was intended to replace the mosaic of trade agreements between the EC and the non-member Mediterranean countries signed in the 1960s. The Community offered those countries that could not become full members of the Community trade agreements characterized by free trade in industrial goods, some access for agricultural produce and financial co-operation. Agreements were signed with the Arab Maghreb (Morocco, Algeria, and Tunisia) in 1976, with the Arab Mashreq (Egypt, Jordon, Syria and the Lebanon) in 1977 and with Israel in 1975. In the aftermath of the Iberian enlargement, new agreements were signed with Tunisia, Egypt, Jordon, the Lebanon and Israel in 1987 and with Morocco in 1988.

The southern enlargement of the Community (Greece, 1981; Spain and Portugal, 1986), by making the Community self-sufficient in many of the products sold by the countries on the southern shores of the Mediterranean, poses a major challenge to the Community's 'global policy'. Even before enlargement, the Maghreb and Mashreq were disenchanted with the EC for a variety of reasons. The Community negotiated 'self-limitation' agreements curtailing their exports of sensitive textile and clothing products, one of the few sectors in which they could compete successfully in the EC market. The protectionist CAP and the unfavourable treatment of North African migrant workers also contribute to the tension in the relationship.[25] Migration is likely to be a source of even greater tension in the future, for population projections suggest that the working-age population in the North African countries is set to increase from 67 million in 1990 to 106 million by the end of the decade. Such large population increases will lead to a significant labour surplus in North Africa. Within the EC there is a division between those member states that are willing to open up the EC market, at least substantially, to the produce of those countries and those member states that want to base the Community's policy on budgetary transfers or aid. Britain, The Netherlands and Germany favour opening the market, whereas the Mediterranean member states do not want to make further trade concessions. Because the financial provisions of the 1987 and 1988 agreements, pledging 1,600 M ECUs in aid, are due to run out in 1991, the EC must reconcile its interest in stability and prosperity on its southern shores with the capacity of the Mediterranean member states to protect their 'insider' status.[26]

EPC and the Middle East

The Middle East, one of the first topics treated in EPC, remains a core issue. The Arab-Israeli war of 1973 and the ensuing oil embargo presented the nascent structures of EPC with their first major challenge. In July 1973 the Italian and Irish governments proposed that the political directors should take a long-term view of the Middle East crisis, but because of deep-rooted policy differences, this did not prove possible. As a result, the Europeans had not laid the groundwork for a concerted response to the Arab-Israeli war and the oil embargo. In December 1973, a group of Arab ministers turned up at the Copenhagen Summit to ask for a dialogue with the European Community. The Arabs were motivated by a desire to counterbalance the influence of the two superpowers in the region. The United States reacted unfavourably, fearing that the Europeans wanted to strike individual deals with the Arabs. EPC had the appearance of being an 'un-American' activity.[27]

The member states felt that they had to respond to the Arab request for dialogue, although they remained deeply divided on the issues at the centre of the Arab-Israeli conflict. The dialogue began in 1975, organized through a series of committees dealing with economic issues, but stalled in 1978 with the signing of the Camp David Accords. By 1980, the Middle East had re-emerged as a major issue on the EPC agenda. The shared experiences of political co-operation during the 1970s led to a convergence of views among the member states which enabled them to agree to the Venice Declaration on the Middle East in June 1980. Traditionally pro-Israeli countries, such as the Benelux, Denmark and the Federal Republic progressively moved closer to those countries pursuing a pro-Arab stand.

The Community's approach rests on two principles: that resolution of the conflict requires a recognition of the right of the state of Israel to secure borders, but also the right of the Palestinian people to 'exercise fully its right of self-determination'.[28] The Declaration emphasized the need to associate the PLO with any future settlement. The Europeans wanted to distinguish EC policy from the pro-Israeli policies pursued by the United States and to give support to the moderate Arab states. The Venice Declaration remains the core of the Community's *acquis politique* on the Middle East.

Although the Venice Declaration may be seen as a high point of EPC in so far as it produced a common position on one of the big questions of world politics, the EC is not a major force in the Middle East. According to Allen and Smith, the Europeans were 'unable to produce any credible initiatives on the ground'.[29] During the 1980s, the United States continued to play the most influential role in the Western response to events in the Lebanon and the wider region. The US bombing of Libya in April

1986, as revenge against the Libyan support for terrorism, left the Europeans on the sidelines. The bombing raid was conducted by US forces based in Britain but without consultation between the US and Western Europe. Britain allowed its facilities to be used for the raid, whereas other Western European governments refused over-flight facilities to the US planes on their way to Tripoli.[30] The British Foreign Minister did not inform his counterparts in other member states about his governments' decision, even though there was an EPC ministerial meeting before the raid took place. Until 1988 Britain also vetoed re-establishing links with Syria because of its alleged terrorist activities. This hampered the revitalization of the Euro-Arab dialogue for some time.

The Gulf

The UN Security Council responded to the 1990–1 Gulf crisis with an unprecedented show of solidarity. There was unanimous agreement to enforce a strict sanctions policy against Iraq. This was followed by an ultimatum to Iraq to withdraw from Kuwait by 15 January 1991. At the invitation of Saudi Arabia and the smaller Gulf states, a large multilateral force led by the United States was stationed in the Gulf region. The initial purpose of the force was to deter Iraq from further incursions into the territories of its neighbours and to enforce UN sanctions. With the refusal of Iraq to withdraw from Kuwait by the UN deadline, war broke out in the Gulf.

The nature of the Gulf crisis required the European response to go beyond mere declaratory statements. The contradictions in Western Europe's machinery for dealing with international crises, particularly of a military kind, were exposed. EPC cannot deal with defence, and NATO does not have a competence for action outside the NATO area. Countries initially responded individually to the crisis. Britain followed its 'Atlanticist' instincts by immediately deploying sizeable forces in the Gulf with the US. France, after some hesitation, decided to send naval and ground forces but emphasized the independent nature of its force. A meeting of the Western European Union (WEU), three weeks after the Iraqi invasion, which was attended by all EC states except Ireland, arrived at a wider consensus. Italy, Belgium, Spain and Greece (a non-member of the WEU) used the meeting to announce their dispatch of naval forces to the Gulf. An EPC meeting held the same day as the WEU gathering resolved not to comply with the Iraqi demand for the closure of embassies in Kuwait and stated that any harm done to a citizen of any member state would be 'considered as a most grave offense directed against the Community and all its member states and will provoke a united response from the entire Community'.[31] In the days before the UN Security Council deadline, there were clear tensions among the member states as they grappled with the growing realization that the use of force in the Gulf looked likely. France continued to seek a diplomatic solution after the other member states in EPC had decided that such a course was fruitless. France did not consult with its partners, although its final diplomatic initiative was a foreign policy matter of general interest. In the last few hours before the UN deadline expired, Britain and France clashed on the issue in the Security Council.

Once hostilities broke out in the Gulf, the diversity of responses to the use of force showed just how far short of a common foreign and security policy EPC falls at present. The UK was the only country to commit its forces to the war effort without reservations. France initially restricted the use of its air force to targets in Kuwait, although it later expanded their remit to targets in Iraq itself. Italy joined the hostilities after two days. The smaller states with a military capacity in the region did not engage in hostilities. Belgium refused to sell ammunition to the UK for use in the Gulf. For the first week of the war, the German Chancellor and Foreign Minister were virtually silent on the issue; they were torn between strong anti-war sentiments in the population and the need to reassure the US and the allies of their support. In response to pressures from their allies, Germany has agreed to make a financial contribution to the war effort and to station air forces in Turkey, a NATO state with a land border with Iraq. The Gulf War clarifies in a very real way, the difficulties facing the member states as they attempt to negotiate on a common foreign and security policy in the Political Union Intergovernmental Conference. The incentive for such a policy lies in developments in the former Soviet bloc and in the USSR itself.

THE NEW EUROPE

Eastern Europe and the Soviet Union

The revolutions in Eastern Europe and instability in the Soviet Union pose an immense challenge to the EC. Economic and political turmoil in the East could unhinge the Community's recently regained internal dynamism. The desire of the Eastern and Central European countries to 'rejoin' or 'return to' Europe raises the delicate issue of enlargement and the boundaries of the Community's political system in the 1990s. Difficult issues concerning market access, financial transfers and free movement of people will have to be confronted.

For a long time, relations between the Community and Eastern Europe were hampered by the Soviet Union's unwillingness to recognize the EC as such. President Gorbachev's accession to power opened the way for more normal relations between the then blocs, underlined by the signing of a joint EC-COMECON declaration in June 1988. This enabled the Community to establish diplomatic relations that same year with the USSR, the German Democratic Republic, Bulgaria, Hungary, Poland and Czechoslovakia. So-called first-generation trade agreements were concluded with Hungary (1988), Czechoslovakia (1988), the USSR (1989), Poland (1989) and the GDR (1990).

The rapid collapse of communism in 1989 demanded a more substantial response from Western Europe and the United States. At a meeting held in June 1989, the industrialized countries (Group of 24) decided to embark on an extensive programme of aid for Poland and Hungary, the two countries at the vanguard of the reform process. The decision of the Group of 24 to give the EC Commission the co-ordinating role in the development of the aid package highlighted the importance of the EC in the new Europe and the success of the Delors Commission in establishing its credentials. The United States was happy to see the EC assume a major role in promoting economic and political reform in Eastern Europe.

The Commission embarked on its new role with zeal. It undertook a series of fact-finding missions to Poland and Hungary, made contact with the relevant international agencies, notably the IMF, the OECD and the 'Paris Club' of creditor nations. Five major priorities were identified for the programme, now known as PHARE:

1 food aid and the restructuring of Polish agriculture.
2 improved access for Polish and Hungarian goods to Western markets through the abolition of quantitative restrictions and the extension of the generalized scheme of preferences to their goods.
3 the promotion of investment in Poland and Hungary. A stabilization fund was set up for Poland, followed by the decision of

the European Council in Strasbourg (December 1989) to set up
a European Bank for Reconstruction and Development.

4 vocational training for executives, managers and students, especially in financial and banking services.

5 The improvement of the environment.[32]

The Group of 24, under the auspices of the Commission, has
agreed the major elements of the programme. The European Bank
for Reconstruction and Development (EBRD) and the European
Training Foundation play a key role in the Western response. In May
1990, the EC established the TEMPUS programme, which is designed
to provide mobility grants for students to study in the Community.

As the process of reform spread within Eastern and Central
Europe, Yugoslavia, Czechoslovakia, Bulgaria, Romania and the
DDR asked to be involved in the PHARE programme. In February
the Group of 24 agreed to extend its operations geographically,
although the countries were not formally admitted until June, when
the Group met at ministerial level. Five criteria govern accession
to the programme: the establishment of the rule of law, respect
for human rights, free elections, political pluralism, and progress
towards a market economy. The extension of the PHARE programme
to the countries of Central and Eastern Europe poses a problem of
financing. When the programme was launched in 1989 it involved
just two countries, Poland and Hungary. By the end of the year,
there was a long queue waiting at the door. The Group of 24 and
the Community are mobilizing additional monies.

The EC is regarded as a key element in the emerging European
order. The role of the Community as an anchor and zone of stability
was emphasized at the Strasbourg European Council (9 December
1989) in the following terms:

> In this time of profound and swift change, the Community is –
> and must also be in the future – a firm point of reference with
> a strong power of attraction. It remains the cornerstone of a
> new European architecture and, in its desire for openness, – the
> stabilising influence in a future European balance.[33]

Jacques Delors stated in the Commission's 1990 Programme that the
Community had to 'devise new forms of co-operation' to provide for
'genuine dialogue and economic and political consultation' with the
countries of the East.[34] The EC is once again being called upon to
play an important role in promoting peaceful inter-state relations.

A commission document of 1 February 1990 sets out the EC's strategy in response to the European Council's call for an examination of the 'appropriate forms of association with the countries which are pursuing the path of economic and political reform'.[35] The point of departure for relations is the network of trade and co-operation agreements, the so-called first-generation agreements, negotiated by the Community in 1989 and 1990. The Commission envisages 'second-generation' agreements to take the form of association agreements, called 'European agreements', consisting of trade, co-operation, technical assistance and financial support, joint projects, political dialogue, information exchange and cultural co-operation. To date the EC has managed a credible response to the rapidly changing political and economic landscape of the East. It may find it more testing in the next phase of the relationship. There is the more difficult question of economic and technical assistance for the Soviet Union. The degree of market access that the EC will grant to the Eastern and Central European countries is not yet clear. Financial aid without generous access to the Community market will not solve their economic problems. Yet these countries have a comparative advantage precisely in those industrial sectors – textiles and steel, for example – that are sensitive in the EC. Furthermore, immigration is likely to prove contentious as Eastern Europeans follow the lure of the EC's better-endowed labour market. Difficult economic questions have yet to be confronted in the EC's relationship with the other side of the former Iron Curtain.

A Reassessment of transatlantic relations

Atlantic relations form the closest, albeit uneasy, set of economic and security relationships in the post-1945 international system. The mutual relationship of both the United States and the countries of Western Europe forms a central core of their foreign policies. Disagreements, often amounting to crises, about trade, burden-sharing in the Alliance, nuclear strategy and East-West relations have characterized the relationship since the 1960s. Tensions caused by the global interests of the US versus the regional interests of the Europeans often masked their underlying common concerns. The 1980s were a particularly fraught period. The US under Reagan set out to reassert US military dominance over the Soviet Union by embarking on extensive arms procurement and deployment. The weakening of *détente* was a setback for Western Europe because the

European concept of *détente* embraced more than arms control. Then, when Reagan tried to renew *détente*, at the Reykjavik Summit with Gorbachev in October 1986, it seemed to the Europeans that the American President was prepared to bargain away European security interests by proposing to eliminate nuclear weapons in Europe without consulting his allies.[36]

During the Reagan years there was a widespread impression in the US that Western Europe was unable to face up to the challenges of the twenty-first century. Concern about the 1992 programme and fears of a 'Fortress Europe' again focused US attention on Europe. Initial US hostility to the internal market programme has been replaced by enthusiasm. The need to take Europe seriously was underlined by the profound changes in Eastern and Central Europe. The Bush administration is in the process of elaborating the contours of a 'new Atlanticism' in the aftermath of communism's collapse and in the context of a weakening US economy. Washington, intent on securing a good relationship with the new Germany, was very supportive of unification from the outset.[37]

A series of speeches by President Bush and the US Secretary of State, James Baker, set out the main themes in American thinking about the new Europe. The US sees a new regional system gradually evolving from existing institutions. According to Baker, 'The future development of the European Community will . . . play a central role in shaping the new Europe.'[38] The importance of the EC in the reform process in Eastern Europe can be gleaned from US support for the Commission as the co-ordinator of the Western response. The US is keen to develop strong institutional links with the Community to overcome its reliance on bilateral relations with individual member states. In February 1990, the Irish presidency got American agreement to a series of formal meetings during each presidency, at the level of heads of government, foreign ministers and political directors, with the participation of the Commission. This process may well intensify and could lead to a treaty. A joint declaration on relations between the Twelve and the US, adopted in November 1990, is the first tangible outcome of the process.

The US is less clear-cut about Europe's future security order and the role of NATO. It appears to want to maintain a security presence in Europe, albeit at a reduced effort. James Baker, in his Berlin speech on the 'Architecture for a New Era', stressed that 'America's security – politically, militarily, and economically remains linked to Europe's security'.[39] NATO, the traditional vehicle for the US presence in Europe, would continue to play a major role in Baker's new architecture as a forum for the Western nations to negotiate and verify arms control agreements and to develop a concerted response to regional conflicts. Baker also envisaged NATO playing a political role in building 'economic and political ties with the East'.[40] NATOs' role in the transition towards a new security order in Europe is assured, but its longer-term survival in its present format is less clear-cut.[41] The US is uncertain about the role it would like to see being taken by the Conference on Security and Co-operation in Europe (CSCE). The US acknowledges that the CSCE process should go further, but sees its major role in relation to human rights, confidence-building measures and economic co-operation. There is little US enthusiasm for the CSCE as an arena of collective security.

A Western European security identity

A Western European security identity is a vexed question on the European agenda. The failure of the European Defence Community (EDC) in the 1950s relegated security to the hidden agenda of EC co-operation. Notwithstanding the Atlanticist nature of Western Europe's security, fears of collusion between the superpowers and a US desire to see Western European states doing more for their own defence have contributed to pressures for a European caucus within NATO and for the development of a European pillar of the Alliance. The fluid environment of post-communist Europe again places security and defence high on the European agenda. A common foreign and security policy is the key issue for the Political Union Intergovernmental Conference.

How has Western Europe responded in the past to demands for a Western European voice on security matters?

Defence is a classic example of variable geometry at work. A myriad committees and organizations – the Eurogroup, the IEPG, the WEU – deal with some aspect or other of Western European security. In NATO there is the 'Eurogroup', established by the former British Defence Minister Denis Healey in 1968 to ward off the prospect of US troop withdrawals from Europe. From the outset, the Eurogroup shunned grand designs in favour of a pragmatic approach, intended to promote European co-operation and to present the European contribution in NATO to US public opinion and policy-makers.[42] In 1975 the Independent European

Programme Group (IEPG), was established with French participation, to rationalize arms procurement.[43]

Bilateral defence co-operation is yet another manifestation of variable geometry in this policy domain. There is an intricate web of links developed in the 1970s involving co-operation between the British and Dutch marine forces, and coalitions of smaller countries for arms procurement.[44] Franco-German co-operation in defence matters is qualitatively different from other bilateral arrangements. A Franco-German Committee on Defence and Security, involving foreign and defence ministers, is at the pinnacle of a series of committees dealing with political-strategic issues, military co-operation and co-operation in the arms sector. Links also exist between the defence committees of the Bundestag and the French National Assembly. Beginning in 1985, joint Franco-German manoeuvres and the exchange of personnel became commonplace. At the suggestion of the German Chancellor, Helmut Kohl, a mixed Franco-German military unit was created in October 1988. Defence and security co-operation was put on a legal footing, following the addition of a protocol to the 1963 Treaty of Friendship and Co-operation in 1988.[45]

In 1981, the London Report on EPC accepted that the 'political aspects of security' could come within the ambit of foreign policy co-operation, but a plan advocated that by year the German Foreign Minister, Herr Genscher, and his Italian counterpart, Sig. Colombo, to establish a Defence Council, met with a lukewarm response from the other member states. France and Germany, irritated by their inability to get security and defence matters dealt with in EPC and constrained by the 'French problem' in NATO, (i.e. its insistence on having its own nuclear *force de frappe*) took a decision to reactivate the Western European Union.

The Western European Union, set up in 1954 to accommodate the Federal Republic's membership of NATO had lain dormant for many years. However, in the short run it appeared that a reactivated WEU offered the only institutional framework for closer co-operation on security matters among those countries that favoured such a development. The WEU had the advantage that it already existed, involved France and got around the problem of the reluctant EC countries. Unlike the IEGP, the WEU has a general competence on security matters and a parliamentary assembly. On the other hand, as Wallace pointed out in 1985, the reactivation of the WEU offered 'rich potential for additional duplication, redundancy and institutional displacement' in a field already complicated by variable geometry.[46]

The WEU received its 'certificate of rebirth' from the Ministers of Defence and Foreign Affairs in the Rome Declaration of 27 October, which underlined the determination of the seven member states to 'make better use of the WEU framework in order to increase co-operation between the member states in the field of security policy and to encourage consensus'. The ministers would seek to harmonize their views on

- defence questions
- arms control and disarmament
- the effects of developments in East–West relations on the security of Europe
- Europe's contribution to the strengthening of the Atlantic Alliance
- the development of European co-operation in the field of armaments in respect of which the WEU could provide an impetus
- the implications for Europe of crises in other regions of the world.[47]

Immediate decisions were taken concerning the institutional reform of the WEU, notably the reactivation of the Council, which had not met between 1973 and 1984. The Agency for the Control of Armaments, set up to oversee German rearmament in 1950s, was transformed into a series of agencies dealing with arms control and wider security issues. The accession of Spain and Portugal in 1990 extended the geographical scope of the WEU across the landmass of Western Europe.

In the aftermath of the 1986 Reykjavik Summit between the superpowers, the Western European states felt impelled to speak with one voice on security issues. In October 1987 the WEU states issued the 'Platform on European Security Interests'. The negotiations on the Platform took nine months, which serves to underline the complex and sensitive nature of discussions in this area. The Platform grapples with the European and Atlantic context of security and defence. On the one hand, the signatories state that 'the construction of an integrated Europe will remain incomplete as long as it does not include security and defence'; on the other hand, the 'security of the Alliance is indivisible'.[48] The US, for its part, is ambivalent about the WEU, fearing that it might detract from NATO and might turn into an anti-American cabal.

Since 1984, the reactivated WEU has made an important contribution to forging common positions among its member states on
security issues. It brings France back into the mainstream of debate
in Western Europe about security matters. Because of the limits to
EPC, the WEU serves to fill a void. In 1987 discussions in the WEU
about the war in the Gulf led to the dispatch there of ships from
Britain, France, Italy, Belgium and The Netherlands. Although it
was not a joint manoeuvre as such, the image of a European presence
was manifest. The agreement in the WEU Council in August 1990
to co-ordinate Western European naval deployments in the Gulf
can be seen as 'an assertion of European security interests and
the co-ordination of European security policies'.[49] The WEU did
not, however, lead to common positions about the use of force once
hostilities broke out.

The WEU is hampered by the artificial distinction between the
political and economic aspects of security dealt with in EPC and the
defence aspects. The former Secretary-General of the WEU, Alfred
Cahen, envisages the WEU as a transitional measure and argues that
'what is taking place within Western European Union should have
been happening within the context of the Twelve' and 'if at any time
all the Twelve were ready unreservedly to accept a full European
security dimension, WEU would have to be prepared to merge into
the mainstream of the European construction process which the
Twelve represent'.[50] The collapse of communism and the Gulf crisis
is testing EPC's constraints as never before. The Italian presidency
of the Council proposed the merger of the WEU and the EC in a
discussion paper issued in September 1990. A Franco-German paper
on political union (February 1991) sees the Western European Union
drawing progressively closer to the European Community during
the 1990s. The Brussels Treaty, on which the WEU is based,
can be modified in 1998 when it is up for possible revision. The
need to broaden the security dimension of EPC finds favour with
a majority of the member states. The communiqué of the Rome
Summit (October 1990) noted that there was a 'consensus to go
beyond the present limits in regard to security'.[51]

The Conference on Security and Co-operation in Europe

President Gorbachev's desire for a 'common European home' and
James Baker's 'new architecture' express Europe's search for a
new regional system to replace the post-war order. There are

no ready-made institutional models. The system will evolve from existing institutions. The breathtaking speed of change and the complexities of the task are stretching existing institutions to the limit. The Conference on Security and Co-operation in Europe (CSCE) is seen as a central feature of Europe's new political and security order. The CSCE is a legacy from the first period of *détente* or the 'era of negotiations' in the early 1970s. The Helsinki Final Act was signed in 1975 after three years' intensive East–West negotiations. The work of the conference was divided into four baskets, namely principles governing relations between states, economic co-operation, co-operation on human rights and follow-up measures to the conference.

From the outset the CSCE involved all European countries (with the exception of Albania), the US and Canada. Albania attended the Paris CSCE Summit meeting in November 1990 as an observer. The CSCE became a permanent feature of East–West relations, surviving the onset of the second cold war (1979–86). Since 1975 there have been three review meetings: Belgrade (1977–8), Madrid (1979–84) and Vienna (1986–9). A number of expert meetings on particular aspects of the CSCE were held in Athens (1984), Ottawa (1985), Berne (1986); a cultural forum in Budapest (1985); a meeting on economic co-operation in Bonn (1990); and the Conference on Confidence and Security-Building Measures and Disarmament in Stockholm (1984–6).[52]

Characteristics of the CSCE

Before examining the potential role of the CSCE in the new Europe, it is necessary to outline its main characteristics. First, the CSCE is a process of multilateral negotiations among thirty-four countries. The calendar of periodic review meetings gives the process a rhythm of activity and the appearance of permanence. Second, the CSCE operates on the basis of consensus between sovereign independent states. Respect for all states – large and small – is formally guaranteed. Third, neither the Final Act nor the follow-up documents are based on law. The CSCE codifies politico-moral norms for relations between states, underpinned by references to the UN Charter. Fourth, the continuity of the process gives rise to 'rules of the game' and norms of behaviour in negotiations. Formal procedures and informal meetings in the corridors oil the process. Fifth, the scope of co-operation is comprehensive; practically all areas of international life fall within the ambit of the process. Sixth, groups play a dominant role in the process. The European Community received its first experience of collective diplomacy at the CSCE. The neutral and non-aligned group (NNA) mediated between the Warsaw Pact and NATO states on many issues.

As a forum for East–West dialogue the CSCE was at the mercy of relations between the superpowers and the general tenor of East–West relations. The follow-up meetings were characterized by procedural wrangles and disputes about the human rights record of the Eastern bloc countries. However, its existence kept dialogue going, especially during the second cold war. The Stockholm Conference on Confidence and Security-Building Measures (1984–6) took place and reached a successful conclusion despite considerable tensions in East–West relations. The Vienna Review meeting (1986–9) benefited from the thaw in US-Soviet relations. It was followed by the successful launch of the Conventional Forces in Europe (CFE) negotiations, aimed at the reduction of conventional forces. The CFE Treaty was signed at the Paris CSCE meeting of November 1990. The treaty reduces one of the major sources of tension in Europe since the war, namely the Warsaw Pact's overwhelming superiority in conventional forces.

The role of the CSCE

The Paris CSCE Summit formally ended the cold war and saw the beginnings of a new regional system for the European continent. The CSCE became the obvious arena for the construction of new relationships in Europe. It was the only pan-European and pan-Atlantic forum available. The German government places the CSCE at the centre of its plans for the new Europe. Genscher, Germany's Foreign Minister, has great faith in the CSCE process.[53] It offers a ready-made forum for the legitimation of German unification within a wider European context. Following German unification, the Soviet Union has a clear interest in strengthening the CSCE in order to maintain a role for itself in the future security order of the Continent.

The 'Paris Charter for a New Europe' was signed by the thirty-four states attending the CSCE Paris Summit. The document consists of three parts covering

● democracy, peace and unity

- future directions of the CSCE
- CSCE structures.[54]

The first part of the document establishes the principles that should govern the political, economic and legal systems of the participating states and inter-state relations. Particular emphasis is placed on human rights, economic freedom, the freedom to choose security arrangements, friendly relations between states and confidence-building measures. Part two deals with the different aspects of CSCE policy co-operation. The final part of the document provides the CSCE with its first institutional basis. It was agreed to hold periodic summit meetings, yearly meetings of foreign ministers, and meetings at senior official level. Although there was agreement on the value of a parliamentary assembly under the auspices of the CSCE, no decision was taken on the form of such an assembly. The CSCE is given a small secretariat, located in Prague, consisting of a director, three administrators and a small number of technical staff. Two CSCE institutes were agreed upon: a conflict-prevention centre in Vienna and a free election bureau in Warsaw.[55] Thus, in the medium term the CSCE is likely to build on its involvement in confidence-building measures, arms control and the principles governing relationships between states. The CSCE can contribute to European security but is far from a security order. The CSCE must build-up a capacity for mediation and the peaceful settlement of disputes. Conflicts in the new Europe are more likely to stem from ethnic and national rivalries than from East–West antagonism. In the near future the CSCE is more likely to be one of the building blocks in a slow transition to a new security order than an arena for collective security.

CONCLUSIONS

The EC is an important actor in the international system, buttressed by an increasingly complex and extensive range of foreign policy activities. The Community's external relations and EPC endow it with an institutional structure and policy instruments to pursue an independent diplomatic personality. Yet the EC does not have a common foreign policy. The Community's activities in the international arena are fragmented and partial, resting on the foreign policies of twelve states. The limits imposed in EPC discussions of security are a major constraint on the development of the Community's foreign policy. There are intense pressures on the EC, both from the international system and from the internal workings of the Community, to intensify and strengthen its international capacity.

The importance of the EC in establishing a stable and prosperous Continent following the 1989 revolutions is borne out by its role in economic assistance to the Eastern and Central European countries. Association agreements are a first step in 'rejoining' Europe. In the aftermath of the collapse of the Berlin Wall, the EC has regained its original role in promoting peace and stability in inter-state relations. As the reform process continues, the EC may be confronted with very difficult choices about market access and the reform of internal EC policies. Yet if Western Europe does not give sufficient economic and technical assistance to the East, it will be confronted with mass immigration from these countries.

The end of the cold war brings with it the challenge of creating a stable security environment for the Continent. This must accommodate the disintegration of the Warsaw Pact, the decline of Soviet power and the fact of German unification. The Conference on Security and Co-operation in Europe (CSCE), a legacy of the first period of *détente*, may in the longer term provide the basis for a Continent-wide security system. The European Community, for long a civilian power, will have to confront the issue of defence and security in the 1990s.

NOTES

1 B. Meissner, 'Gorbachev in a dilemma: pressure for reform and the constellation of power', *Aussenpolitik*, 1990, vol.41, pp.118–34.
2 M. Malcolm, 'The common European home and Soviet European policy', *International Affairs*, 1989, vol.65, pp.659–76.
3 Address by Mikhail Gorbachev, President of the Supreme Soviet, Council of Europe, 6 July 1989.
4 M. Cox, 'From the Truman Doctrine to the second superpower détente: the rise and fall of the cold war', *Journal of Peace Research*, 1990, vol.27, pp.25–41.
5 For an account of the East European revolutions see T. Garton Ash, *We the People: the Revolution of '89* (Cambridge: Granta Books, 1990).
6 Article 113, Rome Treaty (EEC), 1957.
7 J.H. Weiler, 'The evolution of a European foreign policy', in I. Greilsamer and J.H. Weiler (eds), *Europe and Israel: Troubled Neighbours* (Berlin: de Gruyter, 1988), p.239.
8 EC, *Report on European Political Co-operation adopted by the Foreign Ministers* (London Report), 13 October 1981.
9 EC, Single European Act, Article 30, 6 (c).
10 For an account of EPC procedures see A. Piipers, E. Regelsberger,

W. Wessels (eds), *European Political Co-operation in the 1980s* (Dordrecht, 1988) or P. Ifestos, *European Political Co-operation: Towards a Framework of Supranational Diplomacy* (Aldershot: Gower, 1987).

11 EC, Single European Act, Article 30, 3 (a).

12 E. Regelsberger, 'The European foreign policy in the test', College of Europe, Bruges, 1989.

13 EC, Council Regulation (EEC) 877/82, 16 April 1982.

14 W. Wallace, 'Introduction' in C. Hill (ed.), *National Foreign Policies and European Political Co-operation* (London: Allen & Unwin, 1983), p.14.

15 R.H. Ginsberg, *Foreign Policy Actions of the European Community* (London: Adamantine Press, 1989), p.180.

16 EC, Preamble, First Lomé Convention, 1975.

17 For a detailed summary of the development of the Lomé system, see M.Lister, *The European Community and the Developing World* (Aldershot: Avebury, 1988).

18 J. Notzold and K. von der Ropp, 'Lomé IV: A chance for black Africa's return to the world economy?', *Aussenpolitik*, 1990, vol.41, p.184.

19 J. Moss and J. Ravenhill, 'The evolution of trade under the Lomé Conventions: the first ten years', in *Europe and the International Division of Labour* (London: Hodder & Stoughton, 1987), p.113.

20 A. Hewitt, 'ACP and the developing world', in J. Lodge (ed.), *The European Community and the Challenge of the Future* (London: Frances Pinter, 1989), p.290.

21 Notjold and von der Ropp, op. cit., p.189.

22 See M. Holland, 'Three approaches for understanding EPC: a case study of EC-South African policy', *Journal of Common Market Studies*, 1987, vol.25, pp.295–314.

23 B. Laffan, *Ireland and South Africa* (Dublin: Trocaire, 1988), pp.49–78.

24 EC, *Declaration on Southern Africa*, European Council, Dublin 25/26 June 1990.

25 For an overview of the Community's Mediterranean policy see K. Fetherstone, 'The Mediterranean challenge: cohesion and special preferences', in J. Lodge (ed.), op. cit., pp.186–201.

26 EC Commission, *Redirecting the Community's Mediterranean Policy*, Sec (89) 1961 final, 23 November 1989.

27 D. Allen and A. Pijpers (eds), *European Foreign Policy Making and the Arab-Israeli Conflict* (The Hague: Nijhoff, 1985).

28 EPC, *Venice Declaration* 12–13 June 1980, EC Bulletin no.4, 1980.

29 D. Allen and M. Smith, 'Western Europe in the Atlantic system in the 1980s: towards a new identity', in S. Gill (ed.), *Atlantic Relations* (New York, St. Martin's Press, 1989), p.100.

30 Ibid., p.101.

31 *Irish Times*, 23 August 1990.

32 EC, Commission Information Note, *PHARE*, April 1990.

33 EC, European Council, Strasbourg, 8/9 December 1990.

34 EC, Commission Programme, 1990, p.6.

35 EC Commission, 'The development of the Community's relations with the countries of Central and Eastern Europe', Doc., Sec (90) 196 final, 1 February 1990.

36 J. Scharp, 'After Reykjavik: arms control and the allies', *International Affairs*, 1987, vol.63, pp.239–58.

37 R.D. Hormats, 'Redefining Europe and the Atlantic link, *Foreign Affairs*, 1989, vol.68, pp.71–91.

38 Address by the US Secretary of State, James Baker, to the Berlin Press Club, 13 December 1989, p.3.

39 Ibid.

40 Ibid.

41 S.R. Sloan, 'NATO's future in a new Europe: an American perspective', *International Affairs*, 1990, vol.46, pp.495–511.

42 P. Williams, 'NATO and the Eurogroup', in K.J. Twitchett (ed.), *European Co-operation Today* (London: Europa Publications, 1980), pp.39–44.

43 Ibid.

44 W. Wallace, 'Relaunching the Western European Union: variable geometry, institutional duplication or policy drift', in P. Tsakaloyannis (ed.), *The Reactivation of the Western European Union: the Effects on the EC and its Institutions* (Maastricht: EIPA, 1985), pp.38–9.

45 P. Schmidt, 'The Franco-German Defence and Security Council', *Aussenpolitik*, 1989, vol.40, pp.360–71.

46 Wallace, 1985, op. cit., p.40.

47 WEU, *The Reactivation of WEU: Statements and Communiqués 1984–1987* (London: WEU, 1988).

48 Ibid., pp.31–45.

49 Editorial, *Financial Times*, 23 August, 1990, p.14.

50 A. Cahen, former Secretary-General of the WEU, in an address to the Royal Institute for International Relations, 23 February 1989, p.15.

51 EC, *European Council Communiqué*, Rome, 27/28 October, point 1.

52 For an overview of the CSCE process see K. Mottola, *Ten Years After Helsinki* (London: Westview Press, 1986); and K. Dyson, 'The Conference on security and co-operation in Europe: Europe before and after the Helsinki final act' in K. Dyson (ed.), *European Détente* (London: Frances Pinter, 1986).

53 Speech by the Foreign Minister of Germany, Hans-Dietrich Genscher, WEU Assembly, 23 March 1990, p.4.

54 CSCE Summit Final Document, *Agence Europe*, no.5375, 22 November 1990.

55 Ibid.

TOPICS FOR DISCUSSION

1 Trace the evolution of the EC's role in the international system.
2 Is EPC a Western European foreign policy in the making?
3 What is the EC's role in the New Europe?
4 Should the CSCE be transformed into a system of collective security?

FURTHER READING

Gill, S. (ed.) *Atlantic Relations: Beyond the Reagan Era*, New York: St. Martin's Press, 1989. An excellent analysis of recent trends in Atlantic relations.

Ginsberg, R.H. *Foreign Policy Actions of the European Community: the Politics of Scale*, London: Adamantine Press, 1989. This volume assesses the development of the EC's role in the world from a theoretical perspective. It has the advantage that it examines both EPC and the Community's external relations.

Nicoll, W. and Salmon, T.C. *Understanding the European Communities*, London: Philip Allen, 1990. Chapter 4 of this book provides a thorough synopsis of EPC.

Pijpers, A. Regelsberger, E. and Wessels, W. (eds) *European Political Co-operation in the 1980s*, Dordrecht: Nijhoff, 1988. The editors of this volume provide an extensive account of the development of EPC from a policy and institutional perspective in the 1980s.

Rollo, J.M.C. *The New Eastern Europe: Western Responses*, London: Frances Pinter, 1990. An up-to-date analysis of the issues facing Western Europe in Eastern and Central Europe.

Articles

Froment-Meurice, H. and Ludlow, P. 'Towards a European Foreign Policy', CEPS Annual Conference, 29 November 1989.

Hassner, P. 'Europe beyond partition and unity: disintegration or reconstitution?', *International Affairs*, 1990, vol.66, pp.461–75.

Hintermann, E. 'European defence: a role for the Western European Union', *European Affairs*, 1988, vol.3, pp.31–8.

Hoffman, H. 'A New World and its Troubles', *Foreign Affairs*, 1990, vol.69, pp.115–22.

Hormats, R.D. 'Redefining Europe and the Atlantic link', *Foreign Affairs*, 1989, vol.69, pp.71–91.

Malcolm, N. 'The Common European Home and Soviet European Policy', *International Affairs*, 1989, vol.65, pp.659–76.

Notzold, J. and Rummel, R. 'On the Way to a New European Order', *Aussenpolitik*, 1990, vol.41, pp.212–24.

Schopflin, G. 'The End of communism in Eastern Europe', *International Affairs*, 1990, vol.66, pp.3–16.

Tucker, R.W. '1989 and all that', *Foreign Affairs*, 1990, Fall, pp.93–114.

Chapter 7

The domestic dimension of co-operation and integration

The dynamics of integration have not displaced the state, and national governments are still the pivots of political activity, although the existence of multiple regional organizations has altered the external and domestic environments of Western European states. Participation in the process of integration represents an acceptance of limited sovereignty. The EC creates obligations that limit a state's freedom of action. The voluntary pooling of sovereignty is a hallmark of the Community. An appreciation of the national or domestic dimension of the EC is necessary if one seeks to understand and explain the dynamics of integration. This chapter assesses the salience of the Franco-German axis for the development of the EC and gives an overview of the interests in and attitudes towards integration among the member states.

The Community's political system rests on the political and constitutional systems of its twelve component parts. For the member states, participation in the EC adds an extra and complicating layer to domestic policy-making. The formal decision-making process in Brussels is but the tip of an iceberg that extends down into the national polities. A complex web of relationships between national agencies, Community officials and interest organizations moulds the policy process and policy outcomes. The Community's distinctive characteristics are its multi-levelled and multi-cultural nature.

National governments are heavily involved in the Community's decision-making processes. The twice-yearly meetings of heads of state and government, together with a plethora of Council of Ministers' meetings bring members of national governments into frequent contact. Formal EC meetings are underpinned by widespread one-to-one meetings and contacts. National officials play a critical role in the myriad committees and working groups that characterize all levels of the Community's policy process. Although the experience of working in the Community has not led national officials to transfer their loyalty to the supranational level of policy-making, as was anticipated in early neo-functionalist writings, the ingrained habit of working together induces a willingness to compromise in the constant search for acceptable policy results.

A distinctive feature of the Community's policy process is the dominant role exercised by negotiations. Decisions are the product of an extensive and complex process of negotiation between national governments, Commission officials and the European Parliament; negotiations do not stop once a decision has been reached in Brussels. The implementation and execution of EC legislation frequently involves negotiations between the Commission and national implementing agencies. The latter are not free agents; national interest groups often will use their involvement in transnational groupings and their access to national political leaders to influence the implementation process.

The management of EC business in the national capitals has given rise to new administrative arrangements to foster inter-departmental co-ordination and to ensure that the policy responses presented in Brussels are relatively coherent. Some states more than others place a premium on presenting a united front in EC negotiations. National governments must respond sector by sector and item by item to the agenda as it evolves in the Community. Moreover, they must develop policy positions on the future development of the EC and the institutional balance. Political and official responses to a particular Commission proposal depends on a variety of factors, most notably the economic interests at stake, traditional ways of doing things, the ease with which an EC directive can be implemented, the cost of implementation, the attitude of the relevant interest groups and the sensitivity of an issue in domestic political terms. Officials who are dealing with Brussels all the time have a good feel for what is technical and non-controversial, on the one hand, and what is political, on the other. For example, a health and safety directive for workers may be technical in one country but highly political in another if it has implications for relations between employer groups and the trade unions.

The interests pursued by governments in the EC have a structural and political dimension. A country's general economic position – the balance between agriculture, industry and services, the pattern and structure of trade, the level and nature of unemployment – and its geographical position (at the centre or periphery of the Community) mould national and sectoral responses to integration. Domestic political conditions and political preferences also contribute to national policy stances. The stability of government, the proximity of a national election, the congruence between national goals and the development of the Community, the status of the EC as an issue in domestic politics, and attitudes towards co-operation and integration are all components of the so-called national interest presented in Brussels.

THE ANATOMY OF POWER IN THE EUROPEAN COMMUNITY

The European Community brings together twelve countries of varying sizes, different levels of economic development, and distinctive historical experiences. Table 7.1 provides a brief survey of a number of important economic indicators for the Twelve EC member states. There are four large states in terms of population:

Table 7.1 The member states: some indicators

	(1) *Country Pop.* *1987*	*(2)* *Per Capita GDP PPP* *1989*	*(2)* *Unemp. %* *1988*	*(3)* *Per capita Social Benefits* *1987*	*(4)* *Share of intra-EC Exports* *1987*
Belgium	9.8	100.3	11.5	111	11.1
Denmark	5.1	107.1	8.5	117	1.5
Germany	61.1	113.5	8.1	128	32.2
> 1990	80.0				
Greece	9.9	51.1	7.4	–	0.5
Spain	38.8	75.6	20.0	53	3.7
France	55.6	108.4	10.7	119	14.7
Ireland	3.5	63.1	18.7	58	1.8
Italy	57.3	102.7	15.0	92	13.7
Lux.	0.4	124.9	1.4	130	–
NL	14.6	102.6	11.3	129	9.2
Por.	10.2	55.5	6.5	30	1.3
UK	56.9	108.2	8.5	96	10.0
EUR 12	323.2	100.0	11.3	100	100.0

Sources: 1. Europe in Figures, 1989/90 edition p.7
2. Irl. National Economic and Social Council, 88, pp.110, 117
3. Eurostat, Rapid Reports, no.3, 1990
4. Cutler *et al*, 1989, p.17. Trade in manufactured goods

the Federal Republic of Germany, Italy, Britain, and France; these are followed some way behind by Spain. None of the remaining states has more than 5 per cent of the Community's population. The level of economic well-being differs from one country from the other. Germany is undoubtedly the predominant trading partner in the EC, having, in 1987, almost one-third of all trade in manufactured goods. Eight of the Twelve member states have per capita incomes on or above the EC average. Spain, Ireland, Greece and Portugal fall well behind in terms of material well-being. Unemployment is a particularly acute problem in Ireland and Spain. Major disparities also characterize the level of social benefits in the member states.

Although the Community is founded on the formal equality of all its member states, a large state–small state divide is evident in the EC. Decision-making rules provide for weighted voting which takes account of the relative size of the member states, and in the Commission, the larger countries have two commissioners. The EC has, so far, operated without a predominant power. German economic power was balanced by France's political influence in the Community of the Six and by French and British military power in the 1970s and 1980s. The governments of these three countries are undoubtedly the most important in the Community. Italy is sometimes, but not always, considered a core country. Spain, as a relatively new member state, has not yet assumed the role that its size will allow. The smaller states are not passive participants in the Community's policy process; they can influence negotiations within and between sectors, but they cannot, either individually or in concert, successfully embark on major political initiatives. Constitution-building must have the consent of the larger member states.

Because the Community is based on a delicate balance between different states, coalitions play an important role in the dynamics of integration. The Paris-Bonn axis, the so-called 'privileged partnership', is one of the enduring coalitions of the Community and for long the centre of EC politics.[1] This axis is sometimes enlarged to form a triad involving Paris, Bonn and London.[2] Britain's unease about the goals of European integration undermines its capacity to forge enduring coalitions with other member states. The Netherlands, Belgium and Luxemburg, given their shared experience in the Benelux, form a small state coalition at the centre of the Community. Other coalitions tend to be sectoral in character: countries that favour the Common Agricultural Policy versus those interested in restricting budgetary expenditure on agriculture, or the peripheral countries, interested in a well-endowed regional policy, versus the richer economies.

The importance of the Paris–Bonn axis as the motor of European integration requires special attention. The decision to establish the ECSC in 1951 was based on a realization by the French that integration provided the best anchor for the new and truncated West Germany. The Elysée Treaty of 1963 on Franco-German co-operation provided an institutional basis for the development of an intensive bilateral relationship between these two countries at political and official levels and in the wider society. The Franco-German relationship has not only been critical in fashioning major political initiatives in the Community, but has enabled the two governments to ensure that bilateral disputes on various policy issues did not prevent agreement in the wider forum. This relationship has been as much about managing divergent interests as about pursuing joint interests.[3] Nevertheless, jointly promoted initiatives from these two countries stand a good chance of success. During the 1970s the Paris–Bonn axis was cemented by a very close personal relationship between Chancellor Schmidt of the Federal Republic and President Giscard d'Estaing of France. Although relations between President Mitterrand and Chancellor Kohl have not been marked by the same level of intimacy, major policy initiatives in the 1980s bear the stamp of Franco-German accord. The impact of unification on Franco-German relations is a major issue in the Europe of the 1990s.

THE MEMBER STATES

Given the breadth of Community policy-making, it is not feasible to chart national responses to the entire gamut of EC policies. Rather, it is intended here to provide a necessarily brief overview of the significance of integration for each member state and of the main interests pursued in EC negotiations. The attitude of the member states to the development of the Community provides a key to assessing its future prospects. Marquand distinguishes between a 'maximalist' and a 'minimalist' path towards integration. The 'maximalist' Community is a Community that is transformed into an economic and monetary union and a political union. A 'minimalist' Community has a narrow policy scope and a largely intergovernmental policy process.[4]

The Federal Republic of Germany

European integration offered the Federal Republic a vital opportunity to rehabilitate itself after the war. According to Bulmer and Patterson, participation in European integration not only benefited the international standing of the new state, but also acted as a pillar of the West German political system.[5] Integration is woven into the polity of the Federal Republic. For historical reasons, the Federal Republic never attempted unilaterally to exercise power commensurate with its status as the EC's premier economy.

From the outset, the political leaders of the West German state favoured integration, while at the same time eschewing a unilateral leadership role, accepted their role as the paymasters of the Community budget and promoted economic liberalism within the Community. Bonn's European policy often appears contradictory because the management of EC business is highly fragmented at the level of central government and within the *Länder*. Powerful autonomous ministries frequently pursue conflicting policies in Brussels. For example, although the reform of the Common Agricultural Policy was a major German goal in the 1980s, Ignaz Kiechle, the German Minister for Agriculture used the veto to block agreement on cereal prices on the eve of the important Milan European Council in 1985. The needs of Bavarian cereal producers took precedence over coherence in German policy.[6]

In the early 1980s a certain disillusionment with the Community as a forum for co-operation became apparent in Bonn. Leick concluded that the Kohl government was attempting to defend its own interests 'with such a lack of concern for others' interests and more ruthlessly than any other Federal Government before'.[7] The *Musterknabe* (model boy) of yesteryear, always on good behaviour, was becoming a somewhat apathetic partner in European construction.[8] Yet the underlying interest in integration reasserted itself when the Federal Republic took over the presidency of the Council in 1988. German support for economic liberalization and the completion of the internal market led the Bonn government to place its weight behind the adoption of the Delors package at the February 1988 Brussels Summit. The German presidency saw agreement on a number of important internal market directives and the decision to establish the Delors Committee on Economic and Monetary Union.

German unification

The re-emergence of the 'German Question' in the international arena in 1989/1990 came as a surprise to the 'Four Powers' (USA, USSR, UK and France) that had had a residual role in Germany since World War II. It was also a surprise to Germany's other neighbours and, not least, to the 'political class' in the Federal Republic itself. At first, the government of the Federal Republic attempted to slow down the process so as to ensure that what was happening in Germany was in tune with events in the Continent as a whole. Speedy unification became inevitable, given the outpouring of people from the GDR and the collapse of its economy. East Germans voted for rapid unification at the first free elections to the Volkskammer in March 1990. West German diplomacy succeeded in getting agreement to the international conditions for unification by embarking on an intensive round of bilateral and multilateral meetings with the Four Powers. Germany regained full sovereignty in a treaty signed on 12 September 1990 by the Four Powers and the two Germanies entitled 'Treaty on the Final Settlement with regard to Germany'. Internal unification took place in two phases. (See Table 7.2.) Both parts of Germany are embarking on an untrodden path; the highly industrialized market economy of the West will have to foot the bill for the modernization of an economy with an obsolete industrial base, weak infrastructure and almost nonexistent environmental standards. The challenge goes far beyond economics. The different social, political and cultural experiences of the two parts of Germany since the war make real unification an uphill struggle.

As German unification became inexorable, the traditional maxims of many states' foreign policies were severly tested. From the outset, the German Foreign Minister, Hans-Dietrich Genscher, placed unification in the context of political change in the Continent as a whole. At a meeting of the Western European Union in March 1990, Herr Genscher spelled out his formula for unification in the following terms:

> We seek the process of German unification in the context of EC integration, the CSCE process, East-West partnership for stability, the construction of the common European house and the creation of a pan-European peaceful order. We Germans do not want to go it alone or to follow a separate path. We want to take the European path.[9]

German unification posed least problems for the United States; it could be viewed as a victory for the capitalist West, one more proof that the West had won the cold war. Britain was initially less than enthusiastic in its support, wishing, rather, to bolster the *status quo*, which in effect meant no changes in NATO deployments in Germany. Remarks made by the Minister for Trade and Industry, Nicholas Ridley, in the *Spectator* magazine in July 1990 (which led to his resignation from the British cabinet) suggest that there is an undercurrent of unease in Britain about Germany's potential power. Accusations that Mr Ridley was merely echoing views held in the British establishment, and especially by the then Prime Minister, Margaret Thatcher, led to a serious governmental crisis.[10]

German unification poses the most profound challenge to the foreign policies of France and the Soviet Union. The anchoring of the Federal Republic in Western European integration formed the linchpin of French foreign policy in the post-war era. The French reacted to events in Germany by attempting to slow down the pace of unification; but in the end, the French bowed to the pressure of events. The tepid French support for German unification and the decision to produce, for deployment in 1992, the short-range Hades missiles, which can reach targets in Germany and Czechoslovakia, suggests that France has difficulty in coming to terms with the changing strategic landscape. On the other hand, the Kohl/Mitterrand resolution on political union, of April 1990,

Table 7.2 Timetable of German unification

9 November	1989	Breaching of the Berlin Wall
18 March	1990	First free elections to Volkskammer
18 May	1990	State treaty signed between the FRG and the GDR establishing a monetary, economic and social union
1 July	1990	Entry into force of Union Treaty
12 September	1990	Two-Plus-Four 'Treaty on the Final Settlement with respect to Germany'
3 October	1990	Incorporation of the former GDR into the FRG as three separate *Länder*
19 November	1990	Conference on Security and Co-operation in Europe (CSCE)–Paris Summit.
3 December	1990	First free all-German elections

is evidence of the continuing importance of the Paris–Bonn axis in the EC. The disappearance of the GDR was a major strategic loss for the Soviet Union because it was the central plank of the Soviet security regime in Eastern Europe. However, the Soviets also bowed to the inevitable and accepted the reality of German unification and the participation of a united Germany in NATO, with transitional arrangements for the 360,000 Red Army troops in the GDR. In return, Germany has pledged considerable economic aid to the beleaguered Soviet government.

German unification and Western European integration

German unification has profound political and economic implications for the Federal Republic and, as a consequence, for the EC as a whole. The impact of unification on the dynamics of integration and the balance of power in the Community of Twelve will work itself out in the first half of the 1990s. One immediate consequence of unification is that the territory of the GDR automatically becomes part of the Community. Put simply, there is a *de facto* enlargement of the Community, complicated by the fact that the economy of the GDR is not compatible with the economy of the other parts of the Community. From the outset, the Commission, under Jacques Delors, was supportive of unification, but sought to ensure that EC interests would be protected in the process. A Commission paper, 'The Community and German Unification', set out in broad outline the transitional problems that are likely to arise as Germany and the Community work towards the full application of the *acquis communautaire* and the adaptation of the external commitments of the GDR to its former COMECON partners.[11] The technical adjustments in laws and policies are, however, overshadowed by the potential impact of unification on the dynamics of integration.

The large population of the new Germany (80 million) and the longer-term prospect that unification will serve to strengthen its economic predominance upset the delicate balance between the Community's middle-range powers. France decided, once it had accepted the tempo of unification, that deeper integration in the Community of Twelve is the best counterweight to the new Germany. In other words, integration would once again serve to anchor and contain Germany. However, the demands of unification on the German polity may mean that Germany becomes less active on the international stage and a less reliable participant in European integration.[12] Unification may also mean that the new Germany will drift to the East in search of markets, and as a natural tendency for a country that finds itself again in the middle of Europe. The cost of unification for the Federal Republic will make it less willing to act as the paymaster of the EC budget, and this will exacerbate tensions concerning redistribution within the EC itself.

The centrality of the EC to Germany remains intact. Germany's interest in an economically vibrant European economy is not undermined by unification. West Germany's experience of federalism, with a diffusion of power throughout the political system, makes it less sensitive concerning sovereignty than its partners with strongly unitary political systems. Since the war European integration has enabled the Federal Republic to pursue its economic goals in an unthreatening fashion. Although there are inevitable fears of a resurgence of German nationalism, there is considerable persuasive power in the assertion that German leaders know that a united, fully autonomous Germany would be frightening for many Europeans; and therefore that Germany can actually exercise power more effectively – without engendering fear within and outside –, as a member of the Community than alone.[13]

As Germany emerges as the single most important voice in the Community, it will still have to rely on support from other states to get its preferred policies accepted.[14] Given Britain's tendency to eschew institutional change, the Franco-German relationship is likely to remain central to EC developments. German political leaders constantly reiterate their support for deeper integration among the Twelve. Chancellor Kohl argues that 'integration and co-operation are the important concepts for shaping tomorrow's Europe' and that 'the future belongs to federalism and the sharing of central and regional power, as a model for Europe of the Twelve and beyond'.[15] Bonn is committed to economic and monetary union and political union. Hesitations by the Bundesbank and the Finance Ministry with regard to EMU have been overridden by the Chancellor. Germany, however, will accept only an EMU that has monetary institutions and a currency as sound as the Deutschmark and with the commitment to price stability apparent in the Bundesbank.

France

Since the days of Robert Schuman and Jean Monnet, France has been one of the main architects of the Community of the Six, and now the Twelve. Integration offered a radical means of containing German economic power within a Western European political framework. The Common Agricultural Policy and association agreements for France's overseas territories formed part of a Franco-German compact that allowed France to accept free trade in industrial goods. General de Gaulle's accession to political power in France led to a change in French attitudes towards the 'Monnet' method of integration. Hostility towards all forms of 'supranationality' and to US dominance of the Atlantic Alliance resulted in the 1965 'Luxemburg' crisis in the EC and France's withdrawal from the integrated command of NATO. Thereafter, a commitment to the maintenance of national sovereignty and a 'Europe of nation-states' became central precepts of Gaullist foreign policy. Although de Gaulle's successor, Georges Pompidou, was a key participant at the Hague and Paris Summits, the legacy of de Gaulle continued to overshadow French policy towards the development of the Community. President Giscard d'Estaing placed considerable emphasis on Franco-German relations and on institution-building in the Community.

When François Mitterrand first came to power in 1981, he showed little sustained interest in European integration apart from calling for the creation of a 'European Social Space'. Concerned with internal French politics and wider North–South issues, European co-operation was not a major forum for France's Socialist President. By 1983, this was no longer the case, as the Community witnessed a profound change in France's approach to integration. The failure of the Socialists' expansionist economic programme gave rise to a reassessment of French economic policy, which in turn led to a French conversion to the idea of an Community-wide internal market and the abandonment of an industrial policy designed to create national champions (i.e. highly successful corporations). French political leaders came to the conclusion that the promotion of French national interests could be achieved only by Europe-wide policies and further integration. The attitudes of the various political parties to the Single European Act show that there is an unprecedented political consensus in favour of integration in France; only the communists, at one end of the political spectrum, and the right-wing National Front at the other oppose further integration.

In 1984, when the British budgetary crisis threatened to damage the Community edifice, President Mitterrand adopted a very interventionist style during the French presidency, holding no fewer than thirty bilateral meetings with his fellow EC leaders during the six-month period.[16] The Fontainebleau European Council brought the budgetary crisis to a painful close and opened the way for the reform of EC policies and institutions.

France is a firm advocate of economic and monetary union as it seeks to redress the asymmetrical nature of the EMS. Speedy monetary union in the early 1990s is given renewed urgency as a means of deepening German ties with Western European integration. Support for an intergovernmental conference on political union stems from a commitment to strengthen EC institutions before further enlargement and to equip the Community to deal with the demands of the new Europe. France is seeking to enhance the Community's capacity to form a cohesive force in international politics and favours the development of a Western European defence identity. France does not want to see the European Community supplanted as the fulcrum of integration efforts in the 1990s. Nor does it want to see Community membership expand to a level where cohesive and decisive action is no longer possible. President Mitterrand's call in his 1990 New Year's discourse for a Europe-wide confederation is an attempt to marry the twin needs of Western European integration and the re-integration into Europe of the Central and Eastern European states.[17]

Italy

Italy alternates between active participation in the development of the Community and a passive role on the sidelines. It has always been overshadowed by the political and economic influence of the French and Germans. Internal political instability and bureaucratic inertia have served to inhibit an active Italian role. Paradoxically, instability increases the salience of the EC for the domestic political system. The Community is viewed as a critical counterweight to governmental instability at national level. Thus, at least at the level of rhetoric, Italian protestations in favour of integration are 'maximalist' and strongly federalist in nature. Italy's pro-integrationist stance is somewhat tarnished by its record of non-implementation of Community law. The Commission issues more 'reasoned opinions' against Italy than against any other country, and the Court of Justice has found against it more frequently than against any other member state. The so-called Pergola Law, passed in April 1987 by the Italian Parliament, is an attempt to improve the level of implementation.

During the 1980s, successive Italian governments promoted reform in the Community, starting with the Genscher/Colombo plan, when the Italian Foreign Minister, Emilio Colombo, joined with his German counterpart to promote the Draft European Act. Signor Craxi's adept management of the Milan European Council in 1985 led to the convening of an intergovernmental conference, despite the reservations of the British, Danes and Greeks. During the conference, the Italian government was fervent in its commitment for greater powers for the European Parliament. It entered a reserve at the end of the conference on the grounds that it would not ratify a text that was not acceptable to the EP. In the end the Italians accepted the text.[18]

Italy's commitment to a federal Europe continues. The Italian presidency of the Council in 1990 saw the convening of two intergovernmental conferences on EMU and political union. The Italian Foreign Minister, Gianni de Michelis, called for a 'great leap forward beyond the horizons of national sovereignty'.[19] For the Italians, this includes a greatly strengthened European Parliament and the necessity of 'dealing with issues of defence, security and foreign policy no longer in a limbo but incorporating them with particular rules into the Community rationale'.[20] Although membership of the European Community and of NATO form the core of Italy's foreign policy, changes in Eastern and Central Europe have led it to forge ties with countries beyond the boundaries of the Community. In November 1989, Austria, Italy, Hungary and Yugoslavia launched the concept of Alpine-Adriatic co-operation. Czechoslovakia has since joined the group. At a summit meeting held in Venice (July 1990) a three-year co-operation plan was adopted.[21] Such regional co-operation is not a substitute for European integration, because for all of the non-member states, participation in the EC is the ultimate goal.

The Benelux

Belgium, The Netherlands and Luxemburg together form the Benelux economic union, a precurser to wider European integration. Their central geographical location and their position between the two large continental powers of France and Germany have moulded their attitudes to the post-war reconstruction of Europe. In the Community of 'Six', the Benelux states favoured a supranational approach to decision-making and endorsed the enlargement of the Community. While they welcomed Franco-German reconciliation they feared and continue to oppose the development of a 'directorate' or an inner group of the larger member states.

Because Brussels is the capital of the Community, with the Commission and the Council secretariat, Belgian officials appear more self-consciously European than their Dutch counterparts. Leo Tindemans, a former Belgian Prime Minister, says, 'The best Belgian policy is European'[22] and a Belgian scholar argues that 'Europe became part of the conventional wisdom . . . one that is not even discussed'.[23] The Schengen Accord is evidence of the commitment of the Benelux countries to deepen integration and, if necessary, to adopt a 'variable geometry' approach. Support for integration has never prevented Belgium and its Benelux partners from protecting their interests. The Dutch stymied progress on a common transport policy for many years, and Luxemburg continues to argue for the maintenance of the EP secretariat in Luxemburg.

Fears that events in Eastern and Central Europe would weaken the drive towards greater Western European integration led the Belgian government to submit a memorandum to its partners on institutional reform in March 1990 before the Kohl-Mitterrand letter on political union. The main emphasis in the Belgian paper is on the effectiveness of EC institutions, the democratic deficit, subsidiarity and external coherence. The paper proposes a significant extension in the use of majority voting, increased legislative powers for the European Parliament, the granting of a right of initiative to the EP, codification of the principle of subsidiarity, a strengthening of EPC procedures and an extension of its scope to include security problems.[24] The Belgian memorandum falls well short of proposing a federal constitution for the EC. Its support for the EP and a common foreign policy places Belgium at the 'maximalist' end of the continuum concerning the future development of the EC. Its commitment to the Delors approach towards monetary union and support for a single currency reinforce its pro-integrationist profile.

A Dutch White Paper entitled *Europe: the Way Forward*, published in June 1990, provides a synopsis of the Dutch government's approach to integration. There is a strong commitment to the development of the EC along federalist lines because, according to the Dutch paper, 'the interests of small countries are best served by international co-operation based on legal structures and open-decision making structures' and that 'an intergovernmental structure can never be as effective in guaranteeing and safeguarding the legal order of the Community'.[25] Dutch fears about the dominance of the larger member states in the Community is deep-rooted. The location of the European Bank for Reconstruction and Development in London and the decision to make a Frenchman, Jacques Attali, its president, are seen by the Dutch as evidence of how the interests of the smaller countries are disregarded by the larger partners.[26]

Although committed to a federal Europe, the Dutch paper emphasizes that integration is a gradual, albeit dynamic, process. A federal Europe will not be constructed in one over-arching blueprint but in stages. The paper argues strongly for a deepening of integration so that the EC can serve as a pole of stability in a continent experiencing great change. Considerable attention is paid to developments in EPC and to the need to strengthen the democratic legitimacy of the Community. There is considerable agreement between the Belgian and Dutch approaches to the future of integration. Their 'maximalist' approach is deeply rooted in their export-led economies and their central geographical position. The loss of sovereignty is not a controversial issue. The pooling of sovereignty in EC institutions is preferable to domination by larger and more powerful neighbours.

Britain

Britain has always been an uneasy, reluctant, even awkward member of the European Community. The reasons for this are deeply rooted in the country's history, geographical location, and administrative and political culture. A preference for a free trade area, rather than a common market, and for intergovernmental rather than supranational decision-making structures led Britain's political class to remain aloof from the EC at the outset. A rapid change in policy once integration was under way did not bear fruit because de Gaulle used his power to veto British membership. Thus the Community's institutional style and the balance of policies were moulded by forces outside British influence. Add to this the psychological environment of British policy-makers, conditioned by the 'special relationship' with the United States, and a world role associated with empire. A pragmatic political culture suspicious of the 'grand designs' and rhetoric favoured by the Continentals, notably the French, help explain the difficulties Britain experienced in adapting to the Community method of integration. A strong unitary state characterized by a centralization of power in Westminster and Whitehall and long experience of single-party government make British politicians very protective of the trappings of national sovereignty and somewhat uneasy participants in coalition-building, a key element in the Community's decision-making style.

Britain's accession to the Community provided an opportunity for the growth of a triangular relationship between the three most important centres of power in the Community: Paris, Bonn and London. Yet after seventeen years of membership, relations with France and the Federal Republic are not comparable to the web of ties that bind the Franco-German axis.[26] A preoccupation with Britain's contribution to the EC budget and a concomitant desire to alter the existing balance of policies led British policy-makers to focus on individual issues. Within two years of accession, a Labour government renegotiated the terms of accession and held a referendum on the issue of continuing membership. While the result of the referendum confirmed Britain's membership of the Community, 'support for membership was wide but did not run deep'.[27] This was true both of the electorate and of the Labour cabinet.

The decision in 1979 not to participate in the exchange rate mechanism of the EMS reinforced the image of Britain as a reluctant partner. It was, however, the budgetary issue that dominated Britain's relations with its partners up to 1984. When Margaret Thatcher became Prime Minister, she made resolution of the budgetary issue a key element of her first term of office. Although the budget conflict paralyzed the Community and led to great acrimony in the European Council, it forced the other member states to face up to the somewhat perverse distributional consequences of the EC budget and the predominance of agricultural expenditure. A series of *ad hoc* repayments to Britain were replaced in 1984 by the Fontainebleau agreement on structural changes to the budget.

The settlement of the budgetary dispute opened the way for reform in the Community. Although Prime Minister Thatcher opposed the Milan decision to convene an intergovernmental conference, Britain participated in the conference with the objective of limiting the extent of institutional reform. Britain was persuaded to overcome its reservations because of its support for the completion of the internal market, its recognition that a greater use of majority voting was necessary to achieve this, and its fears of exclusion from the process if its partners decided to persist with reform.[28]

Although Britain was content with the outcome of the Single European Act, the dynamics of integration forced new issues onto the agenda. Britain is agreeable towards the Community's completion agenda, but the Social Charter, EMU and political union raise issues of principle, and Britain finds itself again at odds with many of its partners on these issues. An address by Margaret Thatcher at the College of Europe in Bruges in September 1988 is set to become a landmark speech in the annals of European integration. Provoked by Jacques Delors' claim that 'in ten years, 80 per cent of economic legislation – and perhaps tax and social legislation – will be directed from the Community',[29] the Prime Minister launched a stinging attack on the Commission, criticizing the tendency to create an 'identikit European personality' and 'centralised decisions in Brussels'.[30] Britain's tendency to see European issues from a narrow technical perspective was evident in her desire to see the Community tackle problems in a 'practical' way. There were echoes of de Gaulle in her call for co-operation between 'independent sovereign states'.[31] The Bruges Group, committed to defend British sovereignty, was established after the College of Europe speech.

Deep divisions on Europe in the Conservative Party and cabinet manifested themselves during the Thatcher reign. Five senior Conservative Ministers –, Michael Heseltine and Leon Brittain (1986), Nigel Lawson (1989), Nicholas Ridley and Geoffrey Howe (1990) – resigned from the cabinet on a European matter. Apart from Leon Brittain and Nicholas Ridley, the others resigned in opposition to Margaret Thatcher's policies on Europe. It was the Prime Minister's isolation at the Rome Summit in November 1990 that heralded the end of her long premiership. Sir Geoffrey Howe resigned from the cabinet following the Summit. His resignation speech in the House of Commons is widely considered to have provoked Michael Heseltine's bid for the leadership, which ultimately led to Margaret Thatcher's resignation and her replacement by John Major, the former Chancellor of the Exchequer.[32]

EMU has been a difficult issue for Britain from the outset. In 1988 Nigel Lawson emphasized that Britain could not accept the 'transfers of sovereignty which is implied in the Delors report' and that the boundaries of economic and monetary union outlined in the report 'would require political union, something which is not on Britain's European agenda'.[33] Nonetheless, Britain later accepted the convening of an intergovernmental conference on EMU and on political union because of an underlying desire to avoid isolation in the Community. On monetary union, Britain has produced an alternative to stages 2 and 3 of the Delors Report (see p.114), the hard ECU plan.[34] How Britain will react if the other member states are prepared to go ahead with rapid moves towards EMU remains to be seen. The approach to the intergovernmental conference on Political Union is likely to reflect policies on institutional change adopted during the negotiations on the SEA. There will be an emphasis on the effectiveness of EC institutions, with little sympathy for enlarged powers for the EP. A strengthening of EPC would be acceptable to Britain provided that the EC does not attempt to interfere directly with NATO's policy domain. A reactive approach to institutional, constitutional and policy development in the Community is the hallmark of British policy.

Ireland

For Ireland, as a small, peripheral Western European state, EC membership offered the prospect of economic modernization and a loosening of its economic ties with Britain. Given the predominance of Britain as a market for Irish goods in the 1960s, it could be argued that Irish policy-makers had little choice once Britain decided to opt for membership. Yet the decision to apply for membership was not merely a passive reaction to a change in British policy but a decision that held out the beguiling prospect of placing Anglo-Irish relations in a wider multilateral setting. Economic considerations, especially anticipated transfers from the Common Agricultural Policy, played a large part in the calculations of the economic benefits of membership. Access to the large Continental market was also seen as a necessary component of an economic strategy that depended on an inflow of external capital to fuel industrialization. Ireland's status as a lesser-developed area within the Community reinforces the importance of economic considerations in attitudes to the EC.

Ireland's non-involvement in World War II, coupled with its geographical location, means that although lip-service is paid to the notion of European union, there is little intuitive understanding of the original motivations that led the countries of continental Europe to opt for integration. The decision in 1949 to remain outside NATO and the importance of military neutrality as a symbol of Irish sovereignty in the political arena and among the wider electorate, make the political development of the Community somewhat problematical for Ireland. That said, as a small state with a limited ability to influence its external environment, Ireland has a keen sense that the pooling of sovereignty is preferable to the maintenance of formal sovereignty without the power to exercise it.

In 1990, the Irish Minister for European Affairs, Maire Geoghegan-Quinn, summed up Ireland's approach to current developments in the Community as being 'conditionally integrationist'.[35] This is an apt summation of Ireland's approach since accession. Irish policy-makers have always emphasized the link between political and economic integration. Political integration must be built on a sound economic basis; the benefits of integration must be evenly spread through all the regions of the Community. Ireland is one of those countries arguing for redistribution and a sizeable EC budget as part of the EMU debate. With regard to political union, Irish policy-makers regard the process as more akin to an SEA 'Mark II' than a quantum leap forward. EPC is likely to prove the most contentious issue for Irish negotiators because of neutrality. Recent events in Eastern Europe and the Gulf crisis make it more difficult to distinguish between the political and economic aspects of security, on the one hand, and the defence aspects, on the other. There are increasing pressures on Ireland to allow security and defence issues to be raised in EPC while operational aspects would continue to be the prerogative of NATO and the WEU. Although successive Irish governments have accepted the logic of European Union and have pledged their involvement in a European defence structure, neutrality has become a sacred cow of Irish life, and it may be very difficult for Irish politicians to sell domestically the political stances they may be forced to take abroad. This is an issue on which future Irish governments may not be able to eat their cake and have it.

Denmark

Although Denmark has benefited greatly in economic terms from EC membership, because of CAP transfers and access to the markets of its larger neighbours, the Danish political class and population have had difficulty in adapting to the Community method of integration for a variety of reasons. First, Denmark, like its Scandinavian neighbours, was a reluctant participant in post-war integration, favouring intergovernmental co-operation rather than supranational integration. Second, Nordic co-operation offered an alternative and sometimes competing arena for co-operation. Third, the decision to opt for EC membership was tied up with trade dependency on the British market. Fourth, as one of Europe's oldest states, it had a strong attachment to national sovereignty and independence. A referendum held in 1972 on the issue of membership resulted in a majority of 62 per cent in favour, but the sizeable 'no' vote and the emergence of a split on the issue in the largest party, the Social Democrats, made EC membership a highly contentious issue in the Danish political system. The emergence of a popular movement against the European Community in the 1979 European Parliament elections and their success in gaining four seats confirmed an underlying scepticism in Denmark on the issue of Community membership.

During the 1970s and 1980s, Denmark pursued a 'minimalist' path of opposing all moves towards further political integration. Domestic parliamentary control, in the form of the Market Relations Committee, is the most stringent found in any member state. Danish interests in the EC are seen in an almost exclusively economic context. Political change in the EC is accepted only if it is necessary to promote economic co-operation. Thus Denmark opposed direct elections to the EP and included a declaratory statement in domestic legislation to the effect that direct elections would not increase the powers of the Parliament.[36] Denmark was a reluctant member of the Dooge Committee and opposed the 1985 IGC at the Milan European Council.

The SEA led to a referendum in Denmark, because the Social Democrats felt that its contents represented an unacceptable transfer of sovereignty. The Conservative Prime Minister, Poul Schluter, fearing a defeat in the Parliament, opted for a consultative referendum on the SEA package. Denmark's continuing membership of the Community was the central issue in the campaign. The government argued that the SEA amounted to no more than a modest adjustment of the institutional structure. The result of the referendum, with a 56.2 per cent 'yes' vote, confirmed Danish membership of the Community. It was something of a watershed in Danish EC politics because, in the words of the political scientist T. Worre, 'Everyone now expects that Denmark is in the Community to stay.'[37] The EC opposition has settled down to playing a more active role in the EC decision-making process in order to thwart integrationist tendencies there.

Although the 1986 majority in favour of the SEA did not represent a new attitude towards integration or a mandate for European union, there have been changes in Danish policy. The Delors Report on EMU found favour in Denmark, and Danish policy-makers find themselves to the fore as proponents of speedy monetary union. Support for monetary integration fits easily within the maxims of Danish EC policy, because a multilateral system of central banks would allow them to regain a measure of control over monetary policy lost to the Bundesbank in the EMS. German unification has also led to a significant increase in support for the European Community in Denmark, with a 7 per cent rise in support for integration in the first half of 1990.[38] The need to contain German unification under a European roof may win over the Danes to a more positive attitude towards the Community.

Greece

Echoes of Denmark's scepticism about the European Community can be found in Greece, the country with the lowest per capita income in the Community. Greek entry into the Community in 1981 was the culmination of a relationship that began with the Association Agreement of 1962, the first such agreement signed by the EC. The military dictatorship (1967–74) stalled the operation of the agreement. With the resumption of democratic government in 1975, the government of Constantine Karamanlis applied for full membership. Although the Community wanted to treat the Greek application in tandem with the Iberian countries, the Council of Ministers was prevailed upon to accept speedy Greek accession in order to protect democratic institutions.

The Socialist government of Prime Minister Papandreou, which came to power in 1981, set out to renegotiate the terms of Greek membership and to get special concessions ahead of the Iberian enlargement. A Greek memorandum of 1982 demanded special treatment for Greece in a range of policy areas. The Commission responded instead by devising the Integrated Mediterranean Programmes (IMPs), designed to promote economic development in the Mediterranean basin. Financial support, in the form of a *1,500 M ECU* loan to avert a balance of payments crisis in 1985, did much to alter the anti-EC stance of the Socialist Party.

Greek opposition to the SEA was overcome with the inclusion

of a section on social and economic cohesion and the subsequent Delors plan of doubling the resources of the structural funds for the peripheral regions by 1992. Notwithstanding significant financial transfers from the Community, the income gap between the EC and Greece widened during the 1980s. GDP per capita declined from 58 per cent of the Community average to 54 per cent in 1989. High inflation, and budget and trade deficits in recent years leave Greece ill-equipped to meet the challenge of EMU without a period of economic stabilization.[39]

Greek officialdom has not yet entirely accepted the rigours of EC law, and its record on implementation is one of the weakest. Adjustment to participation in EPC was far from smooth. The Papandreou government tended to go its own way in EPC on many issues, notably on the Palestinian question. On East–West issues, it generally followed an anti-American line. Its long-standing dispute with Turkey concerning Cyprus tends to overshadow most other foreign policy issues. The Greeks oppose Turkish membership of the Community and work hard to ensure that the question of Cyprus is raised in EPC. A statement on Cyprus in the conclusions of the Dublin Summit (April 1990) that favoured the Greek position on the issue is regarded as a major foreign policy gain by the Greeks. It will prove more difficult to achieve EC-wide support for the Greek Cypriot request for EC membership submitted in July 1990. Greek hesitancy about the development of a European defence identity may be a thing of the past, as there is some suggestion that Greece may join the WEU.

The Iberian countries

The transformation of Portugal and Spain into functioning democracies opened the way for full membership of the European Community. Both countries submitted their applications in 1977, the beginning of a long and somewhat tortuous process of negotiations. The entry negotiations were far from smooth for a variety of reasons. First, their level of economic development was well below the Community average, thus exacerbating problems of economic divergence within the Community. Second, as Mediterranean countries, they produce many goods in direct competition with Italian, French and Greek production. The Papandreou government threatened to veto the Iberian enlargement in 1984 unless Greece was compensated through increased funding from the IMPs. Third, the large Spanish fishing fleet was a threat to existing EC fishing arrangements. Fourth, there were fears that the free movement of workers would lead to a large migratory flow from the Mediterranean to the northern member states. Consequently, the accession treaties included a seven-year transition arrangement for the free movement provisions. Although negotiations were opened with Portugal in October 1978 and with Spain in February 1979, the accession treaties were not signed until June 1985.

Public opinion and the political élites of both countries are favourably disposed towards membership of the Community. Participation in the core West European organization heralds the re-integration of both countries into the Continent's political and economic structures. The Community is perceived as an 'external guarantor' of democracy and a harbinger of modernization. Anticipated economic benefits also contributed to a favourable attitude towards integration.

For Portugal, as one of the poorest and most peripheral members of the Community, EC membership offers considerable economic and political challenges. It spent the first five years of membership adapting to EC structures and will assume the presidency in January 1992, having passed over a previous opportunity because its officials did not feel sufficiently *au fait* with the Community to shoulder the burden of the chair. Membership of the EC had a dynamic impact on the economy in the first years of membership, as Portugal experienced growth rates above the EC average. Foreign investment flowed into Portugal, attracted by its low-wage economy; from a level of Esc. 25Bn. in 1986, foreign investment rose to Esc. 360Bn. in 1989.[40] Consequently the Portuguese do not favour binding social legislation which would increase the costs to industry. There are also doubts about the ability of some sectors of industry to withstand the rigours of increased competition in the post-1992 Europe. Underemployment is a major characteristic of Portuguese agriculture. Productivity is about one-quarter of the Community average but employs 20 per cent of the country's work-force.

Extensive financial transfers from the Community's structural funds, representing 11 per cent of total domestic investment in 1989, are enabling a rapid improvement in the country's infrastructure.[41] There are fears in Portugal that the financial demands of German unification and the needs of Eastern Europe will lead to a reduction in the monies available for the EC periphery. The escudo is not a member of the EMS exchange rate mechanism, and Portugal would not endorse an EMU system that lacked provisions for inter-regional transfers. There are considerable fears in Portugal about the emergence of a two-tier Europe, because in such a Europe Portugal would undoubtedly find itself in the lower tier.

Spain also experienced growth rates above the EC average since accession and sizeable inflows of foreign capital. Unlike those of Portugal and Greece, its industrial structure is not entirely dependent on traditional industries. Its capital-intensive sectors are well placed to take advantage of the market. Like that of Ireland, Spain's per capita GDP is just below 70 per cent of the EC average. Receipts from the structural funds are being used to upgrade infrastructure and to promote industrial development. The Spanish government's decision to take the peseta into the ERM in July 1989 at the end of the Spanish presidency was evidence of a commitment to active and full participation in the EC. Although supportive of EMU as a policy goal, Spain does not favour a rapid timetable. The transfer or sharing of sovereignty is not a controversial issue in Spain. The country's long-serving Prime Minister, Felipe González, is willing to share sovereignty, arguing that 'we cede sovereignty to have a share in decisions'.[42]

THE BOUNDARIES OF THE COMMUNITY

The debate about the next and subsequent enlargements of the EC is clearly under way. The renewed dynamism of the Community, evident in the latter half of the 1980s, has acted as a magnet for non-member countries. The issue of enlargement is often posited in terms of a deepening versus a widening of the EC. In fact the Community will have to do both during the 1990s. The process of deepening is taking place in the intergovernmental conferences, whereas the widening will take place over the next decades. The prospect of a greatly increased membership gives rise to major economic, political and institutional issues, both for the Community and for the potential entrants.

Discussion of future members is best considered in four clusters. First, there is Turkey, which has had an association agreement with the EC since 1963. Turkey's application for full membership was put on hold by the Community in December 1989, when it was decided to delay a decision until the mid-1990s. Turkey's membership raises many issues, most notably the boundaries of Europe, economic divergence and migration of labour. Turkey is a Muslim country which straddles Europe and Asia. Very little of its territory is located geographically in Europe, but from the establishment of the modern Turkish state under Kemal Atatürk, Turkey has seen itself as a Western state. It is a member of NATO and the Council of Europe. A population of 53 million, which is set to increase to 76 million by the year 2000, is regarded in Western Europe as a major stumbling-block. Germany already has a large migrant population of Turkish origin and is fearful of the consequences of free movement of labour. Turkey's level of economic development would also place a major strain on the EC budget, as it would have to be a significant beneficiary of redistributive policies. A period of direct military rule between 1980 and 1983, in addition to continuing human rights abuses, raises questions about Turkey's suitability for full membership. Conflict with Greece about Cyprus further complicates the EC-Turkish relationship. The Turkish application is not likely to lead to a positive response from the Community in the near future, but the EC will not be able to fudge the issue forever.

Second, there are the EFTA states. Austria, with a population of 8 million, formally applied for membership in 1989, and Sweden lodged its application in July 1991. The debate on membership is clearly on the agenda in Norway, Finland and Switzerland, but not in Iceland, which is more likely to seek some form of association. The addition of these industrialized states, already well integrated into the Western European economy, poses few problems of economic adjustment, although there would inevitably be problems with some parts of the *acquis communautaire*. In fact these states might well alleviate the strain on the Community budget. The problems lie more in the political realm. These states, for a variety of reasons, have always spurned the Continental model of integration. They are used to a high degree of autonomy in decision-making and will find it difficult to adjust to the Community way of doing things, including majority voting. Their political cultures – and in Switzerland's case its constitution, – will come under strain. There is also the issue of Austrian, Swedish and Swiss neutrality. Both Austria and Sweden have declared that full membership should not impinge on their traditional foreign policies. Yet the Community is attempting to establish the groundwork for a common foreign and security policy in the Political Union Intergovernmental Conference. How to reconcile the pressures towards 'speaking with one voice' with three, if not four, neutrals is a fundamental political issue that must be addressed in the 1990s. The Irish model is not appropriate because Ireland's political classes have accepted the logic of political union and stated on many occasions Ireland's willingness to participate in a full political union including defence, should that evolve. The fact that Irish public opinion would be adverse to such a development is another matter. The Austrian application is somewhat of a test case, because accession negotiations should begin sometime in 1993, when the outcome of the Intergovernmental Conferences is known.

Third, there are the so-called 'orphans' (Cyprus with 0.7 million inhabitants and Malta with 0.3 million). Both have applied formally for membership. The Cypriot application is complicated by the continuing division of the island. There is also the issue of according two such small states full representation in the Community's institutional framework. An arrangement based on partnership is more likely in these cases.

Fourth, there are the states of Eastern/Central Europe: Hungary with 11 million people, Czechoslovakia with 16 million and Poland with 38 million people. For these countries involvement with the EC means 'rejoining Europe'; it symbolizes the end of their isolation from the West. The time-scale for membership is impossible to determine because it will depend very much on the process of political and economic reform. It is simply too early to tell if these states will be able to overcome the legacy of forty-five years of communist rule. Their relationship with the Community will be evolutionary, beginning with the negotiation of 'European' Agreements in 1991/92. The Commissioner responsible for external relations, Frans Andriessen, suggested in May 1991 that some form of affiliate membership might be feasible for a transition to full membership for the countries of Eastern/Central Europe.

The question of enlargement is an issue for the 1990s and the first decade of the next century. There will be a slow but steady increase in membership, provided that the very real economic and political difficulties can be overcome. Of all the potential entrants, only Norway could be absorbed quickly and easily into the Community. The remaining EFTA states, because of neutrality, pose a fundamental dilemma about the long-term evolution of the Community. Turkey, the 'orphans' and the countries of Eastern/Central Europe present serious economic problems. There is also an underlying issue concerning the decision-making capacity of a Community of some fifteen or twenty states. Additional members bring increasing complexity, more commissioners, parliamentarians, a larger Council and more working languages. Without reform, the Community's institutional structures would have difficulty in coping with the pressure of increased numbers around the table. The debate about the competences of and relationships between the institutions is likely to continue during the next decade.

CONCLUSIONS

An understanding of the interests and policy preferences of the member states is essential to a balanced analysis of the EC. National governments and administrations have adapted to an additional level of policy-making, and another level of government. Some governments adopt a more pro-active approach to the development of the Community. Since its foundation, the Franco-German axis has been central to the politics of the EC. The extent to which this relationship is altered by German unification is a matter for the 1990s. While Germany is likely to emerge as the single most important voice in the Community, the habit of working with France will no doubt persist. Policy-making in the EC depends on a convergence of interest among the member states. Franco-German agreement on a major issue usually gets the support of the Benelux states and Italy. The 'inner Six' continue to form the core of the Community. The UK is the 'odd one out' among the larger member states. It is least comfortable with the Continental tendency to establish broad political and economic goals without working out the practical details at the same time. The smaller, lesser-developed states attempt to ensure that the balance of policies in the Community is not entirely focused on the core economies. Enlargement of the Community will bring the domestic politics of an increasing number of countries into the day-to-day business of the Community. How the Community manages new entrants will determine

in large measure how effective a body it will be in the next
century.

NOTES

1 For a seminal study on Franco-German relations, see M. Simonian, *The
   Privileged Partnership: Franco-German Relations in the EC 1969–1984* (Oxford:
   Clarendon Press, 1985).
2 R. Morgan and C. Bray, *Partners and Rivals in Western Europe: Britain,
   France and Germany* (Aldershot: Gower, 1986).
3 M. Butler, *Europe: More than a Continent* (London: Heinemann, 1986),
   p.132.
4 D. Marquand, 'Maximalist or minimalist? Britain's European options'
   in W. Wallace (ed.), *Britain in Europe* (London: Heinemann, 1980),
   pp.25–6.
5 S. Bulmer and W. Paterson, *The Federal Republic of Germany and the
   European Community* (London: Allen & Unwin, 1987), p.6.
6 G. Hendricks, 'Germany and the CAP: national interests and the European Community', *International Affairs*, 1988/89, vol.65, pp.75–87.
7 R. Leick, 'Germany – the European egoist', *European Affairs*, Spring
   1987, pp.55–61.
8 W. Wessels and E. Regelsberger (eds), *The Federal Republic of Germany and
   the European Community: the Presidency and Beyond* (Bonn: Europa Union
   Verlag, 1988).
9 Quoted in *The Irish Times*, 24 April 1990, p.5.
10 *The Independent on Sunday*, 15 July 1990.
11 EC Commission Document, *The Community and German Unification*, Sec.
   (90) 751 final, 20 April 1990.
12 P. Hassner, 'Europe beyond partition and unity: disintegration and
   reconstruction', *International Affairs*, 1990, vol.66, p.463.
13 R.O Keohane and S. Hoffman, 'Institutional change in Europe in
   1980s', in R.O Keohane and S. Hoffman (eds), *Decision-Making and
   Institutional Change in the European Community* (Place Westview Press,
   Boulder: Colorado, 1991), p.26.
14 This point was made by Professor W. Paterson at a UACES Conference
   on the Irish presidency, King's College, London, 24 October 1990.
15 Interview with Chancellor Kohl in *The Financial Times*, Special Supplement on Germany, 29 October 1990.
16 D. Levy, 'Foreign policy: business as usual?' in S. Mazey and M.
   Newman (eds), *Mitterrand's France* (Beckenham Kent: Croom Helm,
   1987), p.179.
17 O. Weaver, 'Three competing Europes: German, French, Russian',
   International Affairs, 1990, vol.66, p.484.
18 R. Pryce (ed.), *European Union* (Beckenham, Kent: Croom Helm,
   1987), p.266.
19 Quoted in *The Irish Times*, 11 September 1990, p.9.
20 Ibid.
21 Christoph von Marschall, *Suddeutsche Zeitung*, 3 August 1990.

22 Quoted in *La Belgique et la Dévelopement de la Communauté Européenne*, 1982, p.13.
23 M. vanden Abeele, 'La Présidence du conseil des ministres des communautés européennes: rapport national sur la Belgique, in C.O. Nuallain (ed.), *The Presidency of the European Council of Ministers* (Beckenham, Kent: Croom Helm, 1985), p.23.
24 Belgium, Memorandum on Institutional Relaunch, *Agence Europe*, no.1605, 29 March 1990.
25 Netherlands, *Europe: The Way Forward Accelerating, Strengthening, interweaving*, Dutch Ministry for Foreign Affairs, June 1990, p.3.
26 *Financial Times*, 5 September 1990.
27 E. Butler and V. Kitzinger, *The 1975 Referendum* (London, 1976), p.280.
28 S. George, *An Awkward Partner: Britain in the European Community* (Oxford: Oxford University Press, 1990).
29 EP, President J. Delors' address to the European Parliament, *Official Journal* Annex Debates of the EP, 1988–9, no.2–367/140.
30 Address by Prime Minister Margaret Thatcher, College of Europe, Bruges, 20 September 1988.
31 Ibid.
32 *Financial Times*, 14 November 1990, p.1.
33 *Agence Europe*, no.4998, 19 April 1989.
34 S. Collignon, 'The EMU debate: a common or a single currency?', EUI, *European Trends*, 1990, no.3, pp.61–5.
35 Address by the Minister of State for European Affairs, Maire Geoghegan-Quinn, Patrick Magill Summer School, 12 August 1990.
36 J. Fitzmaurice, 'National parliaments and the European Parliaments: the Danish Folketing' paper presented to a workshop, EUI, Florence, October 1989.
37 T. Worre, 'Denmark at the crossroads: The Danish Referendum of 28 February 1986 on the EC Reform Package', *Journal of Common Market Studies*, 1988, vol.27, p.385.
38 *Financial Times*, 14 August 1990.
39 EC Commission, *One Market, One Money*, European Economy, no.44, October 1990, p.220.
40 *Financial Times*, 22 August 1990.
41 Ibid.
42 Interview with Felipe González, *Financial Times*, 17 December 1990, p.36.

TOPICS FOR DISCUSSION

1 Why is the UK reluctant to accept a deepening of integration?
2 How important is the Franco-German relationship to the politics of the EC?
3 On a continuum of 'minimalist' to 'maximalist', where would you position the various member states?

4 How can small states exert their influence in the EC?

FURTHER READING

Bliss C., and Braga de Macedo J., *Unity with diversity within the European Economy: the Community's Southern Frontier*, Cambridge: Cambridge University Press, 1990.

Bulmer S., and Paterson W., *The Federal Republic of Germany and the European Community*, London: Allen & Unwin, 1987. This book provides an excellent overview of the FRG and the EC prior to unification.

Coombes D. (ed.), *Ireland and the European Communities*, Dublin: Gill and Macmillan, 1983. Ireland's first ten years of membership.

George S., *An Awkward Partner: Britain in the European Community*, Oxford: Oxford University Press, 1990. An analysis of Britain's approach, government by government, since accession.

Morgan R., and Bray C., *Partners and Rivals in Western Europe: Britain, France and Germany*, Aldershot: Gower, 1986.

Nicoll W., and T.C. Salmon, *Understanding the European Communities*, London: Philip Allan, 1990. Chapter 5.

Simonian H., *The Privileged Partnership: Franco-German Relations in the European Community 1969–1984* Oxford: Oxford University Press, 1985.

Twitchett C. and K., *Building Europe*, London: Europa Publications, 1981.

Articles

Bulmer S., and Paterson W., 'West Germany's role in Europe: 'man mountain' or 'semi-Gulliver'?', *Journal of Common Market Studies*, 1989, vol.28, pp.95–117.

Hendriks G., 'Germany and the CAP: national interests and the European Community', *International Affairs*, 1988/89, vol.65, pp.75–87.

Worre, T, 'Denmark at the crossroads: the Danish referendum of 28 February 1986 on the EC reform package', *Journal of Common Market Studies*, 1988, vol.26, pp.361–400.

Chapter 8

Europe – a period of transition

The states of Europe are faced with the formidable challenge of re-establishing a regional system to manage inter-state relations for the continent as a whole. Superpower hegemony is at an end. The new system is taking shape in an environment of considerable turbulence because of the collapse of communism in Eastern/Central Europe. The future shape of the Soviet Union is far from clear, as the decline from empire continues and as the Union itself disintegrates. Although the 'Iron Curtain' is no more, the legacy of forty-five years of communist rule and Soviet domination engenders a marked contrast between Western Europe and Eastern Europe, a contrast that has its roots in pre-World War II Europe. Western Europe is characterized by integration, high levels of material well-being and political stability, whereas the states of the former Eastern bloc are characterized by political turbulence, the destruction of civil society by communism, economic stagnation, an outmoded industrial structure, pollution and a revival of ethnic and nationalist tensions. The concept of a 'common European home' from the Atlantic to the Urals may prove to be illusory. Institutional arrangements to manage inter-state relations in the new Europe are likely to emerge in a piecemeal fashion, much like the aftermath of World War II.

The new European architecture is being built on three pillars or forms of integration and co-operation, namely economics, politics, and security. The complex agendas of inter-state relations are being addressed in a number of different forums: the EC, EFTA, Norden, the Council of Europe, NATO and the CSCE.

ANALYSING INTEGRATION AND CO-OPERATION

A central point of this book is that the European Community has emerged as the core regional organization in Europe. The form of integration launched by Schuman in 1950, characterized by a transfer of powers from the member states to the Community level, has proved more robust than the more limited forms of intergovernmental co-operation found in other Western European organizations. The voluntary pooling of sovereignty is the distinguishing feature of the European Community. Since its inception the Community has seen an expansion of its policy scope and membership, albeit in a halting and tardy manner. Other Western European organizations – notably the Council of Europe, EFTA and Norden – have found themselves reacting to or adapting to the development of the Community. It is the only post-war organization that has established a political system beyond the level of the participating states. Yet it is one that rests on the national political and constitutional systems.

Analysing the changes in the European Community during the 1980s and in the wider Continent poses a major challenge to students of politics, economics and society. No one theory or approach to the study of integration and co-operation could capture the complexities of formal and informal integration in Western Europe. It is therefore argued in this book that a multi-levelled approach is necessary. Chapters 3 and 6 highlighted the significance of the Community's external environment for its development. Changes in the international political economy posed and continue to pose major competitive pressures for European industry. The collapse of communism in Eastern/Central Europe and continuing turbulence in the former USSR have altered the context in which the EC will develop in the 1990s.

External challenges create incentives for greater cohesion and deeper integration but do not ensure that this will occur. There must be a convergence of views among a sizeable number of member states about how to respond to external challenges or common policies will not emerge. In other words, domestic politics in the member states must create the conditions out of which a response can be fashioned. Chapter 7, on the domestic dimension of integration, stressed the continuing importance of national governments and domestic politics in the dynamics of integration. Yet for all governments, membership of the European Community is central to their strategies for managing their national economies in an increasingly interdependent world. By the end of the 1980s the EC was once again viewed as an important arena for problem-solving by all member states. We should not underestimate the extent to which the member states have accepted an additional layer of government and politics. So-called 'European' policies are part and parcel of the routine of public policy-making. The member states have been willing to sacrifice formal sovereignty in order to increase their influence. Britain, and to a lesser extent Denmark, are increasingly the only states that regard the protection of formal sovereignty as a core political value.

Successful treaty change in the 1980s has led to renewed emphasis on traditional approaches to the study of the EC, notably neo-functionalism and federalism. Concepts such as supranationalism and spillover are again of value in explaining the post-SEA era in the EC. The return to majority voting in the Council and the apparent assertiveness of the Commission have strengthened the supranational character of the Community's law-making system. The capacity of individual national governments to prevent agreement is greatly reduced. The sheer volume of legislation flowing through the Community's policy process does not allow individual states to weigh up the merits and problems of each proposal over a long period. The process of bargaining and coalition-building is a more complex business than heretofore.

There is ample evidence of sectoral spillover in the 1980s. Concern with the free movement of professionals led to policies on student mobility in the form of ERASMUS. COMETT is the result of the technological challenge to Europe from Japan and the United States. The freeing of capital movements as part of the internal market programme increases the pressure for an economic and monetary union. Community policies in the social domain and on the environment stem not only from the desire to create a 'people's Europe' but also from the need to ensure that lower standards are not a source of competitive advantage in the free market. Linkage between sectors is not just a matter of automatic spillover. The history of the Community offers ample evidence of deliberately constructed bargains between states. The SEA itself consists of many bargains across sectors and on institutional issues. Thus intergovernmental bargaining remains central to the dynamics of integration. Each round of constitutive bargaining can be successful only if the ingredients of a successful package can be fashioned.

Although the EC lacks the attributes of full statehood, its political and judicial systems have some federalist characteristics. It is a multi-levelled system of policy-making characterized by joint decisions or 'co-operative federalism'. Continuing debates about policy competence can be found in most federal systems, even when the division of powers is constitutionally guaranteed. The Community's legal order and the judicial review of the Court of Justice are federal in nature. Even the style of politics, characterized by compromises and ambiguous outcomes, can be found in federal systems of government. What the EC lacks, of course, is the reservoir of political authority found in well-established federal states in which legitimacy flows directly from the people. The Community's political system has not yet managed to reconcile integration with democracy.

The concept of differentiated integration is of continuing relevance in analysing the dynamics of integration and co-operation. The SEA did not look for a uniform body of law to apply in all circumstances. Member states are allowed to have higher standards in environmental policy and in relation to working conditions. The needs of the lesser-developed parts of the Community must also be taken into account in the internal market programme. Thus, although the *acquis communautaire* remains central, there is a recognition that there must be some sensitivity to the very different circumstances of the member states.

Notions of 'graduated integration', 'variable geometry' and 'two-speed or multi-speed' integration are likely to be hotly debated in the 1990s, especially in relation to economic and monetary union. The political consequences of a 'multi-speed' EMU are difficult to determine at this stage. It could well be that the level of economic divergence is so great in the present Community that a uniform EMU is not possible in the forseeable future. Political union, also might, be characterized by 'variable geometry' if neutral Ireland opts out of commitments in the security field. The prospect of further entrants adds to the potential diversity of the Community. This brings us to the key question for the 1990s, namely the economic and political capacity of the Community.

A Question of capacity

The EC is a central pillar in the construction of a new European order. It constitutes an anchor of stability in a rapidly changing continent. The key question for the 1990s is whether or not the EC can amass sufficient political and economic capacity to manage the multiple challenges facing it. The Community's renewed dynamism and assertiveness, apparent in the latter half of the 1980s, should not blind us to its weak capacity during much of the 1970s and early 1980s. The member states are still torn between pressures for further integration and the desire to maintain autonomy, between the benefits and the costs of collective action. The Community is still a 'would-be polity'. The tension between sovereignty and integration, so apparent in the history of the EC, remains as the Community and the member states embark on a further round of constitutive bargaining. The challenge of the post-1992 era, economic and monetary union, and policy integration raise important issues about the division of policy competence between the EC and the national polities. The likely establishment of a European system of central banks raises questions about democratic control in the future economic order, and internal developments in the Community have important implications for the external world. The Community is being called on to play a more active role in Eastern/Central Europe and in the international system more generally. The EC cannot simply restrict its attention to the crowded internal agenda.

Although relations with the rest of Europe may absorb the Community's energies, the wider international agenda poses its own dilemmas. The collapse of communism and the war in the Gulf challenge the traditional maxims of transatlantic relations. After the destruction of the Berlin Wall, the US began to reassess its relationship with Western Europe. The key issues relate to American involvement in European security and a conflict-ridden trading relationship with the EC. The collapse of the GATT round in December 1990, on the issue of CAP farm subsidies, does not augur well for transatlantic trade relations. The future shape of US involvement in the defence of Western Europe and in Europe's security system is far from certain. It is not yet clear if the United States will continue to see its interests served by direct involvement in the defence of Western Europe. A reassessment of transatlantic relations is also taking place in Western Europe. The diverse responses to the Gulf War highlights considerable differences among the Western European states concerning their willingness to accept US leadership.

Economic and policy integration

The EC's decision to embark on the completion of the internal market by 1992 gave renewed impetus to economic integration. It led to a reassessment of policies on economic and social cohesion, the environment, social issues and research and development. The dynamic effects of the programme make themselves felt in new production, marketing and distribution strategies adopted by individual companies as they position themselves to take advantage of the wider home market. The strengthening of the Community's role in relation to services extends the reach of the Community's policies beyond the producers of goods. Mergers, take-overs and joint ventures are increasing the ties that bind companies together. As the legislative programme draws to a close, attention is turning to the need for Europe-wide infrastructure, stronger competition policy and even industrial policy. So-called flanking policies in education and training are creating cross-national networks between companies, universities and training institutions. Regional policy and the Community's programmes on research and development have forged ties between individual companies, border regions and regional authorities in the member states. Such networks serve to bind the societies of Western Europe more tightly together.

The decision to embark on economic and monetary union builds on the degree of formal integration achieved so far and represents a significant deepening of integration. Agreement on EMU would amount to the most far-reaching change in the EC since its inception and would have major implications for the autonomy and formal sovereignty of the individual member states. EMU goes to the heart of contemporary politics because economic management is critical to electoral politics. If it is successful, finance ministers will find themselves locked into co-operative decision-making on budgetary matters including fiscal policy. Although in theory such co-operative decision-making will be voluntary, in reality the management of EMU will require a high degree of convergence of economic policies.

Difficult technical and political issues remain to be resolved in the lead up to EMU. Some countries place most emphasis on monetary union, whereas for others a parallelism between economic and monetary union is critical. Preparations for monetary union, including a common monetary institution – the Eurofed – are well advanced. The reports and documents produced so far have not given the same attention to economic policy-making in the Union or to the management of economic policy within it. The Eco-Fin Council may well have to evolve into a centre of economic policy-making if the EMU Intergovernmental Conference does not tackle the sensitive issue of economic management. Although the Eco-Fin Council may fill a gap in the policy process, it does not allow for transparent democratic control. The politics of redistribution and the problem of economic divergence will continue to bedevil the Community. Given the extent of divergence of economic development and performance in the Community, a two-speed or even a multi-speed approach to EMU is likely. A two-speed Community could become a two-tier one, with the lower tier failing to catch up with the upper tier. The peripheral countries will attempt to ensure that economic and social cohesion, a goal of the SEA, will not be forgotten as the core countries forge ahead. It is more difficult for the periphery to get a renewed commitment to cohesion in the present environment. Germany is faced with the public finance costs of unification and redistribution in a wider issue for the continent as a whole. When the 1988 budgetary agreement runs out in 1992, a series of difficult financial issues must be addressed. In fact events in Eastern Europe, German unification and agricultural surpluses have already placed a strain on the budget. The role of public finance in EMU may serve to widen the debate on redistribution beyond the narrow confines of the structural funds.

EFTA and Norden

The renewed dynamism of the EC in the latter half of the 1980s had a major impact on EFTA and Norden. The EFTA countries, a natural part of the Western European market, were faced with the possibility of exclusion or unilateral adaptation to developments in the EC. All of the EFTA countries wanted to protect their access to the Community market and to participate in EC policies on education, training, and research and development. The potential costs of 'outsider' status became apparent. Each EFTA state began to reassess its traditional integration policies. The prospect of an agreement on a European Economic Area that would extend the internal market to the EFTA markets assumed a central place in EFTA thinking. Even before the EEA negotiations opened, Austria decided to opt for full membership and applied in July 1989. During the course of difficult negotiations on the applicaton of the *acquis communautaire* and on decision-making in the EEA, the debate on full membership accelerated in a number of EFTA states. It seems more and more likely that the EEA will be no more than a half-way house on the road to full membership for most EFTA states.

The issues raised by a Scandinavian and Austrian enlargement are more sensitive in the political than in the economic realm. The compatibility of neutrality with the aspiration for a common foreign and security policy will be tested in negotiations with Austria and Sweden. By that stage, there should be one decision-making centre in the Community on foreign policy matters. The distinction between EPC and EC activity will have gone. Countries used to the 'minimalist' strategy pursued by EFTA and its limited institutional reach may find it difficult to adjust to the continental approach to integration. The pooling of sovereignty will not come easily to the Scandinavian states. However, a Nordic bloc in the Community would represent a formidable voting coalition. With a strong tradition of Nordic co-operation behind them, these states will represent an important new coalition in the Community.

The Wider Europe

The EC is one of the key actors in economic co-operation with the former Eastern bloc. The CSCE basket on economic co-operation provides a structure for co-operation, but the EC has the primary policy instruments. The PHARE programme, initiated by the Group of 24 and co-ordinated by the Commission, serves as the main channel for financial and technical assistance although individual countries have bilateral programmes as well. The objective of Western aid is to assist the transition to market economies and to enable the countries of Eastern/Central Europe to overcome the economic legacy of communism. Economic reconstruction requires the establishment of a system of economic law, financial institutions, changes in property relationships, investment in capital equipment, and the restructuring of obsolete industrial sectors. The transition is proving difficult even in Czechoslovakia, Poland and Hungary, which are best placed to succeed. Romania and Bulgaria face more formidable problems. If the problems of Eastern/Central Europe appear difficult, those of the USSR may be intractable.

The EC is committed to signing 'European' association agreements with Poland, Czechoslovakia and Hungary during 1991–2 as a form of expanded co-operation and a framework for closer political and economic ties. For these agreements to be successful, it will be necessary for the Community to take painful decisions on market access – decisions that may harm economic interests in the member states. The question of full membership is uncertain because it is impossible to predict just how the reform processes will go and how long it will take these countries to 'rejoin' Europe economically.

POLITICAL INTEGRATION AND CO-OPERATION

The European Community

The Kohl-Mitterrand resolution of April 1990 calling for an inter-governmental conference on political union to run parallel to the EMU IGC was essentially a strong political statement that the Franco-German axis, for long the motor force of political and constitutional development in the EC, had partly overcome the unease created by German unification. For Germany an acceptance of further integration gave substance to its assertion that unification would lead to a European Germany rather than a German Europe. The other member states – some with great enthusiasm, others with reluctance – agreed to the political union Intergovernmental Conference at the Dublin European Council in June 1990.

The Political Union IGC may be seen as an SEA 'mark II', rather than a substantial innovation in the development of the Community. The agenda for the IGC addresses two main issues, namely the governance of the Union and its international role. Although the ultimate political form of the Union is not being dealt with, there is a perceived need to strengthen the authority and legitimacy of the Union and of EC action. For some member states the effectivness of the Union is paramount, whereas for others political accountability is to the fore.

The policy scope of the Union and the efficiency and effectivness of EC institutions are central to the debate on the authority of the system. The concept of subsidiarity increasingly impinges on all major debates about policy integration. Although it is clear from the preceding discussion that the term is not new in EC parlance, subsidiarity has assumed centre stage only in the last two years. The term encapsulates a growing debate about the appropriate balance between the policy competences of Brussels-based institutions, the member states and regional authorities. Heretofore, the transfer and sharing of competence in the EC has taken place in a gradual manner without serious debate about the Community's policy capacity.

There is general agreement that the principle of subsidiarity should govern the allocation of competences in the Community, and should therefore be enshrined in the Treaty. Endowing subsidiarity with a Treaty basis is far from simple. Invoking a principle does not ensure that it will be respected. Yet designing a system of judicial review is complicated. A European Parliament Report (the d'Estaing Report) draws attention to the difficulty of delineating the principle of subsidiarity because the EC is a 'dynamic, constantly evolving project'[1] Just as domestic politics is bedevilled by issues relating to the appropriate balance between the public and the private, the division of power and competence will remain politically charged in an evolving polity such as the EC. For individual member states, subsidiarity may well be a double-edged sword: useful to invoke against unpalatable policy initiatives but a problem if invoked to restrict policy developments in an area of interest. The debate on subsidiarity is important because it marks a realization of the limits of the EC's policy competence and of the need to assess further transfers of policy responsibilities in a critical manner.

The efficiency and effectivness of EC institutions is a perennial issue on the agenda. Institutional *lourdeur* and a tardy decision-making process contributed to the Community's stagnation of the 1970s and early 1980s. The acceleration of decision-making following the SEA and the prospect of further enlargements draw attention yet again to the institutions. A strengthening of the role of the European Council and the further use of majority voting are envisaged.

The legitimacy of the Union, no less than its authority, are in question. There is a perceived need to transform the Community from a 'producers' and consumers' Europe into a 'people's Europe'. Citizenship and the 'democratic deficit' are the main items on this agenda. A strengthening of the rights of individual EC nationals in the Union as a whole is forseen. The granting of political rights will begin with the right to vote in EP and local elections and may over time be extended to full political participation. The rights of third country nationals, legally resident in one of the member states, is more problematical. Immigration is a politically charged issue in those member states with sizeable immigrant populations. It is estimated that there are some 7.9 million third country nationals resident in the Community. Population growth in North Africa and economic turmoil in Eastern/Central Europe add to the salience of the immigration issue. Because migration policy remains a national competence, it is very difficult for the Community to work out a co-ordinated response to the sensitive political and social issues raised by immigration.

Political accountability continues to be a vexed question in the Community. Its salience is increased by the prospect of a significant transfer of power to an independent system of central banks in EMU. The EP is unhappy with its place in the institutional balance and is seeking full co-decision powers with the Council. Although there is some support for this in a number of member states, it is likely that agreement at the IGC will fall short of this demand. For the first time, the political union IGC is likely to seek to strengthen the role of national parliaments and regional authorities in the policy process.

The profound political changes in Europe, along with the Gulf crisis, provide the motivation for renewed interest in the international role of the Community. There are two main strands in the debate on the Community's international role. First, there is a 'maximalist' approach, which seeks a common foreign and security policy; second, there is a 'minimalist' approach, concerned with improving the internal workings of EPC and the Community's coherence in the international system.

The Gulf War highlighted just how far short of the 'maximalist' position the Community falls at present. Despite the SEA, diversity rather than coherence characterized the member states' responses to the Gulf War. The member states were deeply divided on the legitimacy of using force, on their readiness to use force and on their readiness to be led by the United States. There is a marked contrast between Britain's 'Atlanticist' instincts, France's desire for an independent defence policy, and Germany's conflict between a commitment to the Atlantic Alliance and strong pacifist tendencies in its population. The small member states are equally divided.

The Gulf War demonstrated that the EC does not yet amount to a political union. The gap between its economic weight and political capacity is striking. Concerning the outbreak of hostilities in the Gulf, Jacques Delors, the Commission President, said in the European Parliament, 'To be brutally honest, public opinion sensed that Europe was rather ineffectual.'[2] The British Prime Minister, John Major, said in the House of Commons, that

> Political union and a common foreign and security policy in Europe would have to go beyond statements and extend to action. Clearly, Europe is not ready for that, and we should not be too ambitious when it comes to the intergovernmental conference on political union.[3]

In other words, only a 'minimalist' approach to changes in EPC is possible in the IGC. Advocates of the 'maximalist' approach, on the other hand, argue that the varied response to the Gulf crisis in fact highlights the absence of an adequate machinery for dealing with foreign and security policy in the Community at present. The war is seen as further proof of the need for the Community to strengthen its capacity for international action. Although this argument has some validity, institutions and a prescribed policy process will not on their own deliver a common foreign and security policy. Common policies must rest on a sense of collective interest and shared values rather than on institutional mechanisms alone. Institutions may aid the articulation of shared interests but cannot create them. Does this mean that the goal of a common foreign and security policy is a utopian one?

The Gulf War leaves the negotiators at the IGC with no illusions about the task they have set themselves. This may well serve to sharpen the debate about the possibilities and limits of a common foreign and security policy. Considerable thought must go into what is meant by the blanket terms 'a common foreign and security policy'. Notwithstanding the difficulty of the task, there remain powerful pressures on all Western European states for greater coherence in their international action. In the longer term the Gulf War may well strengthen these pressures. Although the Community and individual member states have an vast array of foreign policy interests, three relationships predominate. Relations with the United States, Eastern Europe including the Soviet Union, the Mediterranean and the Middle East constitute a central core of interests for Western Europe.

Transatlantic relations are in a period of transition. The US may well react to what it considers as less than wholehearted support in the Gulf War by eventually reducing its commitment to Western European security. Or it may feel the need for Western European support as it attempts to work out a strategy for dealing with the

Arab-Israeli conflict in the post-Gulf War era. Western Europe's commitment to a peace conference on the Middle East is favoured by the Arab world, and EPC statements on the Middle East have, since 1980, identified the need for a solution to the problems of the Palestinians. A Spanish and Italian proposal for a Conference on Security and Co-operation in the Mediterranean could well play an important role in the future.

Relations with the former Eastern bloc are critical, because of geographical proximity and the dangers that instability might spill over into Western Europe. The outbreak of a virtual civil war in Yugoslavia between Serbia and Croatia highlights the potential for instability and armed conflict on the Continent. Despite repeated attempts and the presence of EC observers, the Community has failed to curb the fighting. The Community must also face difficult decisions in its relations with Hungary, Poland and Czechoslovakia. For these states, rejoining Europe means membership of the European Community. Association agreements provide only a stepping stone to full membership. The goal of joining the EC is also likely to be adoped by the newly liberated Baltic states. Relations with the disintegrating Soviet Union pose an even greater challenge because of uncertainty about the future political shape of that part of the Continent and the scale of its economic problems.

Thus although, on the face of it, the Gulf War has damaged the prospects for a common foreign and security policy, it has not removed the external pressures for greater coherence in the Community's international profile. In the longer term, it may even add pressures for concerted action in relation to the Mediterranean and dealings with the United States. However, the need to redefine relations with the countries of Eastern Europe and the disintegrating Soviet Union provide the main incentives for a co-ordinated policy response from the Community and the member states.

The Council of Europe and the CSCE

The problems of political reconstruction in Eastern/Central Europe are no less formidable than those of economic reconstruction. The experiences of totalitarian rule, the weakness of democratic traditions and the disappearence of most aspects of civil society under communism leave these states ill-equipped to make the transition to stable democracies. The Council of Europe, as the guardian of Western Europe's political and legal culture, has an important role to play in supporting the transition to democracy and the rule of law. The Convention of Human Rights and other legal conventions will extend shared legal principles eastwards. Membership of the Council will give the countries of Eastern/Central Europe their first taste of non-coercive inter-state co-operation. The Council of Europe Assembly may serve as the nucleus for a CSCE parliamentary forum.

The CSCE provides the pan-European setting for formal multilateral political dialogue for the continent as a whole. Periodic meetings, at the level of heads of government and at Foreign Minister level, provide a useful opportunity to stabilize political relationships in the new Europe. The Charter of Paris enshrines human rights, political pluralism and the rule of law as the guiding principles of government. The translation of the ideals into reality in the longer term is far from certain.

Security co-operation

The decline of the Soviet threat and the acceleration of disarmament have changed Europe's security environment in a profound manner. However, the end of the cold war does not mean an end to security threats. The European continent still has a heavy concentration of troops, tanks and weapons. The disintegrating Soviet Union continues to have a formidable nuclear arsenal. The stability of the Continent demands some counterweight or balance to future Russian power. The Gulf War highlighted the dangers of 'out-of-area' conflicts for Western Europe.

In the aftermath of the revolutions of 1989, the states of the Altantic Alliance, the former members of the Warsaw Pact and the European neutrals are attempting to grapple with the profound changes in matters of security and defence. The CSCE, NATO, the Western European Union and the EC are the main regional components of any new security order. The UN adds a global context to European security.

The role and influence of individual organizations is far from clear. The CSCE has an important role to play in security in the widest sense. It brings the former Soviet Union into the construction of a new security system following its strategic loss of the GDR. Furthermore, it provides a forum for the European neutrals and the states of Eastern/Central Europe on security matters. The principle of friendly relations among states, confidence-building measures, and the Conflict Prevention Centre (see p.173) may, over time, increase confidence and trust among the participating states. An effective CSCE can reduce inter-state and ethnic tensions.

The decline of the Soviet threat clearly undermines NATO's role as a multilateral defence organization designed to contain Soviet military power. It does not, however, mean that NATO's days are numbered. The continued existence of NATO provides the best guarantee of a continued US role in Europe's security. Most Western European states see a US presence as a necessary counterweight to future Russian power. NATO's nuclear arsenal and integrated forces, and the nature of the commitment to mutual defence entered into by the members of the Atlantic Alliance, continue to give the Alliance an important role of deterrence. Moreover, NATO is a useful forum for co-ordinating responses to further arms control negotiations and disarmament in Europe. A major strategic review is under way in NATO as the Alliance adapts to the post-cold war environment.

If, over time, the US decides to reduce its commitment to Europe, the need for a Western European security system may be thrown into sharper relief. The Western European Union and the EC are the two main forums in which this can take place. Although the EC has always been a civilian organization, there are increasing pressures on it to deal with security policy in its widest sense. European integration itself, by creating stable relations among Twelve states, is an important feature of Western European security. Following the outcome of the political union conference, the EC will begin to tackle issues such as arms control, disarmament, CSCE matters, and economic and technological co-operation in the armaments field as part of a developing common foreign and security policy. Put simply, the artificial distinction between the political and economic aspects of security, on the one hand, and the defence aspects, on the other, will be formally removed. Unless NATO is disbanded, however, the EC is unlikely to assume a role in defence.

In the medium term, the Western European Union offers the most effective bridge between NATO and the EC. According to its Secretary-General in 1990, Willem van Eekelen, 'The Western European Union stands at the crossroads of Atlantic and European co-operation. It aims to be both the European pillar of the Atlantic Alliance and the security dimension of European integration'.[4] Although the membership of the WEU does not allow it to play fully this dual role, it includes all of the main Western European states, the core states in security terms. The WEU enables those states in the

EC that want to construct a Western European security identity to proceed without those states that wish to maintain the Community as a civilian organization. France, Germany and Italy seek to establish a formal link between the WEU and the Community. This might well find acceptance at the political union negotiations, provided that it does not undermine NATO in Dutch and British eyes. The US also opposes the development of a Western European security identity outside NATO. For neutral Ireland, and prospective neutral members such as Austria, Sweden and Finland, an 'opting out' clause may be offered. It will take some time for a new security order to emerge from the debate that is currently under way in the EC, the WEU and NATO.

A Europe of concentric circles

As we have seen, the Community is the motor force of economic and political integration on the Continent. The 1992 programme and related policies drive policy integration in Western Europe. The EC is being called on to fill the role of political and economic anchor for Europe as a whole. Financial, technological and managerial aid to Eastern/Central Europe, buttressed by association agreements, are part of the Community's support for the reform process in the former Eastern bloc. Other organizations act in a supporting role. The Council of Europe allows for immediate cultural and legal co-operation among all European countries. The CSCE provides the shaky foundations for a 'common European home'.

The key question is whether the Community can amass sufficient economic and political capacity to meet the twin challenges of internal integration and the demands of the rest of Europe and the Mediterranean for new relationships. On the face of it, there is a tension between the impulse towards deeper Western European integration (Political Union and EMU) and the demands of non-member states. Yet the history of the Community tells us that widening without deepening weakens integration. The Iberian enlargement worked most smoothly in institutional terms because it was accompanied by the SEA. So the Community may have no option but to deepen and widen, more or less simultaneously. Continued prosperity in Western Europe is necessary if it is to have the capacity to aid the former Eastern bloc. There may be no alternative to further economic and policy integration. The pressures for deeper political integration, in terms of both the institutional balance and the Community's international role, are also sizeable. Difficult policy and institutional questions must be resolved. A deepening of formal integration requires a further pooling of sovereignty among states that have already significantly reduced their autonomy.

Yet the Europe of Twelve cannot become an exclusive club. The term 'European Community' is not synonymous with Western Europe nor with Europe as a whole. Europe and a European identity have a wider remit. Enlargement must be tackled by the Community in the 1990s. Those member states within the Community, especially the 'inner Six', that have traditionally pursued policies of deepening integration will try to ensure that prospective member states buy into the new compact established by the intergovernmental conferences.

The Maastricht European Council of December 1991 marked the end of year-long negotiations on political union and EMU. The Maastricht treaty is an interim agreement because many of the issues debated at the IGC will be reopened in the second half of the 1990s. There was, however, substantive agreement on the timetable for EMU. A single currency may be introduced in 1977 if seven states conform to convergence criteria concerning economic performance laid down in the Treaty. If this does not happen, then a single currency will be established in 1999 by those states that are in a position to progress. Because of British reservations about a single currency, a protocol attached to the Treaty allows Britain to opt out of the move to a single currency. The inclusion of a firm date in the Treaty concerning the introduction of one money is the most important decision taken by the member states since the foundation of the Community. It signifies a political commitment to hand over responsibility for exchange rates and interest rates to a European system of central banks. This will alter the environment within which public policy and budgetary politics are conducted in the member states. It further erodes national sovereignty.

The second major decision to be taken at Maastricht was the inclusion of a chapter on a common foreign and security policy (CFSP) in the Treaty. This will replace Title 111 of the Single European Act which codified European Political Co-operation (EPC). The provisions of the Maastricht Treaty differ from the SEA in a number of important respects. First, a series of objectives are elaborated for the Community's foreign and security policy. Second, the institutional capacity of the Community in this field is strengthened. Although unanimity will be the norm for the establishment of general principles and areas of interest, voting may take place concerning the implementation of joint action. Third, the most important development is the abolition of the distinction between the economic and political aspects of security, on the one hand, and the defence aspects, on the other. The Treaty simply refers to 'security' in broad terms. The Treaty also refers to the Western European Union (WEU). Although the latter remains an autonomous organization, it emerges from Maastricht as the implementing arm of the European Union concerning defence and security issues. The member states also undertook to review a common defence policy in 1996. The future shape of a European defence policy and the possible establishment of a means of defence depend very much on what happens to NATO and on developments in the wider continent, especially in the former Soviet Union. There continues to be a deep split among the EC member states concerning an 'Atlantist' or a 'European' defence strategy. What Maastricht does is to establish the framework for the elaboration of a European defence policy provided the member states see this to be in their common interest.

The Maastricht Treaty contains a number of important changes to the Rome Treaty and the Single Act. The Community's policy scope is widened to include new areas of policy and the legal basics of some existing policies is strengthened. The poorer parts of the Community received a renewed commitment to cohesion and the establishment of a cohesion fund. The budgetary implications of this must be negotiated in 1992. Social policy was the most contentious issue at the European Council. Britain refused to agree to a new chapter in the Treaty. This led the other member states to add a protocol to the Treaty agreeing to proceed on matters of social policy on the basis of eleven member states, using the existing institutions. This is a very messy outcome from an institutional and legal perspective.

Institutional changes in the Maastricth treaty allow for more majority voting, one Commissioner per member state and a limited form of co-decision for the European Parliament. Although the Treaty falls well short of the Parliament's demands, it now has the opportunity to further build on the co-operation procedure of the Single Act. Moreover, the life of the Parliament is set to become co-terminous with the Commission from 1995 onwards which will enhance its influence over that organization. The Treaty's institutional changes amount to a continuation of the process that started with the Single Act; they do not represent a root and branch overhaul of the Community's political system. Nor was the word 'federal' included in the Preamble because of continuing British resistance towards clarifying the goal of European integration. Yet political and economic pressures on the Community to further deepen formal integration seem set to continue in the 1990s.

NOTES

1 EP, The d'Estaing Report on 'Subsidiarity', En/DT/83354, 5 April 1990.
2 Jacques Delors, address to the EP, 23 January 1991, p.2.
3 John Major to the House of Commons, quoted in *The Financial Times*, 28 January 1991, p.30.
4 W. van Eekelen, 'The WEU: Europe's best defence', *European Affairs*, no.4, 1990, pp.9–10.

TOPICS FOR DISCUSSION

1 Assess the tension between deepening and widening in the EC.
2 Can the member states achieve a common foreign policy?
3 What are the main issues in the search for a new security order for Europe?

Index